# The South and Film

# The South and Film

*Warren French*

EDITOR

UNIVERSITY PRESS OF MISSISSIPPI

*Jackson*
1981

*This volume is sponsored and authorized*
*by the*
*University of Southern Mississippi*

*Library of Congress Cataloging in Publication Data*

Main entry under title:

The South and film

    (Southern quarterly series)
    Originally published: Southern quarterly, v. 19
no. 3 & 4, spring-summer 1981.
    Includes indexes.
    1. Southern States in motion pictures—Addresses,
essays, lectures. 2. Faulkner, William, 1897-1962—
Film adaptations—Addresses, essays, lectures.
3. Moving-picture industry—Southern States—
Addresses, essays, lectures. I. French Warren G.,
1922-    II. Series
PN1995.9.S66S6    791.43'09'093275    81-14641
ISBN 0-87805-148-1                AACR2

Unless otherwise credited, all illustrations appearing in this issue were
supplied by Movie Star News, New York City.

# Contents

# The South and Film

# Introduction

## "The Southern":
## *Another Lost Cause?*

*Birth of a Nation* established the format for the American (and international) feature film, and *Gone with the Wind* was recently voted the best of all American motion pictures in an American Film Institute poll. Although these two most momentous American films are epic portrayals of the South, neither fostered a genre of imitative films that became a backbone of the industry. The legendary South gave way to the legendary West; and from 1915 to the end of the 1960s the screen's principal contribution to our native mythology was the Western rather than the "Southern."

Sound economic practices, of course, accounted for this situation. "Southerns" in the David W. Griffith-David O. Selznick tradition would have been, because of the period sets and costumes required, extremely expensive. The studios along "Poverty Row" in the 1930s that ground out the hundreds of horse operas that enchanted young audiences at Saturday matinees could never have mounted an authentic succession of Dixie spectaculars.

Undoubtedly there were other reasons why the Western superseded the Southern. "Good guys" (frontier scouts, cowboys, Texas Rangers) and "bad guys" (Indians, rustlers, Mexicans) were easily identified in non-political terms in Westerns; "Southerns" unavoidably involved touchy political issues. Even *Birth of a Nation* and *Gone with the Wind* have been attacked on racial and social grounds. Black-white relations in the South have caused continual controversy of the kind that Hollywood producers wish to avoid in routine productions, and the genteel traditions of the cotton kingdom would have bored urban youngsters attracted by the laconic dialogue and violent freedom of the horse operas.

3

Ironically, *Birth of a Nation* itself paved the cinematic path westward. Although Griffith's epic is usually supposed to have had no sequel, except spiritually in his own overly ambitious *Intolerance*, the pattern and techniques of the prototypical feature film were soon imitated in the until recently largely forgotten *Martyrs of the Alamo*, directed by W. Christy Cabanne, as one of a group of films "supervised" by Griffith for Artcraft. Although Griffith is reputed to have lent little more than his name to this project, Cabanne's film applied the same dramatic action techniques used in the Civil War film to the story of the resolute Texans' defense of their liberties, and this well-received film provided a pattern for endless other variations on the story of the winning of the West. (The Alamo itself has, of course, remained a principal icon of the genre and has given its name to the only film that super-Western hero John Wayne took sole responsibility for directing.)

*Gone with the Wind* came closer to establishing a regional genre. Two rejected contenders for the role of Scarlett O'Hara did play comparable roles—Bette Davis in William Wyler's *Jezebel* (released before Selznick's colossus but prompted by the long excitement over its promotion) and Paulette Goddard in Cecil B. DeMille's sadly neglected *Reap the Wild Wind* (1942), a tale of the Florida keys that is one of the most beautiful and spellbinding of Hollywood studio films.

Even if the market could have absorbed infinite variations on the Scarlett/Rhett story, economic and social conditions again militated against the flourishing of the plantation special. The austerities demanded by World War II, which premiered soon after *Gone with the Wind*, again prevented the production of elaborate costume dramas, and a new national emergency was hardly an appropriate occasion for exhuming sectional conflicts. The demand was for cheap, quickly made films that showed Yankee and Rebel unified against a common foe—the wicked Axis partners. By the time the war was over, increasing racial tensions rendered the glorification of the "old Southland" a risky undertaking (as evidenced by adverse reactions to Walt Disney's syrupy *Song of the South* [1946]), and rather than a nostalgic Eden the South became in the popular arts the "hell" that Fred Chappell describes in "The Image of the South in Film" (*Southern Humanities Review*, 12 [Fall 1978], 303–11)—the decadent backwoods and backwaters of William Faulkner, Tennessee Williams, Carson McCullers and Truman Capote's fictions. (In pushing this dichotomous image of the South too far, Chappell finally, regrettably, presents too superficial a picture of the scene.)

Beginning with *The Little Foxes* and *Tobacco Road* (both 1941), a number of major films that collectively exemplify "Southern Gothic" did flourish, as Ida Jeter points out in an article that follows. (Follow-ups to the first venture into this territory—the transformation of Faulkner's novel *Sanctuary* into *The Story of Temple Drake* [1933] had been frustrated by the adoption of the Motion Picture Producers Code.) The full possibilities of such "Southerns" were not realized, however, until the breakdown of censorship made possible the national distribution of Elia Kazan's *Baby Doll* (1956), despite the fact that it was the first feature film to be condemned in its entirety by the once all-powerful Roman Catholic Legion of Decency. There fol-

Southern Breakthrough—Censorship Breakdown:
Carroll Baker as Tennessee Williams's *Baby Doll*

lowed, among other immoralistic tales, *God's Little Acre, The Long Hot Summer, The Sound and the Fury* (showing little kinship to Faulkner's novel), *The Fugitive Kind, Cat on a Hot Tin Roof*, and that apogee of the decadent sensibility, Tennessee Williams's *Suddenly, Last Summer* (all released between 1957 and 1959).

These films, however, never really constituted a genre; for despite similar settings, the usually lurid tales were too much based on flamboyant individuals (often deranged) rather than stereotypes, and the usually depressing stories did not appeal to the young mass audiences that had for decades supported the Western. The Southern films of the fifties and sixties were not celebrations of a legendary kingdom but alienated artists' vengeance on their homeland aimed at a cynical elitist audience that remained faithful to film when the masses deserted to TV.

There were continuing efforts, however, to establish a popular, sentimental Southern genre. Filmed three times, Edna Ferber's *Showboat* constituted almost a genre of its own and prompted such other nostalgic recollections of the riverboat era as the musical fantasy *Mississippi* with Bing Crosby and W. C. Fields and comedies like *Steamboat Round the Bend* with Will Rogers and Irvin S. Cobb, which J. P. Telotte discusses in his article on John Ford's South.

In another article Wade Austin recalls a persistent effort in the late 1930s and the 1940s to create a genre of "Southerns"—the hillbilly movies that developed, like many others of those years, from popular radio programs. Beginning with *Mountain Music*, teaming Bob Burns and Martha Raye, these films exploited the quaintness of the old-fashioned life reputed still to exist in the rural Southern mountains, especially the Ozarks of Arkansas and Missouri. The genre flourished for a decade and indeed persisted—despite the competition of television—even into the 1950s through the "Ma and Pa Kettle" series, though—as Austin points out—the Kettle films rarely had Southern settings. Again what had begun as a Southern genre had expanded into a farcical portrayal of folksy backwoods life everywhere. The unpretentious pastorals starring Judy Canova and Bob Burns did not outlast the radio shows that promoted them probably because, as Austin surmises, they are too unsophisticated for the taste even of today's drive-in audiences.

Some of their characteristics persisted, considerably jazzed up, of course, in the films of Elvis Presley, which constitute almost a genre built around a performer rather than a setting or type of action. (No other singer has had such an extensive sequence of films produced only to exploit his personality, except Bing Crosby between 1933 and 1941.) Despite Presley's origins, however, his films are only occasionally set in the South. Yet though the boy could be taken out of the region, the region couldn't be taken out of his style. Presley's extraordinary series of 26 rather small-scale, low-budget films made during a period of only 13 years (1956–68) constitutes an important part of the Southern entertainment legacy that has already been examined in the collection of essays on Elvis edited by Jac Tharpe (1979).

Recollection of the hillbilly and Elvis films calls attention to the surprising fact that despite its enormous influence on American popular taste through live performances and radio and television shows like *Hee Haw*, the country music congregation whose temple is the Grand Old Opry in Nashville, Tennessee, has *never* inspired a genre of feature films. Ironically, as Wade Austin points out, a film titled *Grand Ole Opry* in 1940 had nothing to do with the venerable institution and Robert Altman's *Nashville*, examined in detail in Gerard Plecki's account of the director's South, did not use either familiar singers or traditional songs. Opry regulars indeed were outraged by the satirical exploitation of their legends.

The Opry's failure to spawn a genre of films, especially for the drive-in and shopping center trade, is baffling; perhaps it can only be explained by assuming that film producers feel that even fanatical devotees would be reluctant to take the time and trouble to go out to the movies to indulge themselves in entertainment widely available live and through home media. The recent success of *Coal Miner's Daughter*, a kind of modern saint's legend about country singer Loretta Lynn, may lead, however, to a native genre of what director Ken Russell calls "biopics" about prominent country artists, who surely would provide a rich vein of nostalgic material.

Down through 1969, then, the cinematic picture of the South had not been presented like that of the legendary West, backstage Broadway or the big city underworlds, through a steady succession of only marginally different films, heavily dependent on stereotyped plots, settings and characters. Rather the South had provided the setting for occasional lavish and often quite controversial films, not just *Birth of a Nation* and *Gone with the Wind*, but also others—from King Vidor's *Hallelujah* (1929) and *So Red the Rose* (1935), Jean Renoir's *Swamp-water* and *The Southerner* (discussed in Hart Wegner's essay), Elia Kazan's *Pinky* (1949) and *Baby Doll* (1956) to John Huston's *Reflections in a Golden Eye* (1967). This tradition has, of course, continued to the present with such outstanding and controversial films as *Deliverance* (1972), *Nashville* (1975), and John Huston's *Wise Blood* (1979, from Flannery O'Connor's novel).

I have stressed the period 1969–70 in this survey of the South on film for, as we changed decades during one of the most turbulent periods in American history, a very popular, highly controversial and often mystifying film circulated that we now see marked a watershed in movies' contribution to American mythology. In particular, the film offered the prospect of redressing the balance between the West and the South in the "literature" of the screen by suggesting a set of stereotypes particularly congenial to films with Southern settings.

Dennis Hopper's *Easy Rider* is unique among American films as an allegory that was a box-office hit. Since allegory is the projection through iconic figures of intellectual abstractions, generally even successful literary examples like George Orwell's *Animal Farm* and William Golding's *Lord of the Flies* are too thin in characterization and too talky and inflexible in argument to provide the body that a film needs to transcend its shadowy two-dimensionality. Perhaps, however, because the allegory embodied in *Easy Rider* was absolutely central to the crisis through which our youth culture was passing during the activist years, the characters did seem part of the landscape through which they passed rather than simply symbols imposed upon it. There was much in the film for even those who didn't grasp the allegory to enjoy.

*Easy Rider* dramatizes a traumatic reversal in American romance. Traditionally the catchphrase "Westward the course of Empire" has dominated American thinking about our national destiny. Our business was the movement into the setting sun, subjugating the wilderness; and the story of "how the West was won" continued to be a principal staple of our popular literature and film for nearly a century

Turning Point—Western into Southern: Dennis Hopper, Peter Fonda and Jack Nicholson in *Easy Rider*.

after the West that John Wayne and his fellows kept alive had vanished from every place but untenanted Monument Valley.

Since 1970, however, it has been impossible to make credible films about the legendary West except parodies like Frank Perry's *Rancho Deluxe*, Howard Zieff's *Hearts of the West*, Robert Altman's *Buffalo Bill and the Indians*, and Mel Brooks's *Blazing Saddles*. (An attempt in the summers of 1979 and 1980 with films like *Butch and Sundance: The Early Years* and *The Long Riders* has only made the truth of this observation embarrassingly apparent. The Old West of the films had been shot down with Butch Cassidy and the Sundance Kid in 1969.)

The day of the "horse opera" is over, I suspect, because both its bellicosely optimistic assumptions and even its very *props* are too remote from the newest generation of filmgoers. It is very difficult for people who have not lived around horses to empathize with horsemen. The horse had been conspicuous in even our urban life until the 1950s, but it is little in evidence today. Post-World War II youth has grown up, moreover, in a world dominated by motor vehicles. Though these had been around since early in the century, they did not really become commonplace until after World War II. It is scarcely surprising that today's youth should demand that motor vehicles function as principal icons in its personal mythology.

*Easy Rider* did not so much promote this demand as it recorded a transition that had already occurred (like most powerful myths). Captain America and Billy the Kid, the good and bad faces of our long drive westward depart the West for the South, not on horseback, but on the motorcycles of the title, carrying with them as a gift from the last pathetic frontiersmen in isolated communes the seed of their own destruction, LSD. In the traditional capital of Southern decadence, New Orleans (the filmed image of which is affectionately explored by H. Wayne Schuth in our concluding article), and, most appropriately, in a cemetery, they share the potion that might initiate them into a new realm of magic; but in their own fatal words, "We blew it." Wheeling aimlessly through the Southern woods, these exotic displaced icons are destroyed by a shotgun blast from a redneck's pick-up truck.

I cannot digress here into a detailed meditation on the meaning and significance of this fateful journey; but the basic point is that Captain America and Billy discover (as the migrants in John Steinbeck's *The Grapes of Wrath*, for example, had also discovered when they sought to repeat the legendary Westward migration) that the places they might have occupied were already filled. The South had no need nor use for imported symbols and their vehicles; it had already an established and entrenched culture of its own. Pick-up trucks, of course, abound everywhere in the United States today; but nowhere are they more ubiquitous than in the suburban and rural South, where the weather is good for driving all year and the roads are not so crowded and impersonal as California freeways.

Following the domestication of the confrontation between motorized forces in *Easy Rider*, the horse opera as a central focus of American romance was doomed; for the still unattached young people who make up the movies' principal audience could relate meaningfully only to a "gasoline opera" (that had come into being, ironically, just as rising prices and gasoline shortages were beginning to make the old life "on the road" an unavailable dream).

Such a "gasoline opera" is exactly what has been forthcoming. Most of the youthcult films of the 1970s were built around motorized vehicles from motorcycles to diesel trailer-trucks. Whether a continuing genre will emerge from what we will eventually see in perspective as the gropings during the decade for new stereotypes to supplant exhausted ones remains to be seen; but there have been several intriguing starts, and the South has been dominantly featured in them.

For a while it appeared as if a genre were indeed in the making taking its cues from the violent actions and endings of *Bonnie and Clyde* and *Easy Rider*. Trendy American International studios, which had already given us the beach party films, the Hell's Angels' cyclist cycle, and Vincent Price's transmutations of the works of Poe, sensed that the drive-in trade might respond to a series of revelations of the discomforts awaiting the motorized young at the hands of backwoods Georgia lawmen. But after production of *Macon County Line, Return to Macon County* and *Bad Georgia Road* in rapid succession in the mid-1970s, the formula was abandoned, though only in its excesses. While these anti-pastorals about the horrors of the backwoods that reached their apogee in *The Texas Chainsaw Massacre* delighted small cults of alienated urban filmgoers, they proved—like the earlier Southern Gothic films—too revolting for the generally sentimental mass audience that patronizes drive-ins. (Already the genre flourishes only in parodies like *The Rocky Horror Picture Show*.)

The underlying preoccupation of the genre with fast driving and disrespectful confrontations with malign forces of the law was transformed, however, into agreeable family fare by Burt Reynolds, Sally Field and Jackie Gleason in *Smokey and the Bandit*, curiously another film about the sub rosa transportation of another Western cult icon, Coors beer, to a South that finds it a more acceptable magical potion than LSD. Although *Smokey* had not been released when Fred Chappell wrote "The Image of the South in Film," his essay suggests that the trail of such films about "good old boys" versus the law leads back to such moonshine running films as the tragic *Thunder Road* in 1958; but none of these earlier and heavier films enjoyed anything like the smashing success of *Smokey*.

Has the South's turn come at last? If the "Southern" is to replace the Western for a time as a dominant American film genre, I think that this genre will find its prototype in *Smokey and the Bandit*. Even as I write *Smokey and the Bandit II* is already with us, doing even better business during the summer doldrums than its predecessor. Even if the remarkable trio of Reynolds, Field and Gleason tire of such shenanigans, dollar-wise producers are likely to see the wisdom of trying to clone them. Whatever one may think of the Smokey films, they are surely closer to the sensibilities of a truck-loving, beer-loving, Florida-sunshine-loving generation than Burt Reynolds's other efforts to exploit Southern materials in films like *Deliverance* and *Gator* or the "blaxploitation" films like *Mandingo* and *Drum* that Edward D. C. Campbell, Jr., discusses in his article, or the confused effort to fashion a tragic tale of wasted youth out of a popular Southern ballad in

*Smokey and the Bandit:* promotional copy reads "Sheriff Buford T. Justice (Jackie Gleason) dispenses his own peculiar brand of justice."

*Ode to Billy Joe.* (The mass audience wants raffish, upbeat fare; the other "Southern" of recent vintage to bear in mind is the generally overlooked *Harper Valley P.T.A.*, which has spun off a TV series. Ballads about losers may be popular; but for an evening's entertainment most people want winners.) The South's best chance of rising again—this time cinematically—appears to be in resourceful producers' finding new challenges for the "bandits" who have traded their stallions for thundering wheels. For the audiences of the 1980s a motorhome is going to be much more familiar than a plantation house or a sharecropper's cabin, and it is going to be fascinating to see whether the South can manage to maintain the identification it has so far established with a new kind of "road" film.

The plan for this issue is apparent, I believe, from the table of contents. I have remarked upon the way a number of individual essays contribute to the "plot" of this collection. After provocative reconsiderations of some of the major film classics about the South, we return to the subject that I have introduced here of attempts to create a Southern film genre. Then we look at the "vision" of the South projected through the works of three prominent American auteurist directors. Two subjects of inescapable concern in speculations about the South and film today are then introduced—the importance of female characters and the relation of film to the works of William Faulkner. Finally some attention to the complex problem of regionalism in film focuses principally on the efforts to capture the unique qualities of Appalachia. This section winds up the book with two mellow essays on the perils and delights of the quest for "authenticity" when shooting films on regional locations. These essays simply introduce a vast subject. A hundred omissions might be mentioned, but I do particularly regret that a planned section on filmmaking in the South could not be included in this issue. Perhaps another time.

Warren French

# History Written in Jagged Lightning:
## *Realistic South vs. Romantic South in*
## The Birth of a Nation

ROBERT A. ARMOUR

Just before the New York opening of *The Birth of a Nation* in 1915, Thomas Dixon, the author of *The Clansman* on which the movie had been based, arranged for a preview screening to be held at the White House for his old classmate, Woodrow Wilson. When the light came on at the end, Wilson is supposed to have praised the movie as "history written in lightning"; and even though he later repudiated the comment once the film was attacked for its racial content, the remark was widely repeated and taken by D. W. Griffith as the highest of compliments. But Wilson's insight may have been more appropriate than he afterwards thought. Lightning is beautiful and inspiring, but it is jagged and capable of doing much damage. Like lightning, *The Birth of a Nation* is a mixture of the beautiful and the fearful.

Actually Griffith's goals were rather lofty; he had no clear intention to offend the black race, but instead to portray accurately the war from the Southern point of view. William K. Everson points out that it is a contradiction in terms to believe that a Southerner can be impartial about this war, but we know that Griffith believed that his film would give a balanced view of what happened.[1] The print of the film compiled by the American Film Institute has Griffith's disclaimer of racial slurs just after the intermission; a title claims that the film is a historical presentation of the Civil War and Reconstruction. Lillian Gish recalls that Griffith repeated the same theme the first time he told his company of actors what he intended: "I'm going to use it [Dixon's *The Clansman*] to tell the truth about the War between the States. It hasn't been told accurately in history books. Only the winning side in a war ever gets to tell its story."[2]

This idea contains the conflicting drives that molded Griffith's con-

14

cept of the film. On one hand he wanted to be factual and to tell the truth. He knew that his medium had the potential for documentary effects even though he had never heard the word *documentary* applied to film. He had a sense of fairness which he believed guided him to a balanced view of Lincoln, the North, and black people. But on the other hand, he was deeply immersed in what Everett Carter calls "the Plantation Illusion,"[3] the Southern myth, which holds that the old South was a place of happiness based on an agrarian life style and a social structure dominated both by tradition and by white aristocrats. Until 1915 the illusion was largely a literary motif popularized by writers such as John Pendleton Kennedy, William Alexander Caruthers, John Esten Cooke, Thomas Nelson Page, and Mary Johnston; but Griffith adapted its conventions to the screen. His film, then, becomes a jarring combination of romanticism and realism not uncommon in the naturalistic fiction and art of the first decades of this century.

The realism probably resulted from his sense of his medium and his fairness; the romanticism came from his background. He was the son of a Kentuckian whose Civil War exploits had become family mythology. Colonel "Roaring Jake" Griffith had been an unsuccessful physician, gold prospector, politician, and farmer before the war provided him with his chance for excitement and personal glory. During the war he rose in rank from sergeant to colonel and probably spent the last few weeks of the encounter in the presence of the retreating president of the Confederacy. His finest moment, according to the mythology, came near the end of the war when he led his cavalry troop in a charge while wildly driving a buggy, a vehicle forced upon him by wounds received in an earlier engagement. No historical evidence supports this legend, but the story of the charge became one of the colonel's favorite entertainments for his children. The father did not make significant contributions to the labor effort around the farm, but he did love to entertain the family at night with tales of his war exploits and with readings from popular poetry. A cousin added to the family folklore with stories of the operations of the Ku Klux Klan. Clearly, David Griffith's love for narrative form, for sentiment and, most important of all, his love for the South were shaped early by the stories he heard around the house.[4]

The romantic South of Griffith's imagination is characterized by a title early in the film which describes Piedmont, South Carolina, the home of the Camerons, as a place "where life runs in a quaintly quiet way." Griffith carefully draws images of this quaintness and quiet. He shows the older Camerons at home, happily surrounded by children and pets. As the white masters of the plantation wander about their estate, showing it to visitors from the North, the visuals reinforce the feelings of peace and correctness believed by Griffith to characterize the pre-war Southern society. The slaves, overjoyed to have the whites visit them in the quarters, dance a jig to the pleasure of everyone. As the whites pass through their fields, the camera emphasizes the cotton and its black pickers, the economic foundations of the old South.

The cornerstone of the quaintness and quiet is social structure, structure which maintains class distinctions and upholds correct behavior. The most noxious social image in the film was the role of the blacks in the structure of society. To Griffith the turmoil associated with the freeing of the slaves was the effect of the breakdown of traditional classes and behavior. Griffith's racial attitudes were shaped in Kentucky early in his life; his birth in 1875 came at a time when Reconstruction was still a painful topic for Southerners. There are stories of his friendship for and generosity toward black people he knew personally, but his ideas on race were both patronizing and separatist. A shot near the opening of the film establishes the racial stratification. First we see a wagon of blacks, with children gaily falling in and out, which is juxtaposed with a view of whites with solemn dignity in a fine carriage. The demeanor of the participants and the status of their dress and vehicles delineate class distinctions and social roles. The blacks are portrayed in the films as either good (loyal to their masters or employers and happy with their lot) or bad (drunks, rapists, and power hungry). From Griffith's perspective the images of good blacks toadying to their masters and of the bad blacks drunkenly trying to run the state legislature or lusting after white women are based on historically accurate incidents, although others have questioned the validity and typicality of these images.

Robert Henderson suggests that part of the film's appeal is that it plays to the fears of its white audience that the loss of social structure will lead to the disintegration of the South.[5] These fears were not limited to people living south of Maryland and Pennsylvania, a situation that helps to explain the popularity of the film across the country, even in face of serious opposition from racial and religious groups. Whites in the East and Midwest, especially many of the immigrants who entered this country around the turn of the century, saw in the collapse of the old South the disintegration of their own social values and feared for the survival of their own sense of class structure. The Ku Klux Klan had its followers on both sides of the Mason-Dixon line.

Those fears are expressed most vividly in the metaphor of rape that runs throughout the film: a sign at a rally of freedmen reads "Equal Rights, Equal Politics, *Equal Marriage*" [italics mine]. The most obvious dramatization of the metaphor is the one in which Gus chases Flora, the little sister, who prefers death to dishonor; but there are other suggestions of rape, although none is consummated in the film. Lynch's assault on Elsie Stoneman is a not so subtle reminder to the Northern audience that rape is not reserved for Southern belles and that all Americans need fear violation of one sort or another when the order of our social structure loses its basis. These sexual rapes, as unpleasant as they are, are also suggestive of a more general rape, the rape of the land manifested in the memorable shot of Sherman's march through Georgia to the sea.

Defenders of David Wark Griffith have offered a wide range of explanations for his racial attitudes, none of which entirely satisfies: (1) He used white actors in blackface because there were few black actors in southern California in 1914, and he did use the few blacks he knew. (2) It was possible to save money by having a white man play two roles, one in blackface; but it was impossible to have a black man reverse this process. (3) Griffith liked black people and never intended that the film be interpreted as an attack on them.[6] (4) There are good blacks as well as bad ones in the film.[7] (5) In his later films Griffith was kind to blacks, even showing a white man embracing a dying black comrade in *The Greatest Thing in Life*.[8] (6) Griffith tones down the racism of *The Clansman*, which is the source of the worst anti-black images in the film.[9] (7) Griffith was historically accurate, even if he did overstate the case somewhat.[10]

These explanations dominate the critical writing about Griffith, but they—and the attacks on him for racism[11]—tend to misguide our attention from the other important issues raised by the film and from its contributions to the development of the medium.

The quaintness of Griffith's South is additionally portrayed in other images which support social structure. He shows the value of the agrarian way of life that is centered on the family, and many of the early scenes in the film establish this motif. The Camerons are a family whose concern for each other motivates key scenes in the film: Mrs. Cameron's visit to the Northern hospital in search of her wounded son, Ben Cameron's tender greeting of his sister on his return to Piedmont, and his revenge for her death. The key to the stability of the family is the role of the women, both black and white. Mrs. Cameron is the buttress that keeps her family together and strong. The faithful "mammy" is the one who protects the Camerons from the horrors of the rampaging mobs. The women are held by the men to be objects of veneration and worship, objects to be protected from the harshness of life and death. That the surviving Cameron children find mates at the end of the movie suggests that the family structure has survived the war, and these new families are clearly central to Griffith's vision of the future in the last scenes.[12]

Manners and morals form the spiritual mortar for these families. Margaret Cameron is introduced as a "daughter of the old South, trained in manners of the old school." Early in the film Griffith establishes the graciousness that characterized the South, at least in the version of the South in the Plantation Illusion. The Camerons show great hospitality in entertaining their guests from the North, and Ben Cameron epitomizes Southern manners as he falls in love with a portrait of Elsie Stoneman, whom he has never met, and carries it through the war to give him strength during moments of loneliness. The moral code of the South is evident in Ben Cameron's refusal to shake hands with a mulatto and Flora's preference for death over dishonor. In the scene in the besieged cabin toward the end of the film, the men prepare to use their empty guns as bludgeons on their women so that their honor cannot be taken by the invaders.

There are times when one's honor must be defended, and some of the film's most memorable and self-evident images of the South depict the war and the later creation of the Ku Klux Klan. Even though there is honor in war, there is little glory in Griffith's War between the States. There is excitement in the little colonel's charge across the fields but it is performed in a lost cause. The cost of war is made visible in a shot of the dead upon the battlefield, preceded with a title, "War's peace." Both the Confederate charge and the ride to the rescue of the KKK bring cinematic excitement to the images of the South, but the brutal nature of the battle scenes makes manifest the dualism of romanticism and realism. One moment the charge of the Confederate troops evokes the strongest emotions for a lost cause, but the next moment a scene of the dead on the battlefield reminds us that, to use Griffith's words, "war claims its bitter, useless sacrifice."

His romanticism led him to a personalized view of the South and the war, but Griffith was careful to support this illusion with whatever realism reinforced his vision. His historical research was extensive and, as Lillian Gish says, "this fidelity to facts was an innovation in films." She lists the books he used on the war and the Reconstruction, including Harper's *Pictorial History of the Civil War*, Nicolay and Hay's *Lincoln: A History*, and a book on the Ku Klux Klan by John C. Nester and D. L. Wilson. We know that he consulted Mathew Brady's photographs, maps of major battles, and other records from the Smithsonian. He laid out the battlefields with the help of war veterans who had been in the engagements, and he took great care with accuracy in costumes and ordnance. He used well known photographs and sketches of the war to recreate the scenes exactly. The scene of the surrender, for instance, is set up as he found it in one of the period sketches. The set for the legislature in South Carolina was designed according to photographs provided by a newspaper from Columbia, South Carolina; and the set for the Ford Theatre, scene of the assassination, was a duplicate of the original building. Griffith even had the actors on the stage perform *Our American Cousin*, repeating the exact action when Raoul Walsh, as John Wilkes Booth, duplicated the actions of the murderer.[13]

Griffith's thesis is expressed in the opening title when he explains that the purpose of the film is to demonstrate that "war may be held in abhorrence." This war tore apart a country, led to the senseless deaths of many brave men, disrupted the social structure of the South, and caused the death of "The Great Heart." The romanticism of the Plantation Illusion did not carry over much into Griffith's view of the war. The flag waving and the Confederate charge stir many a Southern heart, but the realism of the horrors of war and its aftermath overpowers those romantic tendencies. The war led to social upheaval that could only be resolved through the birth of the Ku Klux Klan, which was an attempt to restore the old order, founded on the Confederate flag and the Christian cross.

Griffith's conclusion seems to be that the innate dignity and grace of the Southerners were their resources that allowed them to survive the war and Reconstruction. Even though the social structures and way of life of the old South deteriorated with the political changes forced upon the South with defeat, individual Southerners, shored up by values that could not be defeated, found ways to maintain their dignity. The little sister prepares the best possible meal for her brother returning from the war and makes an effort to dress in her finest clothing, even if her accessories are only "Southern ermine" (raw cotton). Immediately after Ben's return the Cameron family go about reconstructing their lives, cleaning up Cameron Hall and taking in boarders. Griffith's concern for dignity is so great that he never shows Ben Cameron personally taking in boarders or even working for a living. After his return Ben rolls up his sleeves and cleans the yard; but as far as we know, he never demeans himself with labor for money, and shortly he is again dressed with his pre-war excellence. In dress, demeanor, and customs, the Camerons maintain their dignity, even under the pressures for social change. In the coda at the end Ben and Elsie and Phil and Margaret are seen on a double honeymoon. This metaphorical union of the North and South is established through the reinstatement of the family as the basic element in the structure of the society.

Griffith's idealized view of the South, founded upon his family mythology and a romantic literary and historical tradition, came into conflict with the documentary potential of film and with Griffith's own desire to tell the truth about the war. The result was bound to be controversial since Griffith used a medium well suited to the factual reconstruction of historical situations to project his own romantic vision, with the result that his subjective vision becomes an inseparable part of the objective history.

NOTES

[1]*American Silent Film* (New York: Oxford Univ. Press, 1978), p. 83.

[2]*The Movies, Mr. Griffith, and Me* (Englewood Cliffs, N.J.: Prentice-Hall, 1969), p. 131.

[3]"Cultural History Written in Lightning: The Significance of *The Birth of a Nation*" in Fred Silva, ed., *Focus on* The Birth of a Nation (Englewood Cliffs, N.J.: Prentice-Hall, 1971), p. 136.

[4]The primary source for biographical information on Griffith is Robert M. Henderson, *D. W. Griffith: His Life and Work* (New York: Oxford Univ. Press, 1972).

[5]Henderson, p. 158.

[6]Everson, pp. 86–87 summarizes the defenses numbered 1–3, although he is not the first to make these defenses; Gish, for example, makes many of the same points, pp. 134–39.

[7]Roy E. Aitken, *The Birth of a Nation Story* (Middleburg, Va.: Denlinger, 1965), p. 60, and Edward Wagenknecht and Anthony Slide, *The Films of D. W. Griffith* (New York: Crown, 1975), p. 60.

[8]Wagenknecht and Slide, p. 60.

[9]Russell Merritt, "Dixon, Griffith, and the Southern Legend," *Cinema Journal*, 12 (1972), 37–38. The relationship of the film to Thomas Dixon's novel is discussed in detail in Joan L. Silverman's accompanying essay, "*The Birth of a Nation*: Prohibition Propaganda."

[10]Aitken, p. 61.

[11]The attacks on Griffith are nicely summarized by Merritt in "Dixon, Griffith, and the Southern Legend" and by Thomas Cripps, *Slow Fade to Black: The Negro in American Film, 1900–1942* (New York: Oxford Univ. Press, 1977), pp. 41–69.

[12]The theme of the family is discussed by Merritt and by Edward D. C. Campbell, Jr., *The Celluloid South: The Old South in American Film, 1903–1978* (Knoxville: The Univ. of Tennessee Press, 1981).

[13]Gish, pp. 136–37.

The wounded "Little Colonel" (Henry B. Walthall) captured by the Union Army at a dramatic high point in *The Birth of a Nation*. (Courtesy of Museum of Modern Art/Film Stills Archive)

# The Birth of a Nation:
## Prohibition Propaganda

JOAN L. SILVERMAN

In discussing the passage of the Prohibition Amendment, historians tend to focus on the relentless lobbying of the Anti-Saloon League which implemented the educational spadework of the Women's Christian Temperance Union. They cite both organizations as representing a last-ditch effort by evangelical small town and rural Protestants to impose their morality on an increasingly urban, non-Protestant America. These groups in their campaign are perceived as taking advantage of a widespread surge of wartime patriotic fervor that sought to conserve grain for humanitarian reasons and simultaneously put the supposedly traitorous German brewers out of business. Moreover, historians point out that rural districts were overrepresented in state legislatures that ratified the amendment and a million men who might presumably have voted for pro-booze representatives were serving overseas without ballots; thus Prohibition was foisted on the American people. Scant attention, however, has been paid to the role of film in promoting negative attitudes toward drink and furthering the Dry Crusade.

From their infancy at the turn of the century, movies were both a school and a social agency. They informed, persuaded, and influenced the native born, and more vividly than any other medium, they pictured American customs and values for the armies of immigrants newly arrived from Europe. According to Lewis Jacobs, film historian, movies were always more than cheap entertainment or an innocent novelty. "They were a powerful medium for disseminating new ideas and attitudes toward government and society, standards of taste, conduct, morals, canons of convention and culture."[1]

The work of filmmaker David Wark Griffith is of particular interest

23

in the promotion of temperance ideology. Raised in Kentucky, Griffith went to work for the Biograph Studio at 11 East 14th Street, New York, in the summer of 1908. While not actually inventing the techniques of fade-out, long shot, close-up, flashback and montage, Griffith soon learned to use them for stunning dramatic and psychological effect.[2] He liberated the motion picture from the confines of the stage. Almost alone among his contemporaries, he realized that the camera would have to serve as a substitute for the spoken word of the drama to express the meaning of the story through the gestures and facial expressions of the actors. After 1910, through the use of subtitles, Griffith made doubly certain that his moral-didactic movie sermons were not lost on his audience. Like an old-time spellbinding preacher, Griffith elicited an emotional rather than an intellectual response. "Hard, difficult thought was not a part of D.W.'s makeup," notes film scholar Jay Leyda.[3]

During the next five years, in addition to producing, directing, and writing hundreds of other films, Griffith personally created twelve specifically pro-temperance, anti-drink one and two-reel films and scores of others with strong temperance messages: *What Drink Did, The Drunkard's Reformation, The Crooked Road, The Rocky Road* are sample titles. Generally these ten to twelve minute films followed the stereotyped pattern established by Timothy Shay Arthur's *Ten Nights in a Bar-Room*. Virtue was always rewarded, even if practiced belatedly, and sin punished. For a confirmed alcoholic, the only outcome was death, although salvation could come about through repentance, sudden religious conversion, intense suffering or the redemptive love of a pure woman or an innocent child. There were, however, no racial overtones in these early films; in fact, the few black characters in Griffith's shorts resemble the "good darkies" of *The Birth of a Nation*.

By 1912, these one and two-reel films were beginning to cramp Griffith's creativity. He searched for a subject that would lend itself to a spectacular use of his talents and put him ahead of his European rivals who by this time were making elaborate and expensive multi-reel films. He eventually found his subject in two novels, *The Leopard's Spots*, published in 1902, and *The Clansman*, number four on the best seller list for 1905. Their author, the Reverend Thomas

Dixon, an unreconstructed Southerner, had left his North Carolina Baptist pulpit to write novels aimed at "building anti-Negro, pro-Southern sentiment in the North."[4] One of the ways Dixon achieves his purpose is to seldom mention the word "Negro" without preceding it with the adjective "drunken." Both novels overflow with descriptions of inebriated blacks bringing ruin to the South and its women during Reconstruction. Yet Dixon does not restrict his opprobrium to the freedman alone. Whites who associate with blacks in any way are equally reprehensible. *The Leopard's Spots* features a white villain, Allan McLeod, whose father was a drunkard and is himself a secret operator of a still, a corrupter of youth, and a drunk. In alliance with Negroes, he tries to thwart the full restoration of white supremacy in the South and fails. In this book, Dixon also restores to life the infamous Simon Legree who has quit drink and "set his mind on greater vices." Legree, whose ferocity and cruelty "that years of dissolute habits had fixed" know no bounds, promises the Negroes the vote and urges them to sit under the trees like gentlemen and have their former masters toil in the fields in their stead.[5]

A noble Carolinian, Reverend John Durham worries incessantly about America: "Can you build in a Democracy, a nation of two hostile races?" "Shall the future American be an Anglo-Saxon or a Mulatto?" On his way home one evening his path is crossed by a drunken, burly Negro who calls him a rebel and tells him to get off the road:

> It was his first experience with Negro insolence since the emancipation of his slaves. Quick as a flash, his right arm was raised. But he took a second thought, stepped aside, and allowed the drunken fool to pass. He went home wondering in a hazy sort of way through his excited passions what the end of all would be. Gradually in his mind for days this towering figure of the freed Negro had been growing more and more ominous, until its menace overshadowed the poverty, the hunger, the sorrow and the devastation of the South, throwing the blight of its shadow over future generations, a veritable Black Death for the land and its people. (p. 33)

Before the Invisible Empire of White Robed Anglo-Saxon Knights rises spontaneously to "bring order out of chaos," the author recounts the disenfranchisement of the whites and the enfranchisement of Negroes who carry jugs of whiskey to the polls. "Ignorance and vice" elect over a hundred and ten Negro representatives to ten whites. The new black members are housed in a boarding house: "The room was furnished with six iron cots on which were placed straw mattresses, and six honourable members of the new legislature occupied these. They were close enough together to allow a bottle of whiskey to be freely passed from member to member at any hour of the night. They thought the beds were arranged with this in view and they were much pleased" (p. 110). Under the leadership of Legree, the new legislature steals from every branch of the government, bankrupts the state, triples its debt, and at last ends its session with an all-night drunken revel.

> An appropriation of three hundred thousand dollars was made for "supplies, sundries, and incidentals." With this they built a booth around the statue of Washington at the end of the Capitol and established a bar with fine liquors and cigars for the free use of the members and their friends. They kept it open every day and night during their reign, and in a suite of rooms in the Capitol they established a brothel. From the galleries a swarm of courtesans daily smiled on their favourites on the floor. (p. 117)

*The Leopard's Spots* takes place in the foothills of North Carolina between 1865 and 1900. *The Clansman* is set in Washington before and after Lincoln's assassination and then moves back to the foothills for two years until the rise of the Klan puts an end to the South's desperate hour.[6] Dixon makes frequent references to Negroes' odors—"African perspiration, onion-laden breath, stale whiskey, the reek of vile cigars"—these have "become the symbol of American Democracy" (pp. 155, 263). Before the Civil War an aristocracy of "brains, culture, and blood" ruled the national capital. Now "gangs of drunken negroes, its sovereign citizens, paraded the streets at night firing their muskets, unchallenged and unmolested" (p. 155). Bowlegged Uncle Aleck, an illiterate freedman, organizes the Union League and drinks whiskey bought with League dues. He wears a shoulder-strap laden with six canteens of whiskey. While performing his duties as an election judge, he frequently pauses to slake his thirst.

The madly vengeful partisan Republican leader Austin Stoneman spends his evening at a plush Faro Palace on Pennsylvania Avenue, gambling and drinking champagne in an atmosphere of king's ransom luxury while the "wounded people of the South lay helpless amid rags and ashes under the beak and talon of the Vultures." Stoneman sends black troops to a Southern hotel to be served "as an example to the people of the state." Two Negro troopers, fighting drunk, walk into the hotel and drink ostentatiously at the water cooler, "thrusting their thick lips coated with filth far into the cocoanut dipper." One of them flops down beside a Southern lady, throws his arm around her chair, thrusts his face into hers, and says with a laugh: "Don't hurry, my beauty; stay and take dinner wid us" (pp. 355–56). She screams, as Phil (Stoneman's son who puts his Aryan blood ahead of his father's radical politics) rushes into the room with drawn revolver. He manages to kill one of the Negroes; the other escapes through the open window. Phil is urged to leave town: two hundred Negroes, armed and drunk, are on the rampage. He is arrested and sentenced to be shot and is saved only by the timely intervention of the Klan, "risen from the field of Death" (Preface).

Griffith fused Reverend Dixon's novels into one scenario under the provocative last minute title *The Birth of a Nation*.[7] One of the most controversial and profitable films ever made, it further intensified the image of the ignorant, besotted, lustful black man already so abundant on the printed page.

Griffith took unusual pains with the picture. Every device he had developed in his Biograph years was used to create excitement and tension enhanced by the hyperbolic subtitles. On opening, the film was immediately greeted by protests from the NAACP and its white supporters, followed by picketing, riots, and lawsuits; it was banned in Ohio until 1917. Millions of people swarmed to see it—in many cases to find out what the hullaballoo was about.[8] As a result of *The Birth of a Nation*, motion picture theaters began to advertise in newspapers and newspapers began to review films regularly. More than any picture before it, it made moviegoing a middle-class activity. Soon movie palaces were built in fashionable neighborhoods all over the United States complete with thick carpeting, plush upholstery, bas relief on the walls and ceilings, vast lobbies, oil paintings, improved sanitary facilities, and crystal chandeliers—a far cry from the smelly storefronts of the cinema's early years. These new temples of silent drama even surpassed the legitimate theaters in plush ostentation.[9] The financial success of *The Birth of a Nation* provided the impetus for the change.

This literally fantastic, pseudo-factual film is in two parts. The first part depicts the romantic, carefree antebellum South with its mythically happy, devoted and sober slaves. Then the impact of the Civil War is shown on a Northern family, the Stonemans, and a Southern family, the Camerons. The second, more inflammatory part concerns Reconstruction. In this melodramatic glorification of the Ku Klux Klan, which "saved the South from the anarchy of the black rule," Griffith not only showed former Civil War enemies uniting in a "Holy War to protect their Aryan birthright"; he also made a strong pitch for prohibition.[10] He portrays the newly-freed black as arrogant, insolent, lecherous and drunk. Negro representatives are pictured in the South Carolina Legislature eating peanuts and taking swigs of liquor from a bottle of whiskey concealed under a book. They then remove their shoes and ogle white women in the gallery. Instead of dutifully working in the cotton fields, former slaves spend their time carousing in saloons and demanding equal rights, equal politics, and equal marriage. The villainous and wicked mulatto Silas Lynch, who is the personal protégé of Representative Austin Stoneman (the Thaddeus Stevens character), becomes the Lieutenant Governor of South Carolina after the whites are disenfranchised. He is shown in several scenes drinking champagne boisterously with his tawny courtesans. The subtitle calls him "The Social Lion of the New Aristocracy." He drinks wine in his office as he plans to send a search party to the Cameron house to look for KKK outfits. Later "drunk with power and wine" he tells Elsie Stoneman "See! My people fill the streets. With them I will build a black empire and you as a queen shall sit by my side," in his attempt to seduce her into a "forced marriage."

The "renegade" Gus, the Cameron's former servant, becomes a militia man. He causes the little colonel's younger sister, Flora Cameron, to hurl herself off a cliff in terror of his lustful pursuit. ("For her," reads the subtitle, "who had learned the stern lesson of honor, we should not grieve that she found sweeter the opal gates of death.") Gus hides out in "White-arm Joe's gin mill"—a black saloon. Klansmen come searching for Gus "that he might be given a fair trial in the dim halls of the Invisible Empire." Gus is seen at first hiding under a table, near some beer barrels. Later, he joins in a free-for-all with whiskey bottles as weapons. One man is thrown out of the window and several flee; a chair is broken on the bar. Shooting starts and Gus kills the local blacksmith (head of the search party) and almost succeeds in escaping from the saloon. After his trial (not shown), his body, face up and open mouthed, is dumped on Lynch's porch. A paper pinned to him bearing a skull and the letters KKK indicates the responsibility for his murder. In contradistinction to Gus, the "good" Negroes inspired by Uncle Tom, shown first as slaves and later as servants to the Camerons, are portrayed as sober, industrious, cheerful and devoted.

Griffith's message in *The Birth of a Nation* was unmistakable: Blacks should be kept in their place and should know their place. When they have access to liquor, they give themselves airs, seize political control, prey on white women. When they have access to liquor, they stop working and go on rampages. Drink inflames their bestial sexuality and criminality, and threatens the hallowed Southern social order.[11] The passage of a national prohibition amendment, Griffith implies, is necessary to quell racial unrest and its attendant evil, miscegenation.[12] Moreover, Prohibition will help the black man to help himself. Enforced total abstinence will bring back the contentment, happiness and industry so prevalent among Negroes in the good old antebellum days.[13] The powerful, indelible screen images in *The Birth of a Nation* helped pave the way for the Eighteenth Amendment.

## NOTES

[1]Lewis Jacobs, *The Rise of the American Film: A Critical History* (New York: Harcourt, Brace, 1939), pp. 12, 21, 77.

[2]For a study of Griffith's work at Biograph, see Robert M. Henderson, *D. W. Griffith: The Years at Biograph* (New York: Farrar, Straus and Giroux, 1970) and Kemp R. Niver, *D. W. Griffith: His Biograph Films in Perspective* (Los Angeles: Roche, 1974).

[3]Jay Leyda, "The Art and Death of D. W. Griffith," from the *Sewanee Review*, 57 (1949), rpt. in *Focus on D. W. Griffith*, ed. Harry M. Geduld (Englewood Cliffs, N.J.: Prentice-Hall, 1971), p. 166. See also Henderson, p. 172.

[4]Dixon is quoted by Arthur S. Link, *Wilson: The New Freedom* (Princeton: Princeton Univ. Press, 1956), p. 252.

[5]Thomas Dixon, Jr., *The Leopard's Spots, A Romance of the White Man's Burden— 1865–1900* (1902; rpt. Ridgewood, N. J.: Gregg Press, 1967), pp. 86–87.

[6]Thomas Dixon, Jr., *The Clansman, An Historical Romance of the Ku Klux Klan* (1905; rpt. Ridgewood, N. J.: Gregg Press, 1967). Page numbers appear in the text, Preface unpaged.

[7]The film opened originally on February 8, 1915 under the title *The Clansman*, but changed to *The Birth of a Nation* just prior to its New York opening.

[8]See Roy E. Aitken, *"The Birth of a Nation" Story* (Middleburg, Va.: Denlinger, 1965), pp. 56–67 and Jacobs, p. 168.

[9]Benjamin Hampton,*A History of the Movies* (1931; rpt. New York: Arno, 1970), pp. 137–38.

[10]The quotations are from the film's subtitles here and below.

[11]Even Booker T. Washington in a letter to the Board of Temperance in 1914 observed that "strong drink is one of the chief causes of Negro crime in the South." His home county of Macon, Alabama, where blacks outnumber whites more than five to one is dry: the sheriff and his single deputy do not have enough work to keep them busy; *Cyclopedia of Temperance, Prohibition and Public Morals*, ed. Deets Pickett (New York and Cincinnati: Methodist Book Concern, 1917 ed.), p. 292.

[12]Although a number of Southern states had passed prohibition statutes by 1915 and 1916, the Drys regarded a national law as a necessity to protect the Negroes from the "energetic exploitation of wholesale liquor dealers of Cincinnati, Louisville, and Jacksonville" who shipped booze into dry states, Pickett, pp. 291–93.

[13]The *Cyclopedia* comments that in counties where prohibition is law those Negroes "who formerly raised a hound dog and a whiskey habit are now raising a family of pigs and a new appetite for industry," Pickett, p. 293.

# *Jezebel* and the Emergence of the Hollywood Tradition of a Decadent South

IDA JETER

David O. Selznick was still searching for the right Scarlett O'Hara in March 1938, when Warner Brothers' drama of the old South, *Jezebel*, premiered at Radio City Music Hall. Advance publicity portrayed the film as a Warner Brothers *Gone with the Wind*. The trailer declared: "From the picturesque glamour of the old south a great actress draws the scarlet portrait of a gorgeous spitfire who lived by the wild desire of her untamed heart. . . . The story of a woman who was loved when she should have been whipped. . . . Jezebel. Pride of the south that loved her. Shame of the man she loved."[1]

This promotion invites the audience to draw upon a popular system of representations (images, symbols, myths, narratives) that convey meanings about the South. The image of the South from which Warner Brothers drew its picturesque glamour constituted a familiar set of motion picture conventions in the 1930s. Its iconography includes mint juleps, stately mansions with white columned porticos, landscaped lawns and gardens, and fields of cotton in which contented darkies labor. This environment connotes an agrarian economy and patrician way of life. Additional associations are the cavalier and belle, genteel customs, the code of chivalry, leisure, hospitality, and faithful slaves. Occasionally this culture is violent, the code duello dictating the means by which one's honor is protected. Especially in the 1930s, the Southern belles were, to varying degrees, constrained by social conventions.

Between 1929, the Wall Street crash and roughly the inauguration of sound film, and 1941, the beginning of World War II, the Hollywood motion picture industry exhibited approximately 75 feature-length fiction films about the South.[2] These films presented a great diversity

31

of periods, locales, subject matters, and treatments. Nevertheless, as Peter Soderberg observes, nostalgic films about a grand old South or genteel Southern customs prevailed.[3]

These dominant representations of the old South of 1930s Hollywood films subsumed two themes. The first portrayed the North as commercial and egalitarian and the South as agrarian and aristocratic. Positive and negative connotations clustered around both representations; however, the national preference tended toward the more genteel, less materialistic South. The Yankee was mercenary and competitive. The popular conception of the Civil War emerged from the divided cultures thesis. The capitalist, industrializing North defeated the brave and noble South. A reconciliation between North and South could be forged, however, in a shared national sympathy and respect for the humiliated region and white supremacy. Such a reconciliation was frequently achieved through the narrative device of a romance or marriage between a Northerner and Southerner or a friendship cemented between previous foes. Some 1930s films which utilized this device tended to depoliticize the war and minimize its effects on both sides. Yet, the tendency to tilt the scales toward the South became increasingly apparent toward the end of the decade when films such as *Gone with the Wind*—inspired by the astonishing success of the novel—offered the Southern experience of war and Reconstruction: devastation, social upheaval, gallantry and courage. Indeed, the South's defeat in war and humiliation in the ill-conceived, if not corrupt, Reconstruction were generally offered as the primary reason for the South's continuing economic and social decline. The nostalgia for this dead culture frequently bore a bitter critique of modern mass society.[4]

Gradually, however, a new view of the South emerged and tended to eclipse all the other conventions. After World War II, Hollywood's Gothic portrait of decadence and depravity in the South, old and new, became a tradition that developed into a still flourishing genre. This paper proposes that *Jezebel* is part of a transition from the nostalgic romanticized renditions of the old South to the Gothic genre and examines the film's complex relationship to this emerging Hollywood convention.

## The Decadent South

The decadent South as an established convention in literature and theater appeared in the late 1920s. The quintessential element in this drama is decay, described by Richard A. Palmer as

> the one inescapable force with which every Southerner must contend. . . . It is both an external dramatic event and an integral aspect of the aristocrat's personality. . . . It is, in short, any event which upsets the delicate world of the aristocrat, which demands that he take steps to repair the crumbling foundation of his archaic society, steps inhibited by his own internal decay. The drama of the decadent south shows, therefore, the struggle of the aristocrat to overcome the breakdown of his society by mastering the weakness he has inherited by his membership in that same society.[5]

In the dramas of the decadent South represented by Lillian Hellman and Tennessee Williams, the new order which wrests control from the gentry is composed of an avaricious middle class. Miscegenation, incest, and sexual perversion may be associated with the decline of the aristocrat. Gothic motifs and themes of degeneracy connected with Faulkner, Caldwell, and later Tennessee Williams found the basis for the post-World War II motion picture representations of the South.

The films about a decadent South are extremely diverse in the 1930s. The industry had not yet established the conventions for the decadent motif. Of course, some subjects were unacceptable for adaptation in this mass medium. Although some 1930s films which are part of the Gothic genre still draw upon the divided cultures thesis that the industrial North defeated the agrarian South, the region's problems also tend to be internal to the social structure and imbedded in Southern character and attitudes. Many of the films tend to be positive in their assessment of the possibility for regeneration of the Southerner.

The two films, *The Story of Temple Drake* (Paramount, 1933) and *Carolina* (Fox Film Corp., 1934), which preceded *Jezebel* constitute perversions of their original sources, Faulkner's *Sanctuary* and Paul Green's play *The House of Connelly.* A brief explanation of a few of the changes in the adaptations will define some of the conventions which *Jezebel* manipulates.

In *The Story of Temple Drake* Temple goes to Memphis with the Popeye figure, who is not impotent, and stays with him not so much out of fear as attraction. The attorney who loves Temple finds her to ask her to testify in a murder trial. Moved by love, she protects him from the gangster. Later, he persuades her to testify by encouraging her to live up to the Drake family name and draw upon her pride in its honorable traditions. Temple admits her transgressions. She is redeemed by confessing her sins and is restored to a legitimate family tradition.

Both *Carolina* and *The House of Connelly* are about poor aristocrats who concentrate so upon their past glories that they cannot cope with their present conditions. The only way Mrs. Connelly sees out of their quandary is for her son, Will, to marry a wealthy woman. But Will chooses the daughter of a Pennsylvania tenant farmer, Patsy Tate in the play and Joanna in the film. Here the similarities between the film and play end.

The play is Faulknerian. Profligate Will confronts the family with its history of "rottenness, injustice," and miscegenation. He believes that "All the Connellys have doomed us to die. Our character's gone. We're paying for their sins." Mrs. Connelly restores the family strength when she explains that Will's father "had a hard struggle, over himself, and the world around him. He failed, struggled again, his face set upward—on—no whining—no tears—of weakness."[6] Uncle Bob, accused of miscegenation, encourages Will to marry Patsy and commits suicide. Will's mother collapses and dies. His two sisters, the remaining representatives of the archaic values and pride, are unable to accept his marriage and leave. Will is free to expel the ghosts of the past and with Patsy, a vigorous hard worker, can embark on a new life.

In the motion picture adaptation Joanna offers the Connellys regeneration. The family does not bear a legacy of guilt. Miscegenation is, of course, not mentioned. The only legacy is the Civil War. The Connelly's current condition of poverty, in part, emerges from that conflict and the South's defeat. They were doomed by historical forces, which will, in turn, generate their renewal through Joanna. The Connellys are decadent because they lack the personal and economic means to rebuild their estate and their lives. According to the film's foreword, they "live in the past, resent the present, and fear the future."

The rottenness in the house of Connelly is Mrs. Connelly—a matriarch who controls the lives of her relatives and opposes Will's relationship with Joanna. Uncle Bob commits suicide not because he can no longer confront his own past but because he learns the truth about how he lost the woman he loved during the Civil War. She was a governess in the Connelly's household. His sister-in-law told her Bob had been killed, and she went away. Mrs. Connelly admits her mistake in opposing Will's marriage to Joanna.

Played by Janet Gaynor, Joanna is spunky, simple, sweet—not the ambitious, assertive Patsy. Joanna actually belongs to the South. She respects the Connelly history and traditions. And, she is the granddaughter of Uncle Bob's old love. She brings to the humiliated Southern clan the vitality and astute farming and business sense it lacks. She also fulfills a historical mission by taking her grandmother's rightful place in the house of Connelly. Joanna suggests that the Connellys and their tenants raise tobacco and manufacture cigarettes because more people, including women, are smoking. The film ends a few years after the marriage, with the plantation on a sound footing agriculturally and industrially, the house restored to its previous grandeur and Mrs. Connelly reconciled with her son and daughter-in-law and enjoying her grandchildren.

The Connellys' problem is history combined with their inability to embrace a new order. Joanna, the Northerner who identifies with the South, provides the resources they need for renewal. The regeneration permits the perpetuation of the entire Connelly tradition. The break with the past comes with Mrs. Connelly's admitting her mistakes. It is not a break with the decay and degeneracy that pervade the aristocratic system depicted in the play.

*Jezebel* inherits the theme of redemption, but its assessment of the possibility for the regeneration of the aristocratic culture is much more despairing. Two films which were released after *Jezebel* also limit the probability for renewal.

While Joanna's new order is not that different from the Connelly tradition, the Hubbards of *The Little Foxes* (Sam Goldwyn, RKO,

1941), also starring Bette Davis and directed by William Wyler, represent an order antithetical to the values of the old South. They represent a rapacious middle class. Birdie Hubbard is a pathetic aristocrat frightened of the family into which she married and dependent upon it for survival. Horace Giddens, not an aristocrat by birth but one by demeanor and perspective, opposes the investment in the proposed cotton mill. He will not support his wife and her brothers in their quest for profits—they will wreck the town and live off the wreckage. Of course, the Hubbards prevail. The film, unlike the play, offers some hope for a future South when Alexandra Giddens flees the house and all it stands for with her suitor.

*Tobacco Road* (Twentieth Century-Fox, 1941) is a rather whimsical look at the slightly libidinous, shiftless, ignorant Lester menagerie. The history of Jeeter Lester's family is conveyed in nostalgic terms in the opening sequence. Over the image of a Tara-like house, now dilapidated and inhabited by shoeless undernourished tenants, Jeeter's voice explains:

> This is Tobacco Road today. But a hundred years ago, when the first Lesters come to Georgia, it was different. It run fifteen miles down the ridge to the Savannah River, through the richest cotton and tobacco plantations in the whole south, past big fine homes that the Lesters themselves built and lived in. But that was a hundred years ago. Come a time then when the land fell fallow, and worse and worse—but you think the Lesters would leave it? No! They stayed on, but all that they had and all that they were . . . that's all gone with the wind and the dust. And this is Tobacco Road today.

The Lesters lost their land to Captain John Harmon, whose son, in turn, lost it to the bank, which wants to convert it to scientific farming. The plot centers around Jeeter's efforts to raise enough money to pay rent to the bank and obtain seed and manure. His attachment to the land, however, is subordinate to his lassitude. When Captain John's son, Dr. Tim, fortuitously provides enough money for six months rent and the stake, Jeeter, who is lazy from unproductivity, talks about his great plans while putting the work off until next week. The dignity and strength associated with the old planters and, in some reconciliation films, with their descendents are absent in *Tobacco Road.* Nor does the film allow for change or regeneration. The crackers themselves are simply too indolent.

Films about the South in the 1930s offered multiple perspectives on that region; however, the grand old South remained the dominant image. The emerging decadent South tended to undermine this image. *Jezebel* bears the mark of these conflicting representations.

## Jezebel

Billed in a promotional trailer as an "impassioned romance torn from the Heart of Dixie," *Jezebel* is not just a resurrection of the legend of the old South. Nor is it merely the tale of a gorgeous spitfire. It is a hybrid, one of the earlier representatives of the Gothic films about a decadent South which dominated the post-World War II movie-making era. The following analysis concerns three dichotomies: the North/South; the progressive Southerner/backward Southerner; and the good woman/bad woman. I will look first at the images attached to the first two opposing pairs and then examine their narrative development and intersection with the third.

As in most films about the South, the North/South opposition is embedded in the setting. *Jezebel* takes place in the New Orleans of 1852 and 1853. About the gentry of the old South, the film conveys its manners and lifestyle. *Jezebel* also renders explicit what is frequently implicit in 1930s films—cultural differences between the North and the South.

At Julie's afternoon party Mrs. Kendrick fusses over her daughter Stephanie, constantly correcting her manners and deportment. When Stephanie objects that ladies do not curtsy anymore, Mrs. Kendrick admonishes her: "They do in New Orleans. You've no call to take up Yankee manners." Southerners are well-mannered, excessively polite, and charming. Their conventions are established in the early sequences of the film. Men do not mention a lady's name in a bar. While such an offense is cause for a duel, a lady should never be implicated in a duel. Ladies drink sherry while men consume toddies and juleps. Julie Marsden defies a code which defines proper dress for ladies when she arrives late to her own party and greets her guests wearing a riding habit. She insists on wearing a red dress to the Olympus Ball, where all unmarried girls wear white. Julie opposes conventions which dictate that ladies not enter banks or other places of finance, that they behave like children and pretend not to know

William Wyler (right of camera) directs Henry Fonda
and Bette Davis (in daring red dress) in the famous
ballroom sequence from *Jezebel*.

about such things as duels and Marie Vickers and Galatin Street (New
Orleans' red light district), both referred to obliquely but with meaning.

The Southern codes against which Julie rebels may seem silly to us,
but most Southerners in *Jezebel* accept them. Buck Cantrell thinks
Northern ways are bizarre. He tells Julie they eat horsefeed beans
there and finds it difficult to believe that Amy, Pres's Northern bride
knows nothing about horses and racing.

New Orleans is a beautiful city and Julie's plantation, Halcyon,
offers the typical image—the white columned house with large,

lavishly appointed rooms. Halcyon means calm, peaceful, happy, prosperous. The visual imagery of the South is not one of decay or malignancy. Nevertheless, this environment conveys an alternative set of meanings, which emerge as a contradiction in the genteel southern culture. It is violent. When Julie endeavors to persuade the recently-married Pres that he belongs to the South and to her, she describes an exotic, yet untamed, world.

> Can you hear them? The night noises? The mocking bird and the magnolia. See the moss hanging from the moonlight. You can fairly taste the night can't you? You're part of it Pres, and it's part of you. Like I am. You can't get away from us. We're both in your blood. This is the country you were born to Pres. The country you know and trust. Amy wouldn't understand. She'd think there'd be snakes. Oh, it isn't tame and easy like the north. It's quick and dangerous! But you trust it. Remember how the fever mist smells in the bottoms—rank and rotten? But you trust that, too. Because it's part of you, Pres, just as I'm part of you.

This is a world beyond the control of civilization. Amy understands this when she tells Belle the South is "strange and beautiful and a little frightening. . . . Because of its strangeness and its beauty, I suppose." Julie represents the impulsive, extravagant aspects of a Southern personality bred in an unpredictable, hazardous environment. The inhabitants of Louisiana, for all their grace and charm, are tainted by violence. The state sanctions the murder of fever victims who attempt to escape beyond the fever boundary. And duels, no matter how formalized in ritual, are evidence of a violent lifestyle. Every Southerner in the film seems to accept them. Julie and Pres exploit the threat of duels to achieve their own ends. Duels are an essential part of the narrative—although they are unseen or avoided. The exception, for which we see only the preparation, is when Ted Dillard kills his best friend Buck Cantrell.

Perhaps the most significant contradiction in the myth of the South is the ambiguity centering around leisure and pleasure associated with the agrarian, patrician life. Such affluence can breed indolence and self-indulgence. Much of *Jezebel*'s narrative centers around parties, balls, and preparations for entertaining. The ruling elite drinks and socializes at the St. Louis Hotel, where they apparently discuss two subjects—hunting and horses, their breeding and racing. Only two people associated with the elite work—Preston Dillard, the banker, and Dr. Livingston. In fact, the productive base upon which the gentry lives and which provides its wealth is never shown. *Jezebel* lacks the usual images which many films associate with the plantation—"lovely" shots of slaves working in the fields. Halcyon's field slaves sing for Julie and her guests, but they are never connected with the work of maintaining the plantation.

Preston Dillard, like Julie Marsden, is a maverick—he is a banker. While his peers attend afternoon parties he works at Dillard and Sons Bank, which has international connections with branches in New York, Boston, London, and Paris. As Pres endeavors to persuade the board of directors to finance the Nashville-Pacific railroad with figures on declining river freight and arguments that the Northern cities are redirecting trade to the Northwest, we are introduced to the city's ruling elite. One doodles. Another sleeps through part of the discussion. A third drinks too much and offers absurd reasons for not supporting the railroad: gentlemen with carriages do not need to travel by train and trains scare his horses. The fourth, the one who at least addresses the question of trade, naively assumes the Mississippi River will continue to dominate commerce and closes his mind to the facts. The drinker objects that trains are unhealthy. Dr. Livingston, Pres's ally, warns the board that unless the civic leaders clean up the city New Orleans will suffer through another yellow fever epidemic like the one in the 1830s. The structure of this scene connects commercial expansion and improved sanitation and health care programs.

This sequence establishes a significant characteristic of the aristocrat implicit in some antebellum representations about the plantation South and developed later in representations about a decadent South. This gentry class cannot adapt to change. They assume their world will remain as it is, yet that world is stagnant. It becomes apparent in this sequence that the South itself is divided between forces of expansion, commerce, and progressive reform and the traditional interests which protect the status quo.

Preston Dillard and Dr. Livingston are the two characters who represent vitality and progressive ideas. Their status as members of the landed gentry is ambiguous, but they are not a rising middle class. We assume Pres is a member of the upper class. Dr. Livingston is not included in their social events but is on intimate terms with Aunt

Belle. Even though they are progressive, they still subscribe to the codes of their region. Dr. Livingston perceives "woman as . . . a frail, delicate chalice to be cherished and protected." He and Pres both accept duels. And, Pres believes Julie must wear white to the Olympus Ball.

What at first appears to be arrogance and extreme provincialism proves to have disastrous consequences as New Orleans begins to deal with yellow fever. It confronts disease with fires and cannons that are intended to blow the fever away. It does not clear the swamps or clean the city streets as Pres and Dr. Livingston propose. The city is like an armed camp. Fever victims are banished to a leper colony. Those who attempt escape are shot.

The dinner conversation at Halcyon places the South's backwardness in an even larger context—that of impending crisis with the North. While General Bogardus cannot believe that the North is prepared to deny the South its sovereign rights, Buck Cantrell is prepared to hang abolitionists as traitors. Preston, however loyal to the South, believes "the tide has turned against" them. He reluctantly admits that "in a war of commerce the North must win. . . . It'll be the victory of machines over unskilled slave labor." Slavery's morality is not questioned. Pres only discredits an economic system based on slavery.

*Jezebel* does not reject completely the old South myth. This world, although violent, is beautiful. Many of the people represent the charm and grace Rhett Butler sought. Aunt Belle and General Bogardus are attractive and gracious. Mrs. Kendrick and the bank board of directors are slightly ridiculous in their smug provincialism, but they are never malicious or deliberately perverse. Buck Cantrell's manner and deportment are engaging. Nor are the Northerners mercenary and graceless. Amy is pleasant. Pres, who identifies with Northern commercial interests, agrees with many of the South's codes. *Jezebel* seems to show something between a sentimentalized version of the old South and a fictionalized account of the internal divisions and external forces which contribute to its decline. The narrative structure, however, proposes a different drama when it integrates the two dichotomies, North/South and progressive South/backward South, with a third, good woman/bad woman. Conventions of 1930s drama required that bad women be punished or redeemed. Hence, the resolution of this third conflict has remarkable impact on the image of the South and the other two oppositions.

Initially the South and its customs provide the setting for a drama about two lovers. The South is contrasted to the North principally on the basis of manner and codes to establish it as a distinct culture. So far, no criticism of the South is implicit in such contrasts. The bank board meeting introduced the progressive influences in Louisiana which illuminate economic differences between the North and the South.

Julie originally violates the Southern codes of proper behavior, exploits those codes when it suits her, and seeks to control the relationship with Pres (while, also, desiring his mastery over her). As we may find these codes anachronistic but quaint, her rebellion is not serious—that is, until Pres introduces Amy.

Julie resolves to get Pres back and manipulates Buck Cantrell into being her ally. At dinner the guests discuss the possibility of war while Julie flirts with Buck, makes "knowing" comments to Pres about traitors and old memories, and attempts to sow dissension between the two men over the sectional issues. The North/South opposition is foregrounded and, in conjunction with the progressive Southerner/backward Southerner contrast, incorporated into the personal conflict.

After dinner Julie tries to persuade Pres that he belongs to her and describes the South as "quick and dangerous." Julie, as the product of this environment, represents this view of the South, which increasingly supersedes the alternative views suggested by more agreeable characters as the narrative progresses.

When the guests hear the fever cannons, Buck and Pres snipe at each other over the effectiveness of measures taken to control the epidemic and whether the South could learn other things from the North. Once Pres leaves, the rivalry between Amy and Julie is placed at the center of dramatic action. Amy respects Pres's devotion to the bank and his work. Julie resents it—other things are more important, presumably leisure and pleasure. Buck objects to bankers in general: "They're always trying to get something from someone." Ted, offended at a slur against his brother, challenges Buck to a duel.

Pres and Buck have, during the Halcyon sequences, represented the North/South and progressive/backward oppositions. With Pres's departure and Buck's death these two dichotomies are subsumed in the Amy/Julie conflict, which acquires a moral and spiritual dimension.

Julie has attempted to transgress the more universal moral and religious codes of society which sanctify marriage and the family. And she has caused a man's death. It is no longer a matter of two women, one a Northerner, the other a Southerner, wanting the same man and having opposing views on duty and customs. Although there is still the sectional opposition, Amy now represents virtue, courage, and goodness. Julie is wicked—a sinner.

The denouement of the narrative shifts to Julie's need for expiation. While singing with her slaves, Julie tells Aunt Belle she is wearing white because she is being baptized. After her guests desert her, Aunt Belle tells her she is Jezebel—a woman who sinned in the sight of God.

When Julie confronts Amy in the end to beg for the right to go with Pres to Lazarette Island, she is seeking redemption. The dominance of Amy over Julie in the framing of shots as they talk on the stairs connotes Amy's moral superiority as well as her rights as Pres's wife. Once granted the opportunity to accompany Pres, Julie stands near the door framed in an arch and at a low angle and lit in such a way as to create a slight glow around her head. On the wagon with Pres, a nun sits near Julie, who looks peaceful.

What are we to make of this ending? Does Julie die so that Pres may live and return to his wife and work? What if, against incredible odds, both Julie and Pres live? Will they stay together or will he return to Amy? Frankly, we are not quite sure where Pres stands. Does he love Amy? Or, is he merely living up to his marital responsibilities when he rejects Julie. In the Owen Davis, Sr. play from which *Jezebel* is adapted, Pres admits his love for Julie and they go to Lazarette Island united. Julie does not go with him to atone for her sins. This, of course, could not happen in a 1930s Hollywood production. The Production Code of the Motion Picture Producers and Distributors of America prohibited such adulterous relationships. Hence, the shift from corporeal struggles to the spiritual level. But has the story really been sanitized by this gesture? Is Julie actually pretty cagey and the winner in the struggle for the possession of Pres?

Why does Amy let Julie go? Because Julie wants to be purged and become pure and clean? Because Amy learns that Pres loves his wife? Because Amy suspects that Pres loves Julie? Or, because Julie possesses superior skills in exploiting blacks and is a fighter who can survive in a violent environment? Pres and Julie, two Southerners, remain together not in a bond of love but because only Southerners can cope in their closed, brutal world.

The predominance of the personal over the political results in a lack of closure. Presumably Julie is redeemed. *Jezebel* suppresses the progressive/backward struggle and displaces the North/South opposition onto the good woman/bad woman dichotomy. In so doing, the film allows no avenue for the development of the first two conflicts. They become part of the context for the drama; but since they have been presented in specific terms and integrated with the third conflict, their resolution is implicated in the resolution of the spiritual struggle.

In most 1930s films North/South conflicts at the level of the personal were conventionally resolved through romance. *Jezebel*'s narrative thrust toward redemption deviates from this norm. The Northerner and Southerner are separated, and the two Southerners remain together, although the conditions of the alliance are bizarre. Even so, by 1938, the dominant reconciliation motif addressed the Southern experience of war or proposed the superiority of Southern customs. Such was compatible with the increase in the number of films which proposed the divided culture thesis. The integration of the three oppositions in such a way that the moral/spiritual good woman/bad woman dominates served to invert the popular conception of the divided cultures. If Julie represents the South, it is immoral and must atone for its sins. Redemption becomes the acceptance of the ways of Amy and the North—commerce, industry, progress on all fronts. Such an upheaval in perspectives and values is not even evident in films about the decadent South.

*Jezebel* appears to be a film about a decadent South in the sense that the aristocrat is ineffectual or backward, not forward looking. But the yellow fever epidemic in conjunction with the Amy/Julie struggle launches *Jezebel* in another direction—perhaps two. The yellow fever epidemic was a major issue around which the progressive Southerner/backward Southerner revolved. It is suppressed as an issue in order to become a narrative device which provides the context for Julie's expiation. Obviously, it is assumed that the progressives failed in bringing about improved health care. The Julie/South analogy implies that it is not ignorance or complacency which lead to the destruction of the system. It is an internal corruption—immorality (not yet degeneracy).

Like Temple Drake Julie seeks personal redemption. Unlike Will Connelly, Julie's regeneration is primarily spiritual. It has no impact on the suffering and death around her. Will's union with Joanna provides for the renewal of the Connelly family and, by extension, the South. The suppression of the progressive/backward contrast in *Jezebel* does not permit a regeneration of the Southern aristocratic system.

No film fits neatly into a genre or formula; nevertheless, *Jezebel*'s relationship to the conventional representations of Southern decadence is extremely complex. *Jezebel* bears the traces of the romanticized view of the old South as do most, if not all, representations which treat the aristocrat, even those which present him as degenerate. But *Jezebel*'s South of 1852 is doomed by its own inability to adapt—this before the inevitable sectional conflict which, according to the 1930s motion picture conventions, contributed to the decline of the aristocratic agrarian culture. The few 1930s films which looked at a decadent South shied away from implications of severe internal disorder in the aristocratic system. Because its narrative is organized around redemption, *Jezebel* foreshadows the 1950s representations which explore moral decay in the Southern aristocrat.

### NOTES

[1]A print of *Jezebel*, promotional trailers, and other resource materials relevant to this study are available at the Wisconsin Center for Film and Theater Research at the Wisconsin State Historical Society, Madison.

[2]The filmography was collected from, among other sources, Jack Temple Kirby, *Media-Made Dixie* (Baton Rouge: Louisiana State Univ. Press, 1978); Peter A. Soderberg, "Hollywood and the South, 1930–1960," *Mississippi Quarterly*, 19 (Winter 1965–66), and Paul C. Spehr, *et al.*, *The Civil War in Motion Pictures: A Bibliography of Films Produced in the United States Since 1897* (Washington: Library of Congress, 1961). "About the South" means that the setting is Southern and that this setting

connotes certain types of lifestyles, which in turn contribute to character and narrative structure. There were musicals and dramas featuring black performers and about black life, musical romances and melodramas set in the old South, and comedies and musicals about feuding hillbillies. Melodramas about the inhabitants of mountain or swamp regions of the South emphasized their simple customs and ties to nature in addition to their underdevelopment. These people could be violent, prone to feuds and vigilante actions.

[3]Soderberg, p. 3.

[4]Kirby offers some analysis of both the reconciliation and divided cultures themes. Charles and Mary Beard, *The Rise of American Civilization* (New York: Macmillan, 1930) and *I'll Take My Stand* (New York: Harper and Row, 1930) propose differing interpretations of the divided cultures concept. These generalizations about Hollywood films about the South in the 1930s are drawn primarily from the film texts and accounts of the films in trade journals.

[5]"The Aristocratic Motif in the Drama of Russia and the American South," *Southern Quarterly,* 17 (Fall 1978), 84.

[6]Paul Green, *House of Connelly* (New York: Samuel French, 1931), p. 102.

# Gone with the Wind:
## An American Tragedy

TRISHA CURRAN

Nearly forty years after its first release in 1939 to tremendous critical and popular acclaim, 350,000 members of the American Film Institute voted *Gone with the Wind* the "greatest American movie," ranking it far ahead of *African Queen, Casablanca, Citizen Kane, Grapes of Wrath, One Flew Over the Cuckoo's Nest, Singin' in the Rain, Star Wars, 2001: A Space Odyssey,* and *The Wizard of Oz,* in their "Ten Best" list of American movies. In *Gone with the Wind,* they could find the tragic faith in man of *Grapes of Wrath* and *Casablanca,* the epic quality and production values of *Star Wars* and *2001,* the technicolor magnificence of *Singin' in the Rain* and *The Wizard of Oz,* the technical virtuosity of *Citizen Kane,* and the intimacy and appeal of *African Queen* and *Cuckoo's Nest.* In none of the above could they find the sensational sex and violence so prevalent in popular American films. Indeed, *Gone with the Wind* is comparable to Renoir's *The Grand Illusion* in its depiction of the effects of war on individuals and society, without the obligatory battle scenes associated with war films. But then neither *Gone with the Wind* nor *The Grand Illusion* is a war film. They are people films, personalized reflections of 1930s pacifism, pleas pro pacem, movies to move men, not militias. They were made in the depths of the Depression, on the eve of World War II, "escapes into history"[1] for the economically depressed, the lonely, the war-torn of their own and of future eras. Both films have fared extremely well over the past forty-odd years since their release, helped no doubt by the growing anti-war sentiment that came with the Cold War and Korea and that climaxed with Viet Nam.

No one could ask for a better anti-war statement in a film than that made by Ashley Wilkes at the beginning of *Gone with the Wind* when

47

he tells his war-hungry friends that "most of the miseries of the world were caused by wars and when the wars were over, no one knew what they were about." Throughout the film we see the miseries caused by the Civil War insofar as they affect Scarlett O'Hara, one of the most unsympathetic heroines Hollywood has produced. Thus Scarlett's extreme egocentricity protects *Gone with the Wind* from becoming an anti-war tract, for Scarlett is concerned only with Scarlett. She views the dead and the dying with distance and disdain, and the camera conveys her distance and captures her disdain. The dead are filmed in long-shot, a mass of depersonalized bodies, obstacles that obstruct Scarlett's search for Dr. Meade and her trip to Tara. In a film of so many excesses, the camera's restraint is remarkable.

Also remarkable is the magnificent meshing of the visual and the verbal in the effectiveness of the verbatim literary dialogue, spoken with conviction and radiating believability within the nineteenth-century context of the film. The visual force of the images complements the verbal force of the dialogue; and the visual force of the images complements the verbal force of the explanatory text. The movement of the printed lines combines with the expressive movement of images behind the lines to describe the war that is not seen on the screen, but that causes the suffering that is seen.

Perhaps even more remarkable than the meshing of the visual and the verbal is the meshing of divergent directorial styles. *Gone with the Wind* is a perfect blend of George Cukor's attention to actresses and Victor Fleming's articulation of action. That Cukor was successful in articulating action and Fleming in directing actresses is evident in Cukor's direction of Scarlett's slapping Prissy and killing the Union soldier and Fleming's of Scarlett's realizing her love for Rhett and triumphing over impending despair. Although both Cukor and Fleming favor the unfolding of dramatic action within the flexible frame, Sam Wood's use of crosscutting for Scarlett and Rhett's narrow escape through the rows of burning box cars and exploding ammunition at the Atlanta station is a perfect illustration of the architectural axiom "form follows function," for the form of Wood's crosscutting follows the function of creating excitement in this sequence of the film.

The casting of Clark Gable, Vivien Leigh, Olivia de Havilland, and Leslie Howard likewise followed the function of creating believable screen characters for Margaret Mitchell's creations. So perfect is each of these stars in the respective roles that it is well nigh impossible to conceive of anyone else as the suave Rhett Butler, the spoiled Scarlett O'Hara, the motherly Melanie Hamilton or the wishy-washy Ashley Wilkes. Their acting is magnetic and their screen personages meticulously true to those of their literary counterparts.

In characterizing Melanie as Charles's older sister and Ashley as India's older brother, the film is also remarkably true to the charac-

Melanie (Olivia de Havilland), Ashley (Leslie Howard) and Scarlett (Vivien Leigh), symbols of the vanishing old South, at a happy moment.

teristics of both sibling positions.[2] Melanie, as befits the older sister of brothers, is maternal toward men—the wounded soldiers in the hospital, the hungry soldiers at Tara, Ashley and Rhett. She is optimistic regarding Ashley's safety throughout the war, independent in an unobtrusive way, particularly in relation to the rumors relating Scarlett and Ashley, and uncomfortable with solitude (hence her coming downstairs in her nightgown at Tara before she was well). And Ashley, as the older brother of a sister, is a ladies' rather than a man's man, hence his adoration by Melanie and Scarlett and his lack of stature with Rhett. He is a kind, considerate employer who will neither accommodate nor conspicuously oppose tyrannical superiors (as evidenced by his impotent objection to Scarlett's hiring prison labor in the mill), and a somewhat cavalier caretaker of his own property, evidenced in his inability to make much of a profit from the mill.

Contrary to her actual sibling position in the novel and the film, Scarlett is much more the female only child than the older sister of sisters. Like the stereotypical female only child, she is egotistical, extravagant, heartless, dependent upon her parents, and more interested in remaining a child herself than in caring for her own children. She is unlike an oldest sister who is typically more concerned with her younger sisters, her friends, and her children than with material wealth and prosperity, whose girlfriends are more important to her than her boyfriends, and whose straightforwardness and strictness discourage men from flirting with her. A far cry from this archetype is the Scarlett who steals her younger sister's fiancee in order to get his money and his lumber business, who has no girlfriends, and who flirts constantly. However, like the oldest sister of sisters, Scarlett naturally gives orders and takes charge—witness her restoration of Tara and her management of the mill. Moreover she is tough and enduring ("I'll live through this and when it is over, as God is my witness, I'll never be hungry again" and "I'll go home and I'll think of some way to get him back. After all, tomorrow is another day.") These lines provide the *raison d'etre* of her sibling position as oldest sister of sisters. They could never be as convincing coming from an only child. In the final analysis, Scarlett rings true. And she is still ringing true as the patron saint/bitch-goddess of various groups.

Unmoved by the suffering of her pyrrhic victory, "America first" isolationists have identified with Scarlett's me-first egocentricity, and environmentalists, closing their eyes to her lumber business, have championed her love of Tara. Unabashed by her bitchiness, her cruelness and her dishonesty, feminists praise Scarlett's strength in refusing to subjugate herself to society's expectations, her shrewdness in making her sex work for her, and her success as mover and doer rather than as wife and mother. But growing isolationism, environmentalism and feminism are irrelevant in a discussion of *Gone with the Wind* as "the great American movie." Irrelevant too is the consideration of *Wind* as the great movie event of Hollywood history, with the public's casting of Clark Gable, the fabled search for Scarlett O'Hara, the firing of George Cukor, the hiring of Victor Fleming, the all-time record for box office sales, the prodigious press coverage of each re-release, the blow up to 70mm., and the selling of the television rights—plentiful manifestations of *Wind's* popularity and possible reasons for its primacy in the minds of members of the American Film Institute, but they neither explain nor justify its filmic greatness.

Explanations of, and reasons for, filmic greatness must be statements about the film itself, about its form, for as Ortega has so rightly noted, "a work of art lives on its form, not on its material";[3] Susan Sontag adds, "ultimately the greatest source of emotional power in art lies not in any particular subject matter, however passionate, however universal. It lies in form."[4] *Gone with the Wind* is a powerful, passionate, emotion-packed film because its form is powerful, passionate, emotion-packed—in a word, organic. All its elements are interconnected and none can be changed without making changes throughout the film. They are interrelated and interdependent as the parts of the human body are interrelated and interdependent. Max Steiner's musical score, William Cameron Menzies' design, Jack Cosgrove's photographic effects, Sidney Howard's, Ben Hecht's, Victor Fleming's and David O. Selznick's script, George Cukor's, Victor Fleming's, Sam Wood's, William Wellman's and King Vidor's direction, and David O. Selznick's production are perfectly fused in this famous film. One would expect a hodgepodge of styles given the number of writers and directors; instead one finds a stylistic whole as one watches the story unfold on the screen in a succession of interrelated shots and scenes that effortlessly and elegantly flow into one another, propelled by

vertical forces that further the unfolding of the diegesis, and enriched
by spiral forces that further the unfolding of the emotions. *Gone with
the Wind* is a rich film because it is a rich fusion.

A magnificent spiral force, Max Steiner's musical score fully fuses
with the visuals in depicting the unfolding of feeling. A sprightly
"Dixie" over the opening titles and picturesque scenes of antebellum
plantation life sets the tone for Scarlett's talk of the picnic and party at
Twelve Oaks; and a mournful "Dixie" played by tearful musicians at
the Atlanta station amid cries, screams and sobs of bereaved readers of
the casualty lists underlines the mournful mood of the beseiged
South. An off-screen rendition of Taps mirrors the mis-en-scene of
maimed men lying on the ground at the same station several months
later—the wounded soldiers Scarlett steps over in her search for Dr.
Meade. As the camera pulls out to reveal a screen full of hundreds and
hundreds of dead and dying soldiers lying unattended on the ground
completely surrounding Scarlett, a single crescendo underlines the
depth of the destruction.

Crescendos also inflate to epic proportions Scarlett's excitement on
finding Tara still standing and running to tell her mother she is home;
her strength and determination as she picks herself up from her
prostrate position in the empty garden, raises her fist, and vows never
to be hungry again; her self-control in resolutely walking away from
Ashley after failing to seduce him; her fear, following Ashley's party, as
she and Rhett disappear into the dark at the top of the stairs before he
carries her in to bed; and finally, her self-confidence, strength and
determination as she sits up after Rhett has left her, looks straight at
the camera and says, "I'll go home and I'll think of some way to get
him back. . . ."

The music also mirrors the emotions and meshes with the visuals in
the unfolding of the diegesis. The tune from Bonnie's music box
segues into "London Bridge Is Falling Down" as the blues and beiges
of Bonnie's room become a beige Big Ben against a blue night sky,
music and color having affected the metamorphosis of Atlanta into
London. Likewise a dissolve on color effects the metamorphosis from
Mammy in violet dress and white kerchief at a white curtained window into the young black boys swinging on the ringing bell, silhouetted against white clouds in a violet sky. An important factor in the

narrative force of *Gone with the Wind* is the use of dissolves, with or without corresponding colors. The sheer force of the narrative is dependent on the force of the editing.

Color, dialogue and dissolves all function as directive elements in the metamorphoses of several key scenes involving Ashley's supposed seduction of Scarlett. From a scene of Bonnie (in blue dress with white trim) riding her pony and Mammy (in grey dress with white trim) telling Rhett that "it ain't fittin, it just ain't fittin," the camera dissolves to Ashley (in white shirt and neutral pants) and Scarlett (in white dress with blue jacket) at the lumberyard where they are caught in an innocent embrace, foreshadowed by Mammy's "it just ain't fittin." A second dissolve on white finds Scarlett at home wearing white undergarments and lying in her white bed. Although other colors are introduced in this scene, the cut to the following scene at Ashley's party is made from the white of Scarlett's undergarments to the white flames of the white candles on Ashley's white birthday cake. Mammy's "it just ain't fittin" is silently echoed in the absolute silence of the guests who stop singing in mid-line when they see Scarlett, dressed in scarlet, standing at the door, the color of her dress expressive of her image as a wanton woman.

The contrast in color between Scarlett's black dress and the pastels of the other women at the Atlanta ball expresses her nonconformity with them and prefigures her union with Rhett, his black tuxedo equally expressive of his nonconformity and equally conspicuous amid the grey and gold of the Confederate uniforms. The movement of the camera mirrors the movement of the dance and the ample close shots of Scarlett and Rhett convey their growing awareness of each other and unconcern with everyone else at the ball. In like manner, the panning camera in its connections of returning soldiers with wives and family within its fluid frame expresses the closeness of coming together, of reunion, that it is filming.

Similarly, the sense of confusion felt by people fleeing their homes in the face of a conquering army is marvelously mirrored in a montage of somewhat blurred close-ups of men and women running, screaming from their homes, grabbing their children, carrying their belongings, and pulling their wagons amid the rising dust of the dirt roads as they hurry into the night with little thought of where they are going.

When Rhett tells Scarlett on the road to Tara that he is going to join the army, the low angle shot (of him) conveys his sense of personal satisfaction with his decision as well as Scarlett's dependence upon him as defender and provider. Conversely, the high angle shot as he answers Scarlett's "Why?" with the simple, "Maybe it's because I'm ashamed of myself," conveys his shame.

Elements within the frame also function expressively. Light is used on several occasions to express Scarlett's optimism. During evening prayer at Tara a candle immediately behind Scarlett expresses her hope as she thinks aloud, "I'll tell him I love him and then he can't marry her." On leaving Atlanta during the war, she carries outside a candle to dramatize the optimism of her determination to reach Tara. Finally, the rainbow in the sky just before the travelers sight Twelve Oaks symbolizes her delight at going home. Once home, the darkness and the destruction of her world is conveyed by a view of the night sky through broken window panes behind her, as she learns from Pa that all they have left are worthless Confederate bonds. Likewise, Rhett's near despair as he awaits news of Scarlett's condition after her fall down the stairs is expressed by the bleak view of falling rain outside his open window.

Sound and camera movement combine with musical crescendos to propel the diegesis to its dramatic conclusion. After Rhett has left and Scarlett lies prostrate on the steps, in long-shot, the camera slowly moves in on her as she sits up and the off-screen voices of her father and Ashley get louder and more insistent—"land's the only thing that matters." ... "something you love more than me, Tara." "Tara." "Tara." The voices are loud, the music reaches a crescendo, the camera is close on Scarlett, now sitting upright, despair and depression banished, as she thinks aloud, "Home, I'll go home and I'll think of some way to get him back." Once again she has confidence in her own resources. The music reaches a louder and more triumphant crescendo and Scarlett looks straight at the camera, her face glowing, to speak her final line, "after all, tomorrow is another day." The music, dialogue and camera angle are all expressive of her hope, and direct our identification with her. She is looking straight at us and talking to herself. We have become Scarlett. The dissolve into the stylized shot of Scarlett in silhouette looking at the Tara of her childhood and the camera pull-out to extreme long-shot distance us from Scarlett and Tara, and direct us into our own world. The final crescendo is expressive of our renewed confidence in ourselves. "Tomorrow is another day" for us as well as for Scarlett. We have entered into her life, engaged in her selfishness, enjoyed her come-uppance, and can now continue to live our lives with her confidence. Such is the power of the vertical forces that propel the unfolding of the plot and of the spiral forces that propel the unfolding of the emotions. And such is the power of tragedy.

The popular focus on Rhett's farewell remark, "Frankly, my dear, I don't give a damn," rather than on Scarlett's "tomorrow is another day" has inclined many critics to consider *Gone with the Wind* pathos or melodrama. But it is neither. Pathos evokes sympathy and a sense of sorrow or pity. *Gone with the Wind* does not. We do not feel sorry for Scarlett. In fact, we delight in Rhett's "Frankly, my dear. . . ." Scarlett got what she deserved. In fact, she got off easy. Nor is *Gone with the Wind* melodrama, a drama with sensational, romantic, often violent action, extravagant emotions and generally a happy ending. There is no sensation, little romance, no violence, no extravagant emotions, save the tragic ones of Scarlett's triumph over despair and a hopeful but not happy ending.

Tragedy is an expression of confidence in the tremendous fortitude of man, in his ability to overcome calamities and to triumph over despair, a declaration that "even if God is not in his heaven, at least man is in his world."[5] *Gone with the Wind* is such an expression. God may not be in his heaven, but Scarlett is in her world. She is the tragic heroine par excellence. She not only survives poverty, hunger, destitution and death, but triumphs over them—"I'll live through this and when it is done, as God is my witness, I'll never be hungry again." She is never hungry again, but she loses her father, her daughter, her only friend and her husband. The loss of her husband is her own fault, the result of her tragic flaw of coveting Ashley and ignoring Rhett. It was surprisingly easy for her to come to terms with the fact that Ashley had never really loved her, but Rhett's leaving threatened the existence of her world, "What is to become of me?" Through her confidence in her own fortitude and strength, she triumphs over despair as she had previously triumphed over poverty and hunger and destruction and death: "*I'll* go home and *I'll* think of some way to get him back. After all, tomorrow is another day."

True to tragic form, the ending of *Gone with the Wind* recapitulates the total action. In going to Ashley rather than to Rhett upon leaving Melanie's deathbed, Scarlett repeated a pattern she had followed from the first scene of the film. Although she could have had any man she wanted at Tara and at Twelve Oaks except Ashley, she only wanted Ashley and kept wanting only Ashley through three marriages, indeed until she brought about her own downfall, Rhett's leaving her. This downfall is unusual in tragedy, it is true, especially after all the classic calamities Scarlett had previously triumphed over, but it *is* her downfall nevertheless, and a tragic downfall.

As *the* modern American tragedy, *Gone with the Wind* reaffirms our triumph over despair. Hence its popularity. And hence its primary position in the American Film Institute poll. A true work of popular art, *Gone with the Wind* lives on its form. And it is the unfolding of the form that mesmerizes us with all its technicolor magnificence. There is not and never was any suspense of plot in *Gone with the Wind*. Most viewers knew the ending before they knew the story, and almost all knew the story before they saw the film. They went, not to be surprised by an ending, but to be entertained and enriched by the unfolding of a form; to enjoy again the experience of Scarlett vowing never to be hungry again, of Rhett calmly saying, "Frankly, my dear, I don't give a damn," and of Scarlett regaining her composure and remembering that, "after all, tomorrow is another day." We know the lines by heart. We go to see the unfolding of the form in all the greatness of its vertical and spiral forces, and all the glory of its tragedy. All art is illusion, and the illusion of tragedy, as Charles Morgan notes, is "the greatest illusion of all."[6] *Gone with the Wind* is a great American movie because it is a great American form, and "the great American movie" because it is the great American tragic form.

NOTES

The author wishes to express her indebtedness to Films, Inc., for its courtesy in lending her a print of *Gone with the Wind* to study in conjunction with the preparation of this essay.

[1]Frederick Lewis Allen, *Since Yesterday* (New York: Harper and Brothers, 1940), p. 255.

[2]Walter Toman, *Family Constellation, Its Effects on Personality and Social Behavior*, 3rd ed. (New York: Springer, 1976), pp. 160–88.

[3]Jose Ortega y Gasset, *The Dehumanization of Art and Notes on the Novel* (Princeton: Princeton Univ. Press, 1968), p. 75.

[4]*Against Interpretation* (New York: Dell, 1966), p. 179.

[5]Joseph W. Krutch, "The Tragic Fallacy," *The Modern Temper* (New York: Harcourt Brace, 1929), p. 125.

[6]"The Nature of Dramatic Illusion," in *Reflections on Art*, ed. Susanne K. Langer (New York: Oxford Univ. Press, 1958), p. 100.

# A Chronicle of Soil, Seasons and Weather:
## *Jean Renoir's* The Southerner

HART WEGNER

When Jean Renoir arrived in America on New Year's Eve of 1940, he had directed twenty-six silent and sound films in France, creating pillars of world cinema: *Nana, Boudou Saved From Drowning, Toni, Madame Bovary, Le Crime de Monsieur Lange, Une Partie de Campagne, La Marseillaise, La Grande Illusion, La Bête Humaine,* and *Rules of the Game.* Although his international reputation by then had not yet reached the level of universal appeal that he was to enjoy from the late 1950s on, he was still a formidable "guest" in 1940s Hollywood.

His American productions were uneven and reflected the loss of his creative ensemble and the language difficulties which burdened him, and they showed the stress of his obligations to the plight of occupied France. The films Renoir directed in America, in spite of all their problems, are still an important and integral part of his total work: *Swampwater* (1941), *This Land is Mine* (1943), *Salute to France* (1944), *The Southerner* (1945), *Diary of a Chambermaid* (1946), and *The Woman on the Beach* (1947).

Renoir himself was not satisfied with the less than congenial production conditions at Twentieth Century-Fox and at RKO. He realized that his American films "marked the beginning of a certain evolution in his work."[1] Yet even in moments of bitterness, as in the conversation with Claude Mauriac in 1951 when Renoir stated that he would gladly erase all of his American films, he spared *The Southerner* from his wrath.[2]

The reason critics of the day were less receptive to Renoir's American films was that Renoir had decided not to direct those motion pictures everybody in Hollywood expected of him. He refused to

58

direct films containing "sequences with moustached policemen and gentlemen in velvet jackets and imperial beards parading against a bogus-Montmartre, bogus-café background."[3] Further, instead of making films in the confining environment of Hollywood studios, Renoir decided to make films in the more congenial South.

Renoir confounded his studio when he decided to take *Swampwater*, his first American production, on location. This was not a common practice in 1941, and instead of a predictable glamor spot, Renoir chose the Okefenokee Swamp. It was not easy to understand why a French director with a minimal command of English should choose to take his crew on a strenuous location trip in the South. During the filming of *Swampwater*, Renoir stayed with his company in Waycross, Georgia, whose people "showed us the utmost kindness."[4] He was fascinated by the people of the district, who made their living by selling the skins of swamp animals.

It was not the "magnolia and old lace" South that interested Renoir, but "real people in adversity."[5] With George Sessions Perry's novel *Hold Autumn in Your Hand* he was presented with a Southern theme after his own liking. The film was independently produced for United Artists by David L. Loew, who was also responsible for such prestigious cultural fare as Somerset Maugham's Gauguin biography, *The Moon and Sixpence*, adaptations of Erich Maria Remarque's novels *So Ends Our Night* and *Arch of Triumph*, and of Guy de Maupassant's *Bel Ami*. The other producer, Robert Hakim, was responsible for such 1930s French films as *Pépé le Moko*, *Le Jour se Lève* and had worked with Renoir before on *La Bête Humaine*. These backers created far more workable conditions for Renoir than he previously had found in America.

Robert Hakim had introduced Renoir to the Perry novel and an already existing script. Renoir rewrote the script, which was to become *The Southerner* (1945), incorporating his own views on the South. He was advised on occasion by William Faulkner. The literary material interested Renoir because of its episodic nature, permitting him the freedom to express his ideas about America, the South, and about man and the land in a series of interlocking vignettes.

The film begins with the decision of the Tucker family to give up sharecropping after an uncle, who is dying in the furrows of a cotton field, implores them to start farming on their own. From their beginning as tenant farmers of a field that has lain fallow for years, the film follows the fate of Sam and Nona Tucker, their two children, and a cantankerous grandmother through the tribulations of a complete change of seasons on their cotton farm. Pride and poverty, love and envy, city and country life are contrasted as the Tuckers suffer and at last risk defeat when their only hope—their first crop—is destroyed in a storm.

Renoir's Southern poor are marked by the meagerness of their existence. Sam Tucker's idealism is balanced by the nastiness of the vinegary Devers, a neighbor who has suffered over the years and feels that the Tuckers should suffer as he had when he started farming in a hostile environment. And even Devers, the only person in the whole film who comes close to being villainous, can evoke the empathy of the audience, who recognize how his struggle for survival has made him hard and unforgiving.

Originally Renoir wanted to film *The Southerner* in Texas, but wartime transportation restrictions brought about a compromise California location—a cotton field by the San Joaquin River near Madera. The production company lived in a tent city, and Russian Dukhobors who lived in the area danced and sang in the evenings. For Renoir the filming of *The Southerner* was a relatively happy time: "Our rather somber story was shot in an atmosphere of gaiety."[6]

The casting of the film may not have appeared ideal to Renoir, but it fulfilled his plan to make *The Southerner* both a comeback vehicle, a means to reestablish his reputation in Hollywood as a viable commercial director, and the first of a series of more or less experimental small films which he wanted to create.

Joel McCrea was first cast as Sam Tucker, but he withdrew from the project and was replaced by Texan Zachary Scott, whose first film had been released the preceding year. The other name actors had little Southern background: Betty Field (Nona) was a native Bostonian, whose language in the film never approximates that of a Texan, though she had played rural parts in *Of Mice and Men* and *Shepherd of the Hills.* Beulah Bondi (the grandmother) came from Chicago. Percy Kilbride, later to appear as Pa Kettle, was described by James Agee as "a wonderful portrayer of certain rural types, but it is hard to imagine

"Authentic Southern types" in *The Southerner:* Charles Kemper as Tim (the narrator and Renoir alter ego), Percy Kilbride as Harmie Jenkins, and Zachary Scott as Sam Tucker.

him much south of Connecticut or much west of the Hudson."[7] J. Carrol Naish (Devers) was a New Yorker; Blanche Yurka (Mom), a Czech-American; and Norman Lloyd (Finley), a British character actor. The casting, with its charge by some of a lack of authenticity, caused critical grumbles for years.

Renoir had acted in some of his French films, playing such seemingly peripheral roles (Octave in *Rules of the Game*) as narrator, reasoner, observer and well meaning but clumsy participant. Renoir does not appear in *The Southerner,* but Charles Kemper's Tim resembles Renoir's earlier roles. He is the friendly "city cousin" who wants to help, but he does not really understand Sam Tucker's love for the land that makes him hang on in an all but hopeless situation. He offers to find a job for Sam at the plant where he works, so that the Tuckers would have money for food, but Sam declines.

The *New York Times*, in a generally favorable review, valued the difficulty of realizing such a project through the entertainment medium: "The poor, white sharecropper, probably as unfashionable a subject for screen treatment as could be contemplated, has been given a forthright, sympathetic and seemingly honest expression in *The Southerner*."[8] *Time* concurred and praised it as "the cinema's first whole hearted attempt since *The Grapes of Wrath* to portray in stirring fiction the lives of real people, in a real world, using their courage against real difficulties."[9] *Newsweek* saw it as "documentary in its realism," but faulted the film for failing "to suggest the social economy that accounts for the share-cropper's predicament."[10]

Manny Farber in the *New Republic* praises Renoir's cinematic treatment of the rural poor as "one of the least trashy and commercial movies made in years."[11] He compares the film to other treatments of country life in America and finds little to praise in the production of the last few years: "But unlike almost any other Hollywood director, Renoir tries to make every shot count as much as possible, and the fine naturalistic work he has done here has turned out some of the only true scenes of American country life that I have seen since films like *Tol'able David*."[12]

Farber's comparison of *The Southerner* to Henry King's film is more valuable than those of most critics, who contrasted Renoir's film to Ford's *Grapes of Wrath*. King's film, in which the Griffith influence appears in its purest form, creates a "simple, unextravagant, sincere, and moving tale of Southern life," a critical statement that could easily have been written about Renoir's film.[13]

Less helpful are comparisons of the Tucker family to the Georgian Lesters of Erskine Caldwell's *Tobacco Road*, brought to the screen in 1941 by John Ford. The *New Yorker* made such a comparison calling Sam and his family "Lesters in embryo, or Lesters cleaned up for a medium that can imagine practically everything about poverty except its sour smell."[14] Nor is it any more helpful in understanding *The*

*Southerner* to compare it to *The Grapes of Wrath*, the other Ford film
dealing with a poor Southern family, made one year before the *Tobacco Road* adaptation. It is true that Ford and Renoir admired one
another and Dudley Nichols, writer of many fine Ford films, wrote the
script for Renoir's *Swampwater*, but the rural Americanism of Ford
(extended to include Ireland) and the international and urbane hu-
manism of Renoir are two distinctly separate worlds.

The *Southerner* is neither an attack on the landholding system of
the South nor a sentimental tract about the poor, but a philosophical
observation on the South, on America and on living with the land.
Renoir never intended to make a documentary about the South and to
those familiar with his career this should have been obvious. The
Tennessean James Agee took Renoir to task exactly for that. His
remarkable review in the *Nation* initially praised the film as a "poetic,
realistic chronicle of a farm year's hope, work, need, anxiety, pride,
love, disaster and reward—a chronicle chiefly of soil, seasons and
weather."[15] He praised, as almost all other critics did, the visual
beauty of this film, but Agee had one major reservation: "Physically,
exclusive of the players, it is one of the most sensitive and beautiful
American-made pictures I have seen." (It may be ironic to speak of
*The Southerner* as an "American-made" film with the production,
direction and cinematography in the hands of "foreigners.") Agee
attacks the casting and acting of everyone in the film, with the exception of Zachary Scott, who as a Texan is "basically right, in everything
from cheekbones and eyes to posture to spiritual attitude."

As the critical essay progresses, Agee's tone changes to the extent
that he finally suggests the film should never have been made because
the director doesn't understand the minute particulars of a given area
and its inhabitants. What Agee would have liked—a documentary-
style examination of regional and social-class specifics of poverty and
those who cause it in the South—was never intended by Renoir. Agee
might have wanted something akin to his own book, *Let Us Now
Praise Famous Men*, which was published in 1941, after having been
commissioned five years earlier by *Fortune*. If Agee's texts and Walker
Evans's photography made *Let Us Now Praise Famous Men* "a book of
doom and desperate resignation,"[16] Renoir's film by contrast was a
triumph of individual and familial strength. The faces of Renoir's

Southerners are not etched by wind, heat and the deprivation of
generations as were those of the Rickettses and Gudgers of Agee's
book. Rather, they are the faces of actors attempting to recreate Renoir's vision of the South.

Renoir's *Toni*, filmed in France, came closer to Agee's expectations
and demands, but Renoir was then filming his own people in his own
language in a country whose geographic and ethnographic details
were familiar to him. Jean-Luc Godard astutely noted the relation of
*Toni* and *Swampwater*, an observation which can be extended to
include *The Southerner*: "The principle of *Swampwater* is that of
*Toni*, but with twenty years of experience behind it."[17]

In spite of his social concerns, which are particularly evident in
Renoir's Popular Front era films (*Toni*, *The Crime of Mr. Lange*, and
*La Vie est à Nous*), he always chafed under the strictures of realism: "I
am incapable of doing good work unless it contains an element of the
fairy-tale."[18] If the photos of Walker Evans, Arthur Rothstein, Margaret Bourke-White and Dorothea Lange and the documentary films
of Pare Lorentz, Floyd Crosby, Willard Van Dyke and Joris Ivens
reproduced the realities of life in the 1930s in the depressed South,
Renoir created with *The Southerner* a paean to survival and human
strength. While the documentarists show the escape of the poor from
their land, Renoir's Tuckers reclaim land that has lain fallow. While
Dorothea Lange follows US 80 with her camera to record the human
suffering strewn along the road to California, the Tuckers hang onto
their land, knowing that without it they would be nothing. They are
not revolutionaries, but farmers; there are no speeches like Ma Joad's
or Tom Joad's promise at the end of John Ford's *Grapes of Wrath*
(1941), but possibly a word with God. Above all else, the characters
commune with their land. They lie on it, caress it, love it and die in its
furrows. *The Southerner* is not tied to a specific time or place, the
events are not politicized nor does the film ever become polemical.
The owner of the land does not appear to be a villain; as a matter of
fact, he seems to like Tucker and, aside from the beginning, plays no
part whatever in the film. If there is a single film created by Renoir
during his stay in the United States which expresses his humanistic
beliefs clearly and poignantly it is *The Southerner*.

In *The Southerner* two strands in Renoir's continuing development merge: man's union with nature and the exploration of America, the country, its people and their values. Significantly he chose to locate both of his films dealing with contemporary American life in the South. While many European directors found America's purest expression in the West, Renoir felt a greater affinity to the South and he chose Sam Tucker as the embodiment of Southern ideals and virtues.[19] Even God, who had been conspicuously absent from Renoir's work until then, is invoked in *The Southerner*. Sam Tucker is a man of dignity; he cannot be demeaned; he is not an exploitor of his land and he in turn is not exploited. He is free, in contrast to many Renoir characters of his French period who are caught in the conventions of their social classes. Sam Tucker's freedom almost bears the stamp of a tribute to American democracy and its working on the most basic levels. This praise of freedom should not be overlooked. The film was, after all, made by a refugee from Europe in the war's final year.

Manny Farber noted quite correctly that the movie may not be about the South but about America: "The movie doesn't strike me as being particularly Southern . . . the movie is so divorced, I think, from an identifiable environment that it seems to be taking place in a generalized American farm country."[20] Of course, Renoir's use of Southern specifics in an attempt to create general truths, does not detract from the film as a picture about the South nor as an important milestone in his career.

If *The Southerner* appears less a complete masterpiece than *La Grande Illusion* or *Rules of the Game*, it is because the latter are the crowning glories at the end of a period in Renoir's career, while *The Southerner* bravely presages new developments, forming a bridge between the South of France in *Toni* and the Ganges and Houghly River country of *The River*.

The South provides Renoir with the opportunity to merge Europe, specifically France, and America. In his essay "The Profession of Letters in the South," Allen Tate traces certain Southern attitudes to their French roots, or at least points out close affinities between the South and France: "In religious and social feeling I should stake everything on the greater resemblance to France. The South clings blindly to forms of European feeling and conduct that were crushed by the French revolution."[21]

Surely not everyone in the South or anywhere else for that matter identifies with a Texas tenant farmer and his struggle for survival on his land. Allen Tate sees the patriarchial family working on its own land as an archetype of contemporary Southern thought: "Where else in the modern world is the patriarchial family still innocent of the rise and power of other forms of society? Possibly in France. Yet the 'orientation' . . . the rise of new Southern points of view, even now in the towns, is tied still to the image of the family on the land."[22]

Philip T. Hartung in *Commonweal* saw the subject matter of *The Southerner* less as a merging of French and American thought and images and more as the development of a universal theme: "It is interesting that a French director would be so successful with an American scene and theme, but perhaps it is the universality of the theme—the struggle of the farmer, the fight of a man against nature—which makes it one that could be told by the motion picture in any country."[23] Hartung also stressed the fact that the film, with all of its visual beauty, never romanticizes its subjects. Renoir especially avoids the sentimentalization of the Southern farmer in Millet's manner. In his biography of Auguste Renoir, the director quotes his father in a sentiment surely shared: "I loathed Millet. His sentimental peasants made me think of actors dressed up to look like peasants."[24] Instead, Renoir is satisfied that his actors are actors and this knowledge is shared with the audience.

Renoir's farmers are not more virtuous because they are farmers, but they are farmers because that is what they happen to be suited for. Renoir lets Sam and Tim argue the virtues of farming and manufacturing and each man spiritedly defends his occupation, having to admit the essential worth of the other's occupation. Their different temperaments make Sam a country man and Tim a city man.

Renoir's preference for the South over other regions of the United States is surely related to one of the strongest influences on his filmmaking: the motion pictures of D. W. Griffith. Renoir speaks of close-ups from early Griffith films as having been "imprinted on my memory for life."[25] It would be an oversimplification to reduce Griffith's cinematic universe to a replica of the Civil War South simply because Kentucky was his birthplace, but Griffith himself said throughout his life that his Southern heritage influenced his films. His depiction of Southern idealism and gallantry, finding its finest expression in the "Little Colonel's" charge into the fire of Northern cannons, certainly was not lost on Renoir.

Sam Tucker is close to Renoir's heart. He understands what motivates him—his desire to make things grow—which in turn allows him to live with dignity, however poor he might appear. Renoir observed sagely: "The only happiness in life comes through making something."[26] Tim, the city man, is as much part of the South as Sam is, and their argument over the merits of their respective professions is in reality a discussion between the older agricultural and the newer industrial South.

The South of this film is not an isolated Virgilian Arcadia, but rather "a rich, unusual and sensitive delineation of a segment of the American scene."[27] Sam and Nona are not related to the shepherds and shepherdesses of the idylls and their rustic lives are far removed from the Poussin sentiment "Et in Arcadia ego." Their simplicity is artless and unsentimental; whatever feelings they exhibit are basic, but never simple-minded. The central image of their "civilization" is the ritual lighting of the fire; only then do they become a family, and the ramshackle, swaybacked shed a home.

The image of the lighting of the fire was the essence of love, the home and the community for Marcel Pagnol in his film *The Baker's Wife* and it has a similar function for Renoir's Southerners.[28] As the baker and his wife are united at the end of the film before the relit bakery oven, so are the Tuckers banded together against adversity after the storm devastates their home and fields.

The central image of the destruction of the crops—the bobbing cotton bolls in the flood-swollen river—is also a symbol of faith in Renoir's universe. His father said to young Jean: "One is merely a cork. You must let yourself go along in life like a cork in the current of a stream."[29] This quiet affirmation of life in a film pointedly located in the South, directed by a European in exile and released just as the Second World War ended, voiced a respect for life sadly needed at that time.

Renoir's American productions pleased neither the motion picture companies who employed him nor the film historians who reasoned that the famed French director had fallen prey to the power of Hollywood to subvert and destroy genius. André Bazin lamented the condescension toward Renoir's American films: "Nobody even considers that he might have undergone a positive evolution or a fruitful transformation in America. We thought of his American works as parodies rather than resemblances, when we should have realized that he was taking tentative steps into new stages of development."[30] Some of his titles smacked of melodrama and B-productions; continental culture, so coveted by Hollywood, was not evident in these films. Renoir used mainly American material and his stars were often B-picture journeymen such as Dana Andrews, Charles Bickford or Zachary Scott. But, as Bazin pointed out: "Renoir did not make a break with himself and betray his gifts; he evolved, and Hollywood played a decisive role in his evolution."[31]

## NOTES

[1]Jean Renoir quoted in Pierre Leprohon, *Jean Renoir* (New York: Crown, 1971), p. 134.

[2]Leprohon, p. 141.

[3]Jean Renoir, *My Life and My Films* (New York: Atheneum, 1974), p. 193.

[4]*My Life*, p. 195.

[5]*Newsweek*, 6 Aug. 1945, p. 85.

[6]*My Life*, p. 238.

[7]*The Nation*, 9 June 1945, p. 657.

[8]27 Aug. 1945, p. 22.

[9]21 May 1945, p. 96.

[10]6 Aug. 1945, pp. 85–86.

[11]10 Sept. 1945, p. 317.

[12]*Tol'able David* (1921), considered along with D. W. Griffith's *Way Down East* to be the beginning of American rural films, was shot in the South. Although the producer asked for Pennsylvania locations, Henry King, a native Virginian prevailed and he shot *Tol'able David* in and around Staunton, Virginia.

[13]Lewis Jacobs, *The Rise of the American Film: A Critical History* (New York: Teachers College Press, 1968), p. 373.

[14]18 Aug. 1945, p. 49.

[15]9 June 1945, p. 657.

[16]William Stott, *Documentary Expression and Thirties America* (New York: Oxford Univ. Press, 1973), p. 313.

[17]Quoted in André Bazin, *Jean Renoir* (New York: Dell, 1974), p. 263.

[18]*My Life*, p. 161.

[19]Renoir dealt in a whimsical way with the American West in his *Crime of Mr. Lange*, whose title hero writes an outlandish Western yarn about a fictional Western hero, "Arizona Jim."

[20]*New Republic*, 10 Sept. 1945, p. 317.

[21]Allen Tate, *Essays of Four Decades* (Chicago: Swallow Press, 1968), pp. 520–521.

[22]Tate, p. 521.

[23]*Commonweal*, 1 June 1945, p. 168.

[24]Jean Renoir, *Renoir, My Father* (Boston: Little, Brown, 1962), p. 71.

[25]*My Life*, p. 45.

[26]Charles Thomas Samuels, *Encountering Directors* (New York: G. P. Putnam's Sons, 1972), p. 222.

[27]*New York Times*, 27 Aug. 1945, p. 22.

[28]Segments of *Toni*, the one of his French films closest to *The Southerner*, were filmed in Marcel Pagnol's Marseille studio.

[29]*My Father*, p. 36.

[30]"Renoir, Français," *Cahiers du Cinéma*, No. 8 (Jan. 1952) and in Leprohon, p. 194.

[31]Leprohon, p. 195.

# The Civil War in Early Film:
## *Origin and Development of a Genre*

EVELYN EHRLICH

Despite its former popularity, the Civil War is no longer a major background for film narratives, unlike the Western or, since World War II, the modern war film. Yet, to the first generation of movie audiences, the Civil War was a theme familiar from both literature and drama, one which drew upon an event recent enough to be remembered by many, yet far enough in the past to have lost most of its bitter associations. The Civil War was a favorite subject for many filmmakers during the early silent era and lost its allure only when the first World War displaced its significance as the formative experience in the contemporary American ethos.

The treatment of the Civil War in film was initially drawn from models presented in drama and popular literature. The war had been an apposite topic for late nineteenth-century romantic conventions, combining the valor and gallantry of battle with the personal plight of families torn by sectional differences. Unlike the war with Spain, which never aroused much literary interest, the Civil War was fought on American soil, and even those far from the battle were engaged by the stories of fathers, brothers and sweethearts.

The theme was first taken up by popular fiction in the years after Reconstruction with an emphasis on sectional reconciliation, usually through marriage. Certain conventions in this literature became common in later theatrical treatment, particularly the romanticized images of the antebellum South and the caricatured figures of "uncles, mammies, colonels, gracious ladies and cadets."[1] By the time the theater adopted the Civil War theme in the 1880s, the romanticism and nostalgia for the pre-war period began to be associated with the war itself.

The theater lagged somewhat behind literature in treating the Civil

War theme, but when the cycle began it soon dominated the American stage. The first major success was William Gillette's *Held by the Enemy* in 1886, and from that time until the end of the century the Civil War drama was the most popular subject for the American theater. Among the hits of the period were Bronson Howard's *Shenandoah* (1889), David Belasco's *The Heart of Maryland* (1895), William Gillette's *Secret Service* (1896), James Herne's *Griffith Davenport* (1899), and Clyde Fitch's *Barbara Frietchie* (1899). After 1900, interest in Civil War plays declined, with the exception of William C. DeMille's *The Warrens of Virginia*, which was a huge success in 1907.[2] Many of these plays continued to be produced, however. Thomas Dixon's *The Clansman* in 1908 ran for a respectable 51 performances.[3]

The reconciliation theme which underlay much of the post-war fiction became the central motif of the Civil War play. The model of this type can be drawn from *Shenandoah*, which contains nearly every convention common to the group. The convoluted plot is essentially a love story between a Northern hero and a Southern heroine, balanced by the secondary romance of the protagonists' siblings, with sectional affiliations reversed. The play opens in Charleston on the night of the firing on Fort Sumter, proceeds through the Virginia campaign, at which all the main characters are present including the two heroines, and concludes in Washington shortly after the war, with the reconciliation of all parties.

The standard plot structure of all the plays almost invariably revolves around a Northern officer and a Southern belle who, having fallen in love before the war, find their sympathies torn between love and duty. Occasionally, there is intersectional conflict within a single family—as in *The Heart of Maryland* where the hero's father, a Southern general, must condemn his son, a Union officer, as a spy—but this "divided kinsmen" device, which would become popular in motion pictures, is always secondary to the romance.

The villain, if there is one, is clearly shown to have loyalty to neither side, while the regulars of both armies are brave, loyal and courteous. Most often, it is the girl who proves her love by sacrificing her principles, although in *Secret Service* both man and woman put love before duty. In most cases, the final reconciliation comes at war's end; occasionally, as in *Secret Service* and *Griffith Davenport* the couple reconcile before the hero is sent to a prisoner of war camp.

What is most striking about these plays is the almost total absence of battle and death. Although references to campaigns and off-stage battles are common, the few characters who are killed are invariably secondary. Attention is sometimes given to the destruction of Southern homes, and in *The Warrens of Virginia* a major sub-plot involves finding food for the starving family, but by the 1890s the war has become "a rather exhilirating experience for various sets of genteel lovers."[4] Even in a play like *Griffith Davenport*, which returns to an earlier literary formula of showing the war's effect on a Virginia family, the major concern of the play is the reconciliation of husband and wife.

*Griffith Davenport* introduced another motif that remained undeveloped on the stage but became common in the cinema—the presence of historical characters. The appearance on stage of such figures as Lincoln, Lee and Grant was confined to the biographical dramas then beginning to appear, especially those concerning Lincoln and Lee, who had become nationally admired. In the first draft of *Davenport*, Lincoln was on stage throughout much of the climactic action, but the playwright and star, James A. Herne, feared he was being upstaged by Lincoln's ghost and eliminated the part.[5] Without star egos to contend with in the motion picture, the immediate recognizability of these figures became a virtue, and many a seemingly insoluble plight would be rectified by Lincoln, who emerged as a kind of *deus ex machina* in the cinema stories.

## The Motion Picture, 1897–1910

Motion pictures before 1900 seldom had narratives. They tended to be relatively short (30 seconds to several minutes) recordings of vaudeville acts, sights of distant lands, or events of the day. The films of events, called actualities, attest to the continuing importance of the Civil War in American life, since they often covered the reunions of veterans and the unveiling of Civil War monuments. The earliest known examples of this group of films date from 1897, when the Edison company produced two shorts titled *Grant Veterans-G.A.R.* (Grand Army of the Republic, 30 seconds) and *Amoskeag Veterans, New Hampshire* (one minute).[6] Like most contemporary actualities, these are single-take films that detail the passing parade of veterans and dignitaries.

Although "story" films were produced from the late 1890s on, they did not become common until the middle of the first decade of the Twentieth Century. One of the pioneers of the narrative film was Edwin S. Porter, whose *The Great Train Robbery* became one of the most popular and influential films in the early years of the century. In 1903, the same year of *The Great Train Robbery*, Porter filmed the first story with a subject related to the Civil War, *Uncle Tom's Cabin*.

In spite of the trend away from portraying the bitterness of the war and its ostensible causes, this play was the single most popular vehicle touching on the subject. It had been adapted from Harriet Beecher Stowe's novel by George L. Aiken in 1852, and its popularity endured through numerous travelling companies well into the 1900s. It is not surprising that the first fictional motion picture concerning the war should have been this vehicle, which was also filmed by the Lubin company in the same year as Porter's version for Edison. Both versions were performed by theatrical stock companies, and the Porter version is a condensed recording of the play as performed on stage, each vignette filmed from a fixed camera position, preceded by a title describing the action. Because the film was derived from a popular stage play which audiences no doubt knew, it lacks the innovative technique of *The Great Train Robbery*, although it was equally popular with audiences.

Prior to 1908, there is no record of the existence of additional story films about the Civil War.[7] A 1904 Edison film titled *Military Maneuvers, Manassas, Va.* provides an example, however, of a new trend in motion picture treatment of the Civil War. Kemp Niver describes this film as a reconstruction of a Civil War battle, and thus it provides one of the earliest examples of a type of historic reconstruction which would become popular later in the decade.[8]

Although staged "newsreels" of contemporary events were not uncommon (both Edison and Vitagraph produced films purporting to show battles of the Spanish-American war, which were actually filmed in New York), the practice of reconstructing a historic battle of more than forty years past suggests that the Civil War continued to be perceived, to some extent, as a contemporary event. In part, this sense of currency may be ascribed to the continuing presence of living veterans who had a concrete notion of how such battle scenes actually looked. But perhaps more important, the Civil War was the first American conflict in which still photography had had an extensive role, and even those too young to have had personal experience with battle had strong images of the front shaped by the photographs of Mathew Brady and others. The similarity of the photographic and motion-picture images may have led audiences to expect a greater realism in its Civil War films than they had demanded on the stage. This expectation may also explain the reluctance of motion picture companies to incur the expense of providing large costumed casts in authentic looking locations which the exploitation of the Civil War theme would later require.

Another factor retarding the development of the Civil War film until 1908 may have been the composition, or perceived composition, of the audience. If, as is often stated, early film audiences were made up largely of working class immigrants, the appeal of such a distinctly American subject would have been minimal. The beginning of the Civil War cycle in 1908 corresponded with attempts to broaden the motion picture audience, according to some observers.[9]

The first original Civil War story-film was probably Kalem's *The Days of '61*, released during the first week of January 1908. Although we have only *Moving Picture World's* description (4 January 1908, p. 11), it appears to be interesting for its melding of stage convention with cinematic realism. The film begins with an elderly lady in her garden, falling asleep and dreaming of '61, when "she is chosen as sweetheart to one of the brightest boys at a husking bee.... Her happiness is soon blanched, for there comes a call to arms, when every citizen who has his country's interests at heart shoulders musket and goes to fight for 'Old Glory.' " The ensuing scenes depict the leavetaking, the front line, an ambush, a powder mine, the storming of a hill, combat, the capture of a gun, victory, the wounded soldier's return, the lover's greeting, and a wedding and the last scene is a return to the present as the now aged hero kisses the dreamer. Although the film maintains the structure of the theatrical vignette and essentially concerns the stereotyped romance broken by war, the middle section of the film is devoted exclusively to the reality of the war itself, a surprising departure from stage convention that can only be attributed to the filmmaker's consciousness of film's enhanced ability to capture the feel of battle. Further, the film's political viewpoint is distinctly Unionist, in contrast to the conciliatory positions of most stage plays.

Presumably, the *Days of '61* proved popular with audiences, for more Civil War films soon followed, thirteen in all in 1908. In March 1908, Billy Bitzer filmed *A Famous Escape* (for American Mutoscope & Biograph[AMB]), which was released in April. The company's publicist must have considered the subject matter too controversial to specify either the conflict or the film's bias, for the description of the film in *Moving Picture World* refers to a "story founded on an incident taken from the history of the U.S. during a time of strife." Soldiers captured in battle are taken to a military prison where there are "indignities heaped upon them by their jailers." They dig a tunnel, escape, and return to their own lines. It is difficult to understand the reticence of AMB in specifying the Civil War, for the uniforms plainly identify the protagonists as Union soldiers, the brutal guards as Confederates, and the prison as most likely Andersonville.

Other "realistic" films of 1908 include Lubin's *Scenes from the Battlefield of Gettysburg*, subtitled *The Waterloo of the Confederacy* (August), a re-creation of the battle without an encompassing story line, *Sheridan's Ride* released by Vitagraph in December, another re-creation without fictional plot, *In the Shenandoah Valley*, still another re-creation of Sheridan's ride, by Selig,[10] and *The Life of Abraham Lincoln* (Essanay). The latter, which details in eighteen scenes the Lincoln biography from boyhood to death,[11] may have been produced in response to the success of *The Reprieve: An Episode in the Life of Abraham Lincoln* (Vitagraph, August), a supposedly true incident in which a wife secures a reprieve for her court martialed husband "in a thrilling manner," not specified.[12]

Not all of the early Civil War films eschewed theatrical conventions and melodrama. Edison's *The Blue and the Grey; or the Days of '61* tells the conventionalized story of two West Point classmates who join opposite sides in the war. The wounded Northerner is nursed by the Southerner's sister while the Southerner crosses enemy lines on a spy mission. When he is chased to his Virginia home by Northern soldiers, the wounded Yankee protects his former friend and gives him his

uniform. The Yankee is court-martialed for this act of friendship and is
saved only when his Southern sweetheart appeals first to General
Grant and then to Lincoln. She arrives with his reprieve just as he is
about to face the firing squad. This convoluted tale is plainly in the
William Gillette tradition, one which would become increasingly the
norm for Civil War dramas. In fact, one writer for *Moving Picture
World* complained in 1913 that "our Civil War has furnished the
background for many stirring photodramas, but most of them are
marred by the inevitable trio of young people."[13]

Also noteworthy is the appearance, even in the most melodramatic
plots, of actual historical figures. Although derived from the stage, this
convention became fully developed only in the motion picture.

Another noteworthy departure of many films from stage convention
is the shift in the hero's class. Whereas in the theater the hero was
invariably a top-ranking officer from a genteel background, the motion
picture hero was often an ordinary soldier undergoing the real hardships of battle. This change may be attributed to the characteristics of
the motion picture audience.

Other films of 1908 used the growing popularity of the Civil War as a
mere backdrop for conventional melodrama. One example is *The
Guerilla*, D. W. Griffith's first Civil War film for Biograph, filmed in
October and released in November 1908. This film is interesting
technically in terms of Griffith's development, since it includes a
series of panning shots, as well as parallel editing for the climactic
rescue. In terms of narrative, however, the film lacks any real sense of
historic realism. The story concerns a Northern officer and his
sweetheart, whose home is besieged by ruffians posing as Southern
soldiers. (The film is careful to show the guerillas changing from
civilian clothes into their stolen uniforms, in order to forestall any
suspicion that these men are Southern regulars.) As the guerilla leader
menaces the girl, the faithful black servant (played by white actor
Charles Insley in blackface) seeks out the hero, despite wounds in-
flicted by the guerilla band. The cross-cutting between the menaced
girl and the pursuing hero, which includes shots of a brief skirmish on
horseback that involves fewer than ten men, is less a climax than a
build-up for the final swordfight between hero and villain. It is possible, as suggested earlier, that Biograph was reluctant to make a film

that might provoke controversy and insisted that realistic elements of the war be deemphasized. The Bulletin for the film is revealing in its insistence that "it is an episode that may have occurred during the progress of any civil war, but to give it atmosphere (we) have timed it during the Civil War of the U.S."

If Biograph was reluctant to give offense to either side, that studio was unique in its scruples. Unlike the conciliatory motif taken up by the theater and fiction, the heroes of the Civil War films were identified with one side, and that side was almost exclusively that of the Union.[14] The story told in *A Famous Escape*, for example, was told again in 1909 under the explicit title *The Escape from Andersonville* (Kalem), although by 1909 the South had begun to receive more sympathetic treatment from moviemakers. In February of that year, Kalem opened a studio in Jacksonville, Florida, and its first production was *The Old Soldier's Story*. According to *Moving Picture World*, it was the "first (film) ever made that represents the Southern side, and it is the first one of this type that is made in the South, having the atmosphere of the country throughout." (27 February 1909, p. 235). The film itself is a story within a modern frame of a veteran who reminisces about a spy mission through enemy lines, where he meets General Grant, is chased by Yankee soldiers, and successfully delivers his message. The flashback arrangement may have been inserted in order to distance the audience from the main events of the film, by making them appear as long ago and almost forgotten (the framing story pokes fun at the veteran's forgetfulness.) But 1909 was also the year when Kalem began its popular serial with *Nan, the Girl Spy*, starring Gene Gauntier as a "wholesome Dixie orphan whose patriotism led her to espionage," which continued until 1912.[15]

If motion pictures tended to be more explicit in their political sentiments than the theater, most of the plots continued to be drawn from the Civil War melodramas of the 1890s. A typical working out of the "divided kinsmen" plot line was Selig's *Brother Against Brother*, released in April 1909. The film opens on Kentuckian Allen's wedding day, which is also the day Fort Sumter is fired on. Allen goes to fight for the South, his brother John for the North. When Allen is captured by Northern troops, John helps his brother escape. Later the brothers meet in battle and Allen is killed. At war's end, John confronts his brother's widow, who though bitter becomes reconciled and eventually marries John.

Concentrating on 1908–1909 as the formative period for the development of the Civil War film, leads to a privileging of the work of Griffith, whose films are among the few extant, and whose second Civil War film, *In Old Kentucky* is among the most unusual examples of the group in terms of both plot and technique. The film was made in July and August 1909 (released 20 September) and was the first film in which Griffith began to explore the themes which would culminate in *Birth of a Nation* six years later. The plot itself is unusual in two respects—not only is the hero recognizably the Southerner (Henry Walthall) who is victimized by his vindictive and thoroughly unsympathetic brother (Owen Moore), but the story contains no romance whatever, concerning exclusively the interaction of the two brothers and their parents. Thus, although it is a story film and contains certain melodramatic elements (particularly the final reconciliation scene), the film is essentially part of the "realistic" mode of the reconstructed battles rather than of the theatrical tradition.

Griffith's conscious attempt to invoke the poetic realism of Mathew Brady photographs is particularly striking in a series of shots which begin with a long-shot of a lone sentry silhouetted against a hillside. The succeeding shot includes a slow pan across the hill top to the underbrush where Walthall is hiding, and then a reverse pan back to the sentries who discover Walthall's presence. The following sequence is dramatically unusual, for after a brief chase Griffith cuts to a shot of Walthall and Moore *after* they have recognized each other. Although the original version no doubt contained a title to bridge this jump cut, what would ordinarily be the dramatic center of the film— the meeting of the two brothers—is completely omitted from the action on the screen. In the shot of the two brothers, Moore shows not only a lack of concern for his brother's fate, but gleefully pantomimes his hanging.

The remainder of the film is more traditionally melodramatic. In a scene reminiscent of *Barbara Frietchie* Kate Bruce as the mother holds a gun to her head to prevent Moore from capturing his brother. And the final reconciliation of victorious North and tattered but proud

*In Old Kentucky:* (top) A lonely sentry (Mack Sennett) silhouetted against a hillside; (bottom) Victorious North and tattered but proud South (Mary Pickford front right). (Frame enlargements courtesy of Film Division, Library of Congress)

South is transformed into a *tableau vivante*. Nonetheless, Griffith's personal concerns are manifest throughout.

Although the scope of this study is limited to pre-1910 films, selective viewing of Griffith's later Biograph career demonstrates that his seven Civil War films are always among the most advanced examples of his technique in the period they were made. His next Civil War film, *The Honor of His Family* (made in December 1909 and released in January 1910) is the first of these films that includes a large scale battle using at least 50 men. Although the battle scene is brief in this film (which is about a Southern soldier's cowardice and its tragic repercussions), in succeeding films Griffith increasingly emphasized his battles, striving for the verisimilitude which he later achieved in *Birth*.

To conclude, there were very few direct adaptations of Civil War plays in early motion pictures, possibly because producers wished to avoid the expense of paying royalties to copyright owners.[16] Nevertheless, the popularity of the Civil War subject in the theater was one of the factors that led to its use as a subject in motion pictures.

In many ways the treatment of the subject in the two media was similar. The cinema borrowed many of the romantic conventions of the stage melodrama, emphasizing both the intersectional love affair and post-war reconciliation and the villainy of the individual outcast who was motivated not by the exigencies of war but simply by the desire to do evil. The most popular stories—the intersectional romance, the divided kinsmen, the loyalties torn between love of country and love for an individual family member—appear again and again in both plays and films.

The cinema, however, added to these simple melodramatic stories a realism that it alone could provide. Unlike the theater, the cinema showed battle, hardship and death. Actors chosen for their resemblance to the originals appeared on the screen as actual historical characters. For the first time audiences were able to see the Civil War reenacted as a war, from a distinct political position, and from the point of view of the ordinary soldier. The motion picture did not merely tell a story, with the camera situated on the front lines; it allowed the audience to be at the Battle of Gettysburg or with Sheridan on his ride.

Perhaps it was the cinema's enhanced ability to show the reality of the war itself which doomed the genre's popularity on the stage. In the cinema, the subject increased in popularity over the early years of the century, growing from thirteen Civil War stories in 1908 to twenty-three in 1909 to thirty-four in 1910. Popular interest in the subject increased unabated through the middle of the 1910s, but the essential outlines of the narrative did not change. Counterposing the melodramatic conventions of theater and fiction to the realism of the photographic image, gifted filmmakers like Ince and Griffith synthesized the two components to create definitive cinematic essays on the subject. Whether filmmakers simply overexploited the subject, or *The Birth of a Nation* intimidated later filmmakers from tackling the subject, or, more likely, the first World War changed American notions of war as a subject for "genteel lovers," the cycle began fading out in 1917 and the only subsequent major success in the silent era was Keaton's *The General*, which satirized the earlier romantic conventions of chivalry and heroism.

The Civil War never again emerged as an autonomous genre in the sound period, although the subject provided the background for a number of films, most notably *Gone with the Wind*. The subject nonetheless provides a useful typology for studying the adaptation of a subject from other media for film, particularly since the time span of its popularity is restricted to the formative period of the cinema.

## NOTES

I would like to thank Cooper Graham for assistance in preparing this paper.

[1]Paul H. Buck, *The Road to Reunion 1865–1900* (New York: Vintage, 1937), p. 215.

[2]William Henry Wegner, "The Representation of the American Civil War on the New York Stage, 1860–1900," Diss. New York Univ. 1966, p. 285.

[3]Burns Mantle and Garrison P. Sherwood, *The Best Plays of 1899–1909* (New York: Dodd, Mead, 1944). This was, of course, the principal source for Griffith's *Birth of a Nation*.

[4]Wegner, p. 301.

[5]Arthur H. Quinn, introduction to "The Reverend Griffith Davenport," in Barrett H. Clark, ed., *America's Lost Plays*, Vol. 7 (Princeton: Princeton Univ. Press, 1941).

[6]Paul H. Spehr, *The Civil War in Motion Pictures: A Bibliography of Films Produced in the United States since 1897* (Washington: Library of Congress, 1961) and Kemp Niver, *Motion Pictures from the Library of Congress Paper Print Collection 1894–1912* (Berkeley: University of California Press, 1967). Unless otherwise noted, all titles are from Spehr.

[7]An earlier one-minute Civil War film titled *The Little Reb* has been credited by Spehr to Edison in 1897, but I can find no additional information about this film.

[8]Niver, p. 338. A viewing of the film has raised some question about Niver's

statement, since the uniforms appear to be contemporary and the site is not identifiable. I am indebted to Cooper Graham for all information concerning the Civil War films in the Library of Congress collection.

[9]See, for example, Robert Sklar, *Movie-made America: A Social History of American Movies* (New York: Random, 1975), pp. 18–32. Russell Merritt points out in his article, "Nickelodeon Theaters: Building an Audience for the Movies" (*Wide Angle* 1 rev. ed., 1979, pp. 5–9), that while early theaters attracted a predominantly working-class (immigrant) audience, theater owners and film producers were eager to draw the "better classes." Although their efforts to broaden the composition of the audience did not really succeed until the mid-1910s, such attempts began during the period 1908–1910, which corresponds to the beginning of the Civil War cycle.

[10]It is not clear which version came first, since the Selig film is not listed in *Moving Picture World*.

[11]The description of the film is taken from George Kleine's catalog for 1910, and it is not certain that the film described is the Essanay film of 1908.

[12]*Moving Picture World*, 22 Aug. 1908, p. 145.

[13]Louis Reeves Harrison, "Historical Photoplays," *Moving Picture World*, 17 May 1913, p. 680.

[14]The exception was Vitagraph's *Charity Begins at Home: A Story of the South during the Civil War*.

[15]Jack Spears, *The Civil War on the Screen and Other Essays* (South Brunswick, N.J.: Barnes, 1977), p. 50.

[16]The precedent was set in the famous *Ben Hur* case, in which the film's producers, the Kalem company, adapted Lew Wallace's novel without securing adaptation rights. Kalem was sued for $25,000 and lost the case in 1912. Although the case was still in litigation during the period under discussion, producers had already begun to buy rights for their more prestigious productions. It is not known whether the rights to the Civil War plays were overpriced, or whether producers simply felt these films were not worth the added expense of a well known title.

# The Real Beverly Hillbillies

WADE AUSTIN

From *Birth of a Nation* (1915) and *Gone with the Wind* (1939) to *Thunder Road* (1957) and *Smokey and the Bandit* (1977) the South as a setting and the Southerner as a character type have been fixtures in American motion pictures. In the films mentioned, all big budget or "A" productions, the Southern character went through a considerable evolution. The aristocrats of *Birth of a Nation* and *Gone with the Wind*, doomed by slavery and the Civil War, gave way to the strong willed, taciturn loner of Robert Mitchum in *Thunder Road*, who in turn was replaced by the "good ol' boyism" of Burt Reynolds in several recent films set in the South.

Almost forgotten today, several series of low-budget "hillbilly" films, produced from about 1935 to 1955, presented a more consistent view of the South and the Southerner. These films treated thematically two inherent American myths: (1) The country is better than the city. Country living brings out man's essential goodness; city living destroys it. (2) A country dweller is more than a match for a city slicker, and most city dwellers are slickers; wisdom, along with goodness, comes from the earth.[1]

This characterization was sustained, furthermore, by the presence of Southern-born actors and actresses in starring roles: Bob Burns, Chester Lauck and Norris Goff (Lum and Abner), the Weaver Brothers and Elviry, and Judy Canova. They showed a Southerner who, though uncultured, instinctively did the "right thing," someone who, given to exaggeration, always observed the truth. They portrayed persons open enough to be susceptible to con artists but smart enough to withstand such endeavors. Most of all, the characterizations were presented in a humorous way. This view of the South evolved from an

83

American literary tradition, flourished because of the popularity of radio and the prodigious production of "B" films, and died an ignominious death on television.

Traditionally, the American, especially in the South, has had a strong sense of humor, and the nation has had a long literary tradition of humor. In the beginning, American humor simply reflected the conventions of Europe. Soon native resources capable of enriching the art of humor were incorporated. American landscapes, character types, and language became part of the texture.[2]

Washington Irving's "The Legend of Sleepy Hollow" may be the transition piece in which American humor began to diverge from that of Europe. The seeds of the "frontier humor" of Augustus Longstreet, George Washington Harris, and T. B. Thorpe are present—the atmosphere of fantasy, the character of the rural commoner and the city intellectual, and the conflict of their opposing values.[3] This conflict would broaden considerably to one between city and country and one between the North and the South.

Three of the best examples of "frontier humor" that produced characterizations appearing again and again in the Hollywood Southern "B" film are the horse trader in Augustus Longstreet's "Horse Swap" (1835), the tall-story teller in T. B. Thorpe's "The Big Bear of Arkansas" (1841), and the Sut Lovingood character created by George Washington Harris.

With sure comic insight, Harris created a character who boasts of his scariness, his tendency to flee from trouble, his natural "durn fool spirit," and his petty trickery. But out of the chaos and meanness of Sut's personality and actions, a moral and philosophical order emerges. Ultimately, Sut represents numerous traditional and wholesome values concerning heroism, fertility, masculinity, and femininity—mythic universalities founded upon love, joy, truth, and justice.[4] Such characteristics are the basis for the "hillbilly" characterizations in the "B" films of Bob Burns, the Weavers, Judy Canova, and Lum and Abner.

Bill C. Malone has cited a recording session in 1925 during which the term "hillbilly" was used in association with music of the rural South, although he acknowledges that it has been used in print since about 1900 as a term for a backwoods, rural inhabitant. "Hillbilly" became a generic term for country and mountain music, and eventually a common term for country musicians and fans alike.[5]

By the 1930s radio was enormously popular, especially in the rural South, and "hillbilly" musicians were becoming stars. At the same time, Americans were developing a voracious appetite for motion pictures that would continue until the widespread availability of television in the early 1950s. The "B" film, the low-budget, sixty-minute programmer, helped to satisfy the public craving for movies by making the "double feature" possible, two "B" films for the price of an "A." Some studios, Republic and Monogram, for instance, produced practically nothing but low-budget films, but most of the major studios at one time or another had a "B" unit. "B" films could be produced for a small outlay of capital, and they nearly always made a profit. These films covered every genre—western, crime, musical, comedy—and found a constant market. Westerns did well in the West, Midwest, and South; the crime film and the musical did well in urban areas. Of course, there was a certain degree of overlapping.

After radio popularized "hillbilly" music and performers, Hollywood soon beckoned. "B" film economics depended upon a recognizable product to guarantee sales, and in the 1930s and 1940s radio supplied that product. Gene Autry, the first in a string of singing cowboys, went to Hollywood from radio. Other "hillbilly" performers were to get the call from the movie capital.

Bob Burns was the first Southern performer to answer the call. He played "Arkansas" Smith in Spencer Tracy's *Quick Millions* in 1931. A native of Van Buren, Arkansas, Bob Burns comes directly from the line of "frontier humorists." He called himself the Arkansas Traveler. From his home in Van Buren, he wandered over the state gathering folk songs and tales that later made him famous. Burns took his stage name from Colonel Sanford C. Faulkner who had roamed the South fiddling and singing wherever he could find a crowd. The colonel told a story of an Arkansas traveler who met a hillbilly playing away on a fiddle trying to capture a haunting tune. The traveler knew the tune and when he played it, the hillbilly welcomed him warmly. When Bob Burns learned the tunes, he too was warmly welcomed—first on stage, then in films, and finally on radio. He travelled the Southern low country, playing carnivals and backwoods vaudeville sometimes for as little as three dollars a week. While he was playing mandolin with the Van Buren Silvertone Cornet Band, Burns invented a musical instrument. The band sometimes practiced in a plumbing shop. As a gag one night, Burns fitted two pieces of pipe together with a funnel, trombone style, and blew out a bass tone which seemed to suggest the word "ba-zook-a." Bazooka became the instrument's name and Bob Burns's trademark.[6]

Although he was a ground breaker in bringing a stock "Southern" character to films, Bob Burns had an uneven career in motion pictures. Mostly, he played the sidekick, or pal, to the star. He was Bing Crosby's pal in *Rhythm on the Range* (1936) and Gene Autry's pal in *Guns and Guitars*, a "B" western of the same year. Finally, he did break out of the sidekick type casting. Following a suitable response to the pairing of Bob Burns and Martha Raye in *Rhythm on the Range*, Paramount teamed them in four more pictures: *The Big Broadcast of 1937* (1936); *Waikiki Wedding* (1937); *Mountain Music* (1937); *Tropic Holiday* (1938). *Mountain Music* is a prototypical "hillbilly" film of the type Judy Canova would make again and again at Republic in the 1940s. Martha Raye is a folksy Ozark girl yearning for the bright lights and a man. Bob Burns is the man who thinks Martha is the girl for him as long as he is in a state of amnesia.

"B" films existed because of a specific audience's affinity with a recognizable face, characterization, or plot. So it is hardly possible to distinguish one "B" or one "Southern" from another. Whatever his contribution to the "B" Southern, Burns was there first, and then he went on to a successful career in radio. His bazooka went on to a career, of sorts, on its own. In World War II the U.S. army developed an over-the-shoulder weapon for launching rockets. It was named Bazooka, after Bob Burns' gas pipe and funnel.[7]

Among the dozens of "hillbilly" groups trying for an opportunity in Hollywood in the late thirties was the Weaver Brothers and Elviry (Frank, Leon, and June Weaver). Members of the group possessed a genuine Southern charm, and each managed to project an individual screen personality. Leon is the loquacious, country hick, seemingly easy prey for any city slicker. But that isn't the case. Underneath the hick exterior and country talk is a basic sharpness and understanding of the foibles of human nature. Frank Weaver is the clown of the group, a kind of country Harpo Marx. Like Harpo, he never talked on screen, using, instead of his voice, a variety of whistles, his own and manufactured ones, with which to communicate.

June Weaver's screen characterization is truly that of a liberated woman, way ahead of her time. She is never typed as a hillbilly harridan. She portrays simple but astute country women.[8] In many of the films June's role is strong, sometimes even stronger than the roles of the Weaver men.

The Weavers' film career began with small roles in *Swing Your Lady* (1938), a Humphrey Bogart film for Warner Brothers. Joe Hyams, a Bogart biographer, quotes Bogart as saying this is his worst film. The film represents mainstream Hollywood's assumption that the South was peopled with barefoot, bearded, tobacco chewing, moonshine guzzling, early marrying "hillbillies."

Fortunately, the Weavers landed a contract with Republic Pictures, the largest and the most productive of the "B" studios in Hollywood. Republic turned out pictures in every genre, which were aimed at regional audiences, especially the rural areas of the South and Midwest. Gene Autry was the top moneymaker for the studio when the Weavers arrived, and Roy Rogers was fast becoming established as a popular singing cowboy.

Republic made no effort to promote the Weavers as anything other than what they were—entertainers from a Southern tradition of country music. The films were designed for a rural audience already presold on the Weaver name. In the initial production, the Weavers took second billing to Ralph Byrd, who portrayed Dick Tracy in Republic serials. The trite plot of the film, *Down in Arkansas* (1938), has Byrd as a government agent overcoming the opposition of country folk to a proposed government dam.

In their second film, *Jeepers, Creepers* (1939), the Weavers were top billed. This picture is a good example of Republic's penchant for buying a popular song and building a film story around it, or simply using the song to pull in an audience. This idea would stretch the limits of credibility in *Tuxedo Junction*, a Weaver entry from 1941. The song, a very popular swing tune of the time, bore no resemblance to the film's plot, which had the Weavers using juvenile delinquents to help harvest a "victory crop." There is a certain degree of incongruity in the combination of "hillbilly" entertainers, jazz music, and urban delinquents. What worked for audiences, however, was the warmth of the Weavers, their sincerity, and the perpetuation of the Southern myth—country is better than the city.

By 1940 Nashville's "Grand Ole Opry" was a radio institution, having been on the air in one form or another since 1925. Republic arranged to use the title for a Weaver film, *Grand Ole Opry* (1940), but the film title is deceptive. The film is not about the "Grand Ole Opry" although the show's creator, George D. Hay, and two regular performers, Roy Acuff and Uncle Dave Macon, have bit parts. What a viewer sees is a film with the established Weaver characterizations. They portray officials or leading citizens of a Southern town, which looks suspiciously like California or the studio back lot. Through strength of community and plain virtue, they triumph over an assortment of urban crooks and slickers. They defeat Allan Lane, another Republic cowboy (later the voice of Mister Ed on television), who tries to control state politics.

The essence of the Weaver appeal might be summed up in the title of one of their films in 1940, *Friendly Neighbors*. Frank McDonald, who directed several of the Weaver films at Republic, says of the group that they were "grand, simple, honest, sincere, fun to be around."[9]

Chester Lauck and Norris Goff, both from Arkansas, created two of the most popular Southern characters ever—Lum and Abner. Like Bob Burns's storytelling Arkansas Traveller, the Lum and Abner characterizations descend from the line of the "frontier humorists." The dialects, the tall stories, the convention of the local yokel's besting the city slicker are as common to characters in George Washington Harris and Mark Twain as they are to Lauck and Norris's Lum and Abner.

The genial bickering between the two personalities, the way they said things as opposed to what they said, captured a radio audience in 1931 and held a large part of it until 1955.[10] The setting of the show was Lum and Abner's Jot 'Em Down store in mythical Pine Ridge, Arkansas. Though sketchily described, this general store was a replica of an institution familiar in nearly every rural community through the first half of the twentieth century. It was the place where community gossip thrived and citizens conducted business. Through this familiarity, the Jot 'Em Down store became an essential part of the success

Original hillbilly teams: (top) the Weaver Brothers and Elviry; (bottom) Lum n 'Abner. (From the author's collection)

of Lum and Abner, especially when Lauck and Goff transferred the characters to the screen.

As the show's popularity grew, the characters of Lum and Abner evolved: Lum became the conservative, Abner the adventurer who would gamble on anything from checker games to horse races. Other characters appeared, all played by Lauck and Norris in the beginning: the town patriarch, the town drunk, the village idiot. Rural radio listeners easily saw around them living examples of these fictional characters.[11]

*Dreaming Out Loud*, the first Lum and Abner movie, was released in 1940. The plot is strictly a "B" movie staple: a struggling young doctor romances the postmistress; someone commits a hit-and-run; Lum and Abner solve the hit-and-run. There is the obligatory city-slicker con: Lum and Abner buy several cases of bath salts, not a fast moving item in rural Arkansas. Only the personalities of the characters are able to add any spark to this hackneyed effort.

*So This is Washington* (1943) stands as the only Lum and Abner film worthy of more than passing mention. It takes a satiric look at World War II Washington, touching on the housing shortage and the difficulty the average citizen has in cutting through government red tape. Following a plea by the government for inventions to help win the war, Lum thinks he and Abner have invented synthetic rubber. Between attempts at getting a hearing for their product, the Southerners spend much time on a park bench dispensing advice on a variety of problems to several government officials. Rarely has the Southern character received such generous treatment in the movies.

Lum and Abner never achieved success in films equal to the success of the radio show. Despite the expertise of Hollywood makeup artists, Lauck and Goff looked like what they were: men in their thirties pretending to be elderly men (see accompanying illustration). Moving pictures of Lum and Abner and Pine Ridge, Arkansas, could not compare with the powerful bond of imagination that existed between radio and listener.[12] Still, the Southern charm and sensibility came through on screen.

Judy Canova, the last Southern-based performer to make a "B" film series, had the longest career in Hollywood. She went from a specialty number in *In Caliente* (1935) to fifteen years of starring roles at

Republic Pictures, ending with *Lay That Rifle Down* in 1955. In his book on the movie slapstick actresses James Robert Parrish says of Judy Canova: "The public immediately cottoned to the frenetic mixture of good vocalizing and country bumpkin humor. Canova developed her characterization of the rural miss, a little addled, but a delightfully honest creature. No matter that her manners might need a little polishing or that her guileless nature might embarrass one with its forthright honesty. Here was a fun person who represented the basic stock of American culture. All she asked was to be accepted as one's friend; to be helpful whenever possible; and if lady luck smiled on her, to land a man of her own."[13]

Following the path of Bob Burns and Lum and Abner, Judy Canova found her greatest success on radio. Born and reared in Starke, Florida, near the Georgia border, Canova, with sister Anne and brother Zeke, went from community amateur contests to a radio station in Jacksonville, Florida. She perfected routines built around "hillbilly" accents and studied rhythmic contortion and tap dancing. Although she aspired at one time to a classical music career, Judy had to accept the fact that there was a demand for her "hillbilly" act but not for her attempts at serious music.

After a successful vaudeville career and a Broadway play, *Ziegfeld Follies* of 1936, Canova concentrated on radio and motion pictures. Tiring of brief specialty roles in "A" pictures at the major studios, she accepted a contract from Herbert J. Yates of Republic Pictures in 1940, preferring the stardom offered by that studio's low budget films.

*Scatterbrain* (1940), the first Canova starring film, has a complicated plot in which a girl is "planted" with an Ozark family so she can be discovered to play the heroine in a "hillbilly" movie. By error, Judy Canova, the real "hillbilly," is signed for the role. The New York *Daily News* gave the film a three star review: "The gags are good, the situations are funny, and Judy Canova herself a riot in her first starring role."

In *Sis Hopkins* (1941) Canova was again playing the underdog, this time in a college setting. She is a wholesome, if ignorant, country girl competing with big city snobbery in the person of Susan Hayward. Her sympathetic characterization is an obvious factor in Canova's motion picture success. Audiences responded in the 1940s to the idea of country innocence winning out over city sophistication, to a pleasant, unpretentious country girl or man undaunted by the lack of urban opportunity. After all, isn't country better than city?

Canova became a radio star in *Pudden'head* (1941) and a war time heroine in *Joan of Ozark* (1942) by destroying a Japanese submarine. Again in *Sleepy Lagoon* (1943), she became a heroine by capturing a gang of crooks.

Judy Canova, the not-so-pretty girl with the voice that could sing swing, ballads or opera, conquered vaudeville, Broadway, films, and radio. A large American audience liked the way she played havoc with uppercrust mores and man's pretensions. For many, she represented what is the very essence of what is best about Southerners and Southern life.[14]

A final "B" series deserves mention here—the Kettle films starring Marjorie Main. Strictly speaking, the series was not "Southern." Ma and Pa Kettle were characters in Betty MacDonald's *The Egg and I*, which was set in Washington state. Although the film settings ranged from Washington to Hawaii and to the Ozarks, the stock characterizations and situations from the "Southerns" were present: the "hillbilly," the city slicker, and country values.

Ma and Pa Kettle were supporting characters in *The Egg and I* (1947). Response to the gruff yet tender Ma and the lazy but resourceful Pa was such that Universal pictures decided to produce a series. The resulting films, which continued until 1957, suffered from the benign neglect indigenous to most "B" productions: hack writing, indifferent direction, and skimpy production values. Only the talent and personalities of Marjorie Main as Ma and Percy Kilbride as Pa kept the series going.

The Kettle films bridged the gap between the phasing out of "B" movies by the film industry and the rise of the generally inferior "Southerns" on television, *The Beverly Hillbillies*, *Green Acres*, and *The Andy Griffith Show*. Only the Griffith show presented the Southern character free of the scurrilous "hillbilly" stigma. In the tradition of the Weavers, Lum and Abner, and Judy Canova, Andy Griffith, an actual Southerner from North Carolina, portrayed a rural sheriff, strong, sensitive, and able to hold his own against the inevitable big city adversary.

The Southern character represented by the performers mentioned here is absent from Hollywood films today. There are no "hillbilly" film series anymore. Some "B" films are still being made for the summer drive-in theater trade; and some—like *Macon County Line* and *Harper Valley P.T.A.*—are even about the South. But these films emphasize the same violence and sex as today's costly super spectacles. The South is slowly becoming part of the national community, its regional identity being absorbed by industrialization and urban growth. Perhaps because of the prodigious output of television entertainment, even rural audiences have become too sophisticated for the likes of the Weavers or Judy Canova. A faint glimmer of this Southern character can be seen in some of the films of Burt Reynolds, but Reynolds is more at home on the "Tonight Show" than he would be at the Jot 'Em Down store.

### A Selective Filmography of the "Hillbilly" Motion Picture

1937 *Mountain Music* (Paramount) Bob Burns, Martha Raye, John Howard, George "Gabby" Hayes

1938 *The Arkansas Traveler* (Paramount) Bob Burns, Irvin S. Cobb, Fay Bainter, Lyle Talbot
*Down in Arkansas* (Republic) Ralph Byrd, The Weaver Brothers and Elviry, June Storey

1940 *Friendly Neighbors* (Republic) Weaver Brothers and Elviry, Thurston Hall
*Grand Old Opry* (Republic) Weaver Brothers and Elviry, Allen Lane, Roy Acuff, Uncle Dave Macon
*Dreaming Out Loud* (RKO) Chester Lauck (Lum), Norris Goff (Abner)
*Scatterbrain* (Republic) Judy Canova, Alan Mowbray, Eddie Foy, Jr.

1941 *Arkansas Judge* (Republic) Weaver Brothers and Elviry, Roy Rogers, Spring Byington
*Sis Hopkins* (Republic) Judy Canova, Bob Crosby, Jerry Colonna

1942 *Bashful Bachelor* (RKO) Chester Lauck, Norris Goff, LaZu Pitts
*Joan of Ozark* (Republic) Judy Canova, Joe E. Brown, Eddie Foy, Jr.

1943 *So This is Washington* (RKO) Chester Lauck, Norris Goff, Alan Mowbray

1944 *Goin' to Town* (RKO) Chester Lauck, Norris Goff, Barbara Hale

1948 *Feudin', Fussin', and Fightin'* (Universal) Donald O'Connor, Marjorie Main, Percy Kilbride

1949 *Ma and Pa Kettle* (Universal) Marjorie Main, Percy Kilbride

1951 *Honeychile* (Republic) Judy Canova, Eddie Foy, Jr., Alan Hale, Jr.
1954 *Ricochet Romance* (Universal) Marjorie Main, Chill Wills, Rudy Vallee
1955 *Lay That Rifle Down* (Republic) Judy Canova, Robert Lowery, Richard
   Deacon


## NOTES

[1]Thomas Burnett Swann, *The Heroine or the Horse* (South Brunswick and New York: A. S. Barnes, 1977), p. 104.

[2]Brom Weber, *The Art of American Humor* (New York: Thomas Y. Crowell, 1962), p. xi–xii.

[3]Weber, p. 155.

[4]Weber, p. 265.

[5]Bill C. Malone, *Country Music, U. S. A.* (Austin: The Univ. of Texas Press, 1968), pp. 43–44.

[6]John Dunning, *Tune in Yesterday* (Englewood Cliffs, N.J.: Prentice-Hall, 1976), p. 84–85.

[7]Dunning, p. 85.

[8]Lewis G. Krohn, "The Weaver Brothers and Elviry," *World of Yesterday*, No. 13, p. 24.

[9]Krohn, p. 23.

[10]Charles K. Stumpf, "Lum and Abner," *World of Yesterday*, No. 20 (1979), p. 27.

[11]Dunning, p. 376.

[12]Lewis G. Krohn, "Lum and Abner Placed Pine Ridge on the U.S. Maps," *World of Yesterday*, No. 20 (1979), p. 31.

[13]James Robert Parrish, *The Slapstick Queens* (New York: Castle Books, 1973), p. 208.

[14]See Parrish, pp. 208–13.

# Business and Love in the Post-Reconstruction South: *Warner Brothers'* Bright Leaf

MARTIN F. NORDEN

May 31, 1950, was quite a day for Raleigh. Warner Brothers Pictures, in cooperation with the Raleigh Merchants Bureau and twenty-three other North Carolina cities and towns, had organized an all day series of events, and, in the words of Charlotte *Observer* columnist Dick Pitts, "The Warners publicity staff headed by Herb Pickman really took over the town."[1] The events held that day included a float-filled parade, an afternoon tea, a charity ball, and various forms of street entertainment. Floodlights blazed outside the Ambassador theater, while several on the spot broadcasts covering the day's proceedings emanated from the lobby. Among the prominent people taking part in the day's events were movie stars Patricia Neal and Donald Crisp, novelist Foster Fitz-Simons, broadcast personalities Ted Malone and Tommy Bartlett, several Warner Brothers officials, North Carolina Governor Kerr Scott, U.S. Representative Harold Cooley of Nashville, dozens of area mayors, twenty-four beauty contestants vying for the title of "Bright Leaf Queen," a small band of Cherokee Indians, and a contingent of newsreel photographers and movie magazine writers. In all, an estimated 75,000 people participated in the festivities.[2]

The occasion for this ballyhoo, as unnoteworthy as it might seem today, was the world premiere of a film entitled *Bright Leaf*.[3] Though Raleigh, N.C., might appear an unlikely candidate to host the first public presentation of a Hollywood film, the mystery dissipates with a revelation of the subject of *Bright Leaf*. As columnist Pitts described the film, "It's the story of the building of a tobacco empire in the old south, set against a background of southern mansions, beautiful women, fiery tempers, and courtly manners—the story of the rise and fall of a man in love and in business."[4] Adapted by Ranald MacDougall

95

from Foster Fitz-Simons's best-selling novel and directed for Warner Brothers by Michael Curtiz, *Bright Leaf* is the rags-to-riches-to-rags story of a vengeful capitalist-cum-egoist, and features twin themes of incompatibility: that of power and love, and of personal delusions and real-life situations. Such a story and attendant themes have been explored previously in the cinema, of course, perhaps most spectacularly by Orson Welles with his *Citizen Kane* (1941) and *The Magnificent Ambersons* (1942). While *Bright Leaf* is not as flamboyantly packaged as these earlier films, it nevertheless follows in their tradition. This article will focus on these themes as presented in *Bright Leaf,* with special attention to the ways they are interwoven with certain Southern concerns: the erosion of Southern values and lifestyles in the face of twentieth-century industrial and de-regionalization pressures.[5]

I hardly need to point out that despite the hoopla surrounding its world premiere, *Bright Leaf* is today a largely forgotten film. Its relative obscurity is indeed unfortunate, for, among other qualities, it is one of the exceedingly few films with Southern themes and backgrounds set during neither the Civil War era nor the period reflecting the time in which the film was made. *Bright Leaf* is unique in that its events take place at the turn of the century. It is a "midway" film not only from this perspective, but also in terms of the development of Southern issues and concerns presented in the cinema.

The Civil War era proved to be an early favorite for filmmakers, whether the generic meta-structure was turgid melodrama, as with D. W. Griffith's *Birth of a Nation* (1915), or physical comedy, as exemplified by Buster Keaton's *The General* (1927). It continued to be a promising topic for exploration in the late 1930s and early 1940s, and during that time a relatively new character "type" took on sharp definition: the strong-willed, tempestuous Southern belle. Manifestations of this character appeared in such prominent films of the time as *Jezebel* (1938), *Gone with the Wind* (1939), and *Reap the Wild Wind* (1942). From the post-World War II era through the 1960s, the Civil War began giving way to modern Southern backgrounds. Most of the Southern-oriented films during this time explored various rotten fruits of the Southern heritage: most notably, social injustices committed upon blacks, and modern vestiges of the decaying Southern culture.

A rare transitional film set in the years 1894 to 1900, *Bright Leaf* is unique in its Southern themes. The strain of transition is reflected in the filmmakers' seeming inability to make up their minds on some issues. For example, *Bright Leaf* presents the mostly pre-World War II image of the fiery Southern belle, but she is by no means the center of attention in this film; also, it examines social themes, but not such hot-potato ones as racism and poverty.[6] The social issues with which it deals are surprisingly absent in other films with Southern themes. This absence brings us to the focus of this article: the post-Reconstruction economy and the motivations and ethics of its business leaders.

The issues of business and business ethics arise almost immediately in *Bright Leaf.* In 1894, Brant Royle (Gary Cooper) returns on horseback to his hometown of Kingsmont, N.C.,[7] after a period of six or seven years to claim the cigarette factory left to him by his recently deceased uncle. Through an ensuing conversation between Royle and Calhoun, the probate lawyer, a background story is revealed: Royle and his father had been run out of town years before by Major James Singleton (Donald Crisp), the local tobacco magnate, once the Royle tobacco farm had begun to turn a profit. Royle's recounting of the events has a strongly bitter tone to it: "My father worked that land up from nothin'. Sweated over it fourteen, fifteen hours a day. I know it, 'cause I used to help him. Nobody in the valley grew better bright-leaf tobacco. Then just when it started to pay off, the Major stepped in. It was a nice little farm, once."[8] His parting words to Calhoun foreshadow events to come in the film: "I'd do the same thing to him if I had a chance. Maybe more."

The similarities between Singleton and Royle, hinted at in this conversation, become more pronounced as the film progresses: both share a desire to build up a tobacco empire at any cost, especially at the expense of the other man. A major difference between the two arises very quickly, however, in the form of traditional values. The Major's specialty is hand-rolled cigars, and when a "yankee" from Connecticut named John Barton (Jeff Corey) attempts to sell him on the new idea of a cigarette-rolling machine, he refuses to listen: "I'm afraid I don't believe in cigarettes, much less a machine for makin' 'em. It turns my stomach, sir, everytime I have occasion to witness someone poking one of those vile concoctions into their face. I deal in cigars, sir, nothing less. Let me tell you something. For more than 100 years, Singletons have been growing, smoking, living, and thinking tobacco, and they were cigar smokers to a man. I'm too old a horse to change my gait."

The Major clearly represents a popular view of the Southern business mentality of the times: tradition-bound, largely agrarian, autocratic, close-minded, unwilling to bend with the times. True to his name, Singleton is "single-minded" in his endeavor to continue the tradition of hand-rolled cigars while avoiding both cigarettes and new technology, whatever the cost.

Royle, on the other hand, is far more flexible in his business dealings. During his "exile" from Kingsmont, he has learned modern business practices at the Boston Tobacco Exchange. When Barton turns to Royle with his plans for a cigarette-rolling machine, Royle quickly sees the possibilities, and it is not long before he, Barton, and Chris Malley (Jack Carson), a reformed "snake-oil salesman" whom they take on as a business partner, begin mass-producing cigarettes in Kingsmont.

The company they form, Royle, Inc. (its slogan—"Royle Cigarettes, Fit for a King"), represents the new way of conducting business in the South near the turn of the century. Even its personnel makeup is strongly anti-traditional: a Southern expatriate who learned the tobacco business in Boston, a Connecticut inventor, and a former nation-traveling huckster whose honey-tongue shows no trace of a Southern accent. And the financial backer for this organization is Sonia Kovac (Lauren Bacall), a local businesswoman originally from Pittsburgh, known affectionately by Royle as "Carpetbagger." It is clear they symbolize the growing trend of *de-regionalization* within the South's industrial growth at this time, in addition to espousing the ideas of industrial mechanization and the manufacturing of a product aimed for the masses.

These innovations are not enough, however, to make Brant Royle a truly viable alternative to Major Singleton and the business practices he represents. Far from becoming a revolutionary, Royle attempts instead to model himself after the Major. As is clear when Royle offers the following reason for insisting on having his office face the Single-

Confrontation of the Old South and new: Brant Royle (Gary
Cooper) and Major Singleton (Donald Crisp) meet at an
auction in *Bright Leaf* (Jack Carson looks on)

ton mansion: "I wanted to be able to sit here and see that house.
Singleton's place. When I was a kid, kickin' along in the dust, I used to
promise myself I'd have a place like it someday. And everything that
goes with it." His imitation becomes complete late in the film when he
rejects a Royle cigarette proffered him at a board of directors meeting,
preferring instead to light up a cigar.

In the process of emulating the Major, Royle becomes an even
greedier capitalist. His business tactic is to attend personally the local
tobacco auctions and buy up as much of the plant as possible, regardless of the going purchase rate, thus cornering the market. The execu-

tives of the older cigar companies balk at this tactic, and their hesitancy quickly comes back to haunt them; it is not long before their companies are sucked in by the Royle juggernaut. These takeovers are visualized in *Bright Leaf* in a remarkable and economical way: the factory buildings of three lesser competitors—Pendleton, Phillips & Co., and Devers-Hokins Tobacco Co.—are shown, one right after the other. Each building remains the same when presented, except for the huge sign posted on each structure displaying the company name, which changes via a dissolve-montage from the original name to Royle, Inc. One company name is conspicuous by its absence, and soon it is apparent there is only one holdout left.

The Major realizes he cannot withstand the pressure from Royle much longer. Drawing upon his Southern heritage, he does the only thing he believes is honorable: he challenges Royle to a duel. "Defend yourself," orders the Major, "or I'll kill you where you stand." Royle, however, is acutely aware of the strength of the Southern code of ethics in such situations, as he indicates in his self-revelatory reply: "No, you won't. I might if I were in your shoes, but you haven't got the kind of *courage* it takes to shoot an unarmed man. You're a *gentleman*. You live by a code that doesn't permit such things. That's all you've got left: your gentlemen's code."

Royle's response immediately sets the two men apart. If Royle has become a mirror-image of Singleton, it is just that: an image. There is no "soul" to him, in the sense that he holds virtually no values or ethics, is ill-mannered (a point brought up several times in the film), and feels no responsibility except to himself. (As the business partner Barton caustically comments to him later in the film: "I've learned a great deal from you, Brant. If I weren't an honest man, I might be able to use it.") When out of weakness and frustration the Major shoots, wounding Royle in the arm, Royle shows no sympathy for the broken man: "Now there's nothing left."

Not quite. As an atonement for his betrayal of the code, the Major does one last thing in a remarkably dark and poignant scene. He returns to his carriage and climbs in. Immediately a gunshot is heard in the darkness, and the startled horse hitched to the carriage takes off. The driverless carriage eventually crashes to a stop, knocking over a piece of fence. The Major's body falls out of the rig, his suicide suggesting the apparent end of the Singleton power structure and its opposition to the upstart Royle, Inc. Not quite.

Royle's lack of ethics and responsibilities in his business dealings is tied directly to difficulties in his love life, in particular, to his infatuation with Major Singleton's beautiful daughter Margaret (Patricia Neal). Problems surface early in the film, when Margaret coyly "fails to recognize" Royle after they have run into each other for the first time in six years. Royle tries to jog her memory:

> Royle: My name is Royle. We had a farm not far from your place. You used to come and visit me in the fields.
> Margaret: I don't remember any such thing. And if I did, I wouldn't expect anybody to refer to it.
> Royle: I was just recallin' myself to you. I kissed you. Your father saw us. He broke his cane on me for it. Maybe you'll remember now.
> Margaret: Oh, I do remember you now. You're that bad-mannered, gangly farmer boy that used to pester me. The one I used to laugh about so hard.

This opening round of verbal fencing is illustrative of their relationship, which is based on the paradoxical notions of antagonism and attraction. As the film progresses, it becomes apparent that Royle is completely enchanted by Margaret, and that Margaret is not as cool to Royle as she seemed during this initial encounter. (She secretly confides to her Aunt Tabby: "I'll say one thing for Brant Royle: when he looks at me, I know I'm a woman. It isn't my ruffles that charm him, or the way I crook my finger when I hold a cup of tea. And you'd be surprised just how much that means to me.") Yet it is Royle's attempt at love that eventually ruins him. His love is, quite simply, perverse. Royle does not really love Margaret; he loves what she and the Singleton House represent: the trappings of wealth, class, and respectability. The true desires of Margaret, however, do not manifest themselves until it is clear that her father's fortune (and her potential inheritance) is strongly threatened.

Margaret is a fascinating and mercurial character. She has a polarizing quality to her, as demonstrated in this brief exchange with her aunt:

> Tabby: You're a strange girl. I wish I could understand you.
> Margaret: If you did, I'd do something else so you wouldn't.

She confounds her father with a plan she has: to marry Royle and then exploit him, thus saving what is left of the Singleton estate. The Major is despondent over this scheme: "He's done this to you? He's infected you with his own rot!" Margaret's reply is blunt and to the point: "What do you expect me to do? Stand here and watch you lose everything because you're too proud to admit you're beaten? Well, what about me? What am I supposed to do when all of this is gone? You made me a Singleton. That's all I'm good for. So I know how to behave like a Singleton."

On the one hand, Margaret represents a continuation of the old ways of life in the South. ("You remind me a lot of your father," Royle says to her early in the film.) Yet she is also a modern woman, and feels no reservation or remorse at abandoning tradition and pride when her future security is threatened. Her instincts for selfpreservation are the match of anyone's, and her ferocity surprises even the Major, who laments: "No Singleton ever wert the like of you." In terms of sheer greed and the unfeeling manipulation of others, Margaret and Royle seem a nearly perfect pair, as Sonia Kovac, Royle's business partner and jilted lover, suggests to him: "You and Margaret are alike. You're both greedy; you want something. For you, it's her. But she wants something else: power, like her father. As far as she's concerned, you're just a way of getting it."

Margaret's Southern heritage manifests itself with a vengeance, however, after she learns of her father's death. The suicide clears the way for her to carry out her plans for dealing with Royle, and soon she and her late father's rival marry. He moves in with her at Singleton House (which he renames "Bright Leaf"), but the newlyweds quarrel almost incessantly in the months thereafter. Perhaps through Margaret's calculated efforts, the marital discord distances Royle from the business dealings of his company. He seems completely unconcerned with the anti-trust action which is currently brewing ("Atty General to Smash Royle, Inc!" screams the headline of the local paper), but is finally jolted out of his personal problems when Malley confronts him with the company financial records and shows him that over the past several months Margaret has taken $2,000,000. He also discovers eventually that it was Margaret who leaked information to the U.S. Attorney General regarding the financial dealings of Royle, Inc. He

confronts her with this knowledge, and to his utter surprise, she rather
gleefully acknowledges it:

> Margaret: I wondered how long it would be before you found out what I was
> doing. First I was nervous; I thought surely you'd suspect right away. But
> you're so sure of yourself, that made it easy. Never entered your mind that
> something was wrong. Until now.
> Royle: I've lied to myself from the beginning. After a while that's all there
> was: you lyin' to me and me lyin' to myself. When did it start?
> Margaret: When my father died. On the day he was buried I've thought of
> nothin' else. How to destroy you. How to make you suffer as he did. And I
> have, haven't I? (pause) Now I want a divorce.

This "moment of truth" completely shatters the set of illusions held
by Royle, and he finally comes around to realizing Margaret's true
nature. His response to his recalcitrant wife reveals his new feelings:

> Royle: I've never seen you before the way you really are. This is what I've
> been drivin' myself to get, is it? I feel like I've been wallowing in filth. If
> that's what you wanted, I hope it's made you happy now. Get out of here.
> Margaret: I will. But you'll never forget me. With all of your wealth and
> power, there won't be a day or an hour that you'll get me out of your mind.
> Until the day you die, you'll remember the Singletons. What they've done
> to you.

Like Georgie Minifer in *The Magnificent Ambersons,* Royle "finally got his comeuppance." Undermined by this "Singleton Revenge," a staggering Royle trips over a candelabra, the flames from
which eventually set the entire mansion afire. Royle prevents anyone
from putting out the fire, and watches as the symbolic structure burns
to the ground.

The next morning, Royle pays a final visit to Sonia Kovac, the other
love interest in *Bright Leaf;* it was she who lent Royle the money to
start up what was to become Royle, Inc. She had loaned him the
money out of a misguided love for him, but he had looked upon that
encounter solely as a business deal. Royle has plainly never been
interested in Sonia as a lover; she lacks the class and breeding that he
so dearly cherishes in a woman, and finds in Margaret. To add insult to
injury, Royle is forever denying Sonia her femininity ("Why don't you
stop actin' like a woman?" he demands at one point), but it is always to
Sonia that Royle turns whenever he is desperate either for money or
for some form of affection. A telling scene occurs when Royle is alone

on Christmas, Margaret having gone off to spend the holidays with her Aunt Tabby. He sits at the end of a long table elaborately bedecked with Christmas decorations. A butler enters and begins setting a full-course meal for the solitary Royle, but in a fit of rage he knocks the food off the table and gets up to fix a drink. He thinks of Sonia, and in desperation decides to visit her late that evening, but to his chagrin he is rebuffed. Her rebuke is stinging: "Who are you, Brant? Who do you think you are that you can live in a world with people and have a heart all choked up with money? It's in you like a stone. Go back to your mansion, where you can buy anything. Except the way I loved you once. Go back to *Margaret*. You deserve each other."

Curiously, the three major encounters between Royle and Sonia are on special days: her birthday, Christmas, and New Year's Day. Perhaps the filmmakers were attempting to underscore the point that Sonia is (or should be) special to Royle, but that he acknowledges her uncommonness as infrequently as the occurrence of a holiday. The final time he visits Sonia is on the morning of a date brimming with significance: January 1, 1900, which, apart from its obvious overtones, is the very day after the Singleton mansion burned to the ground. Royle acknowledges his treatment of Sonia and the purging effect the fire has had on him:

> Royle: Seems like I always come to you when I'm hurt. Margaret's left me. Singleton House burned down last night. There's nothing left of it. It meant a lot to me, once. It meant *everything*. I stood there and watched it *burn*, and . . . it meant nothing at all.
> Sonia: Wasn't anything saved? Couldn't they . . .?
> Royle: I let it burn. They coulda stopped it, maybe. I wouldn't let 'em try; I wanted it to burn. Whatever it was that's been eatin' in me all these years seemed to burn out with it. I'm glad to be rid of it. I came here to tell you that. Somehow, after all this time, I've found . . . *peace*, I guess. I don't have to bull my way through, anymore. (pause) I'm leavin' Kingsmont, Sonia.

This last statement is duly realized in the final shot of the film, in which Royle departs Kingsmont the same way he arrived six years before: on horseback and virtually penniless. (The irony of this scene is that earlier in the film Royle had scoffed at Barton's plans to move to Detroit to enter the fledgling auto industry. Said he: "That's your idea of business, is it? The automobiles? [pronounced "auto-MO-beels"] Gadgets for millionaires.") The stark, bare branches of a tree looming behind him accentuate the bleakness of his situation, as he passes a sign reading YOU ARE LEAVING KINGSMONT, HOME OF ROYLE TOBACCO, INC., before turning and riding off into the distance. The Major is dead, Margaret has run off, and Brant Royle has reached rock bottom. Though he has acknowledged the flaws in his character that led to his downfall and seems repentant, there is clearly no hope for Royle to continue as a Southern business leader.

Several conclusions may be drawn from this rather dreary scenario. Regarding the cynical qualities of bitterness, arrogance, self-centeredness, and greed, and the paucity of likable characters (qualities shared with *Citizen Kane* and *The Magnificent Ambersons*, incidently), *Bright Leaf* is completely in keeping with the general thematic trends in the American cinema of its day.[9] Many films of the post-World War II years were marked by considerable interest in the dark and seamy side of human nature, blurred distinctions between "good" and "bad" characters, and depressing endings. Prominent films of the time featuring such qualities include *The Treasure of the Sierra Madre* (1948), *The Lady from Shanghai* (1948), *White Heat* (1949), and *The Third Man* (1949). The reasons for such thematic developments are unclear, but they are generally attributed to post-war pessimism, cold-war anxieties, fear of the bomb, and even the suspicion that one's neighbor might be the new enemy (a "red"), a fear magnified by the inability to ascertain a neighbor's allegiance—his "goodness" or "badness"—merely by his appearance.

More to the point of specifically Southern concerns is the issue of the regional economy. *Bright Leaf* attempts to show that neither Royle's way of doing business nor the Major's can survive alone in the twentieth century. (This point is underscored by the observation that Royle's personal empire was completely destroyed *less than one day* before the start of the twentieth century.) Singleton's approach—gentlemanly, with no interest in mass production, non-traditional (and non-elitist) products, and modern technologies—is too fragile and will be overrun by those who take modern business strategies into consideration. Yet Royle's method—steamroller business tactics untempered by personal integrity and hindered by spiritual blindness—leads to destruction as well. The film implicitly calls for a dialectic or synthesis of the positive aspects of these two approaches, if modern industry is to take firm root in the South. In so doing, the Southern economy would be turning over a new leaf, so to speak, and one that has the possibility of becoming very bright, indeed.

NOTES

[1]Dick Pitts, "The Cinema," Charlotte *Observer*, 2 June 1950, p. 11-A.

[2]Charlotte *Observer*, 28 May 1950, p. 17-B; 30 May 1950, p. 13-A; 31 May 1950, p. 11-B, 1 June 1950, p. 3-F; 2 June 1950, p. 11-A.

[3]*Bright Leaf*, 1950, Warner Brothers-First National, 110 minutes. *Producer:* Henry Blanke. *Director:* Michael Curtiz. *Screenplay:* Ranald MacDougall, from the novel by Foster Fitz-Simons. *Director of photography:* Karl Freund, A. S. C. *Music:* Victor Young. *Leading players:* Gary Cooper (Brant Royle), Patricia Neal (Margaret Single-ton), Donald Crisp (Major James Singleton), Lauren Bacall (Sonia Kovac), Jeff Corey (John Barton), Jack Carson (Chris Malley).

[4]Pitts, p. 11-A.

[5]Though this article is by no means a formal analysis of *Bright Leaf*, some mention of its form is in order. Karl Freund's black-and-white cinematography is, in a word, "lush." Overall, the film is characterized by very opulent settings overflowing with period detail, and equally elegant costuming, recreating a "feel" or ambience not unlike that found in the antebellum portions of *Gone with the Wind*. Also, many deep-focus shots, presumably used to help capture some of the grandeur, are in effect, as are a considerable number of low-angle shots of Brant Royle (accentuating his prominence) and shots featuring dramatic high-contrast lighting.

[6]A word should be said about *Bright Leaf* as a "socio-cultural document" of America in 1950 regarding race. The film is true to the generally conservative white American values and attitudes of the day, in that blacks are virtually invisible. The roles they play in this film are distinctly minor: truck loaders, butlers, bartenders, factory work-ers, redcaps, and the like.

[7]"Kingsmont" is fictitious, though a town named "Kings Mountain" really does exist in the state.

[8]This dialogue quotation and all others are cited directly from the film's soundtrack. All italicized words appearing in these quotations were emphasized originally by the actors concerned.

[9]There are truly few likable people in this film. Several secondary characters (Sonia Kovac, John Barton) are generally positive and virtuous, but they are clearly over-shadowed by the questionable figures of Brant Royle and the Singletons. By today's standards, the Major might come off more strongly as a tragic hero because of his refusal to have anything to do with cigarettes (if for reasons other than health), but to 1950 audiences, his opposition to this popular product must have been one big ironic joke.

# "Burn, Mandingo, Burn":
## *The Plantation South in Film, 1958–1978*

EDWARD D. C. CAMPBELL, JR.

Hollywood in the 1930s—as pointed out in the Introduction to this collection—presented an idyllic South overflowing with wealth and populated by refined ladies and gentlemen surrounded by faithful servants. Scores of films like the musical comedies *Dixiana* (1930) with Bebe Daniels and *Mississippi* (1935) with Bing Crosby, epical dramas like *So Red the Rose* (1935), Bette Davis's Academy Award winning *Jezebel* (1938) and *Gone with the Wind* (1939) provided entertaining escapist fare. The attempt to forget the national Depression dictated much of the productions' format, and images of a grand, vanished South were particularly appealing during hard times.

Signs of change appeared, however, in the 1940s. Only four films set on plantations attracted the usual production and advertising budgets or profits. The first, *The Flame of New Orleans* (1941), was a frivolous comedy by French refugee filmmaker René Clair, starring Marlene Dietrich, turned comedienne since *Destry Rides Again*. *Dixie* (1943), a rousing musical popular with troops overseas, provided another vehicle for the talents of Bing Crosby. *The Foxes of Harrow* (1947) was a potboiler with a rakish Rex Harrison, based on black novelist Frank Yerby's best-selling novel; and, though set in the 1870s, Walt Disney's *Song of the South* (1946), with James Baskett as Joel Chandler Harris's Uncle Remus, evoked such nostalgia that audiences and reviewers firmly believed it to be set in the antebellum period. The romantic contents and advertising for these films closely resembled those of the 1930s.

It would be a mistake, however, to believe that the decrease in "moonlight and magnolia" releases necessarily signalled a change in Hollywood's perception of the region, particularly in regard to the

107

earlier films' overriding racist viewpoints. Rather, the issue of the black-white, slave-master relationship was drawing the attention not of the industry or the audiences so much as the federal government. During World War II, the U.S. Office of War Information applied increasing pressure to refurbish the image of the black. After all, if the nation was to draft blacks or expect them to enlist, and if the U.S. and its allies were indeed fighting a war "to preserve democracy," the image of the South as a region of benevolent, benign planters, pliant fieldhands and devoted houseservants was especially abhorrent. It was, therefore, a subject for the film industry to avoid, revise, or soft-pedal.[1]

The fifties was a period of even fewer films about the slave era, as Hollywood found the subject not worth the risks involved. Motion picture production, as a business first and an art second, was not in the habit of repeatedly raising issues as touchy as the South's peculiar system of bondage and economics was becoming.

Certainly the change in our society was considerable. The single decade after World War II included the integration of the armed services, the instigation of fair hiring guidelines in the federal bureaucracy, and several Supreme Court decisions against discrimination, the most noteworthy being the 1954 *Brown v. the Board of Education* ruling, which ended the concept of "separate but equal." The Congress of Racial Equality, CORE, had by 1947 staged its first "freedom rides."

By 1960, twenty states had enacted fair employment laws. Congress in 1957, 1960, and 1964 passed civil rights acts. The Twenty-Fourth Amendment to the Constitution ended the use of the poll tax, long employed to deny blacks their rightful vote. And the first years of the 1960s were a period of yet more "sit-ins," "freedom rides," and protest marches to Washington and various Southern state capitals. Despite white backlash or vacillation, productions such as *The Littlest Rebel* seemed hardly possible anymore.[2]

In a continuing effort to provide productions using what had heretofore been a consistently profitable setting, the film studios simply eliminated the traditional images of slavery. For example, *The Mississippi Gambler* (1953) and *The Gambler from Natchez* (1954) included only a glimpse of servants in the background; there was no traditional black character development whatever. Warner Brothers' *Band of Angels* (1957) broke ground in exploring the subject of miscegenation, as did the disappointing *Raintree County* (1957). The subject had the twin advantages of appearing liberal in that it was finally being discussed and it most assuredly boosted ticket sales.

Ticket sales by the late 1950s needed all the attention the industry could muster. Films like *The Mississippi Gambler* starring Tyrone Power were the last vestiges of the old days of prosperity. Hollywood faced a changing society and a changing audience. In 1946, only 8,000 American households owned a television. But by 1949, in just three short years, there were 940,000 TV sets. Moreover, during the same period the weekly theater attendance dropped by twenty million. Population patterns changed too. As suburbs grew, the huge downtown theaters could no longer prosper and therefore could not book good films. By 1953, receipts were only half what they were in 1946.

In the face of declining receipts, the difficult political and racial climate, and the changes in urban demographics brought about by white flight or just unchecked development, the motion picture industry dropped the Old South as a theme. The plantation setting was too overworked, had even become trite, and, most importantly, presented too explosive an issue in an era of changing racial relations. Indeed for many, the only use to which the antebellum era could be properly put was in a massive reinterpretation of the black-white relationship. Such an endeavor would well summarize the burgeoning liberal mood and the nation's collective sense of guilt, could attract a growing black audience with films produced especially for the minority community, and could maintain the economic viability of the inner-city urban theatres. Initially, however, the films seemed bent only on undoing what had been at best a regrettably shortsighted interpretation and at worst a pernicious subjugation of a more balanced examination of the slave experience.

The first two films of the reappraisal appropriately enough were adaptations of Harriet Beecher Stowe's abolitionist novel, *Uncle Tom's Cabin*. The very minor production of 1958 was actually nothing more than a re-release of the silent 1927 version with an added introduction by Raymond Massey. The intent was clear enough. An advertisement in the *New York Times* (5 October 1958) encouraged attendance "since integration is a major issue on the current news." Posters further stressed the mission by encouraging one to "Hate Simon Legree, pity Uncle Tom. . . ."

It was not until 1965 that a company broached the subject a second time. Unable to secure American backing for his production, producer Kroger Babb instead filmed *Uncle Tom's Cabin* in Eastern Europe with a large international cast. It was a disaster. Babb employed Yugoslavian cavalry as Southern planters and Serbian farmers as Negro slaves.[3] From there, things only grew worse.

After three years of production, Babb in 1968 insisted that the film was significant. In large advertisements and elaborate articles in U.S. newspapers, he declared that his version of *Uncle Tom's Cabin* presented "the story of slavery in the Deep South with amazing accuracy and tremendous spectacle." Theater posters included claims that the movie "teaches what no teacher can." Unfortunately, he opted more often for brutal spectacle and odd humor rather than accuracy. For instance, in the production the slave Andy is brutally hanged; Napoleon in trying to escape across a river is maimed by alligators. The posters, though, tempted the audience to "come swing with Andy and swim with Napoleon." Another advertisement so radically changed the intent of the movie that one might have thought it a musical comedy: "Tonight have fun, dance with the Natchez folks, sing with Uncle Tom, love with Mr. St. Clair, see the show of shows." Additional captions went to other extremes: "See the hanging of innocent Andy, see the Negro slaves whipped and chained, see Harris dragged behind a horse, see the brutal whipping of black females. . . ."

It was no wonder that the critics and audiences were confused, shocked. Several critics labeled the film "trite."[4] In fact, the film pointed to the problems of reinterpretation. The film attempted to explore new ground in order to attract a new audience, while still offering enough of the formula excitement of action and romance to retain the traditional moviegoer. Babb's production of *Uncle Tom's Cabin* demonstrated the early impossibility of that and signalled the way for yet another attempt, *Slaves*.

The 1969 film *Slaves* ushered in those films which, though still enthusiastically declaring the best of liberal intentions, no longer made any pretense of protecting white sensibilities. The intent now was to make money and to provide the black ticket buyer with an almost visceral experience, a vicarious venting of frustrations through seeing the slave finally turn on his master and wreak havoc. Uncle Tom had at last become Nat Turner.

Though adapted from a 1969 novel by John O. Killens, *Slaves* is nonetheless closely akin to *Uncle Tom's Cabin*. For example, the loyal slave is sold only because his master is indebted to an unscrupulous slave dealer, and the evil Legree-like character is a Northerner aided by black drivers hauntingly similar to those in the novel. The film also displays a remarkable singleness of purpose. Starring Ossie Davis, Stephen Boyd, and Dionne Warwick, the movie was produced by Phillip Langer and directed by Herbert Biberman, once blacklisted in Hollywood for his leftist political leanings. In effect, the company imposed a 1960s social consciousness on an 1850s setting in an explicitly liberal moral and political statement. The producer and director took pains to film the story on actual plantations in Louisiana, and the extras were drawn from an area black Baptist congregation descended from slaves.

The pride of all those involved was evident. At a preview for Baltimore's Johns Hopkins Institute of Southern History, Biberman declared that the picture was "to get at the essence of what slavery was really like—even if it means sacrificing the truth . . . in particular characters and incidents."[5]

The director's effort is especially apparent in the character of Nathan McKay (played by Boyd). The planter is a genuine admirer of African art and culture who often dons native dress and may even truly love his black mistress (Warwick). The point, though, is that for all his appreciation of African culture, he is no less a slave master who is destroying that which he professes to admire. In the end, his true position dooms his society, and the slaves in turn revolt.

What was so unfortunate, however, is that the film's considerable message was masked by the usual requirements of contemporary film needed to attract ticket buyers. The posters and newspaper advertisements were complete with nude pictures of Dionne Warwick being closely examined by her master. Those who were attracted had little reason initially to expect anything more than a seamy picture.

Shrill captions included "See, feel, taste the bloody whip of truth" in a movie which "rips through the moonlight and magnolia to get to the blistering passion of the Old South."

In response, several theater managers who originally had commended the effort later refused to book *Slaves* for fear of racial violence, white as much as black. The critical reaction was bleak as well. With its "R" rating, the film did, however, have an appeal. In Los Angeles, it played at six drive-in theaters simultaneously.[6]

What was most disturbing to many was the answer the film provided to racial injustice. At a time when black organizations were debating whether to work within or totally apart from white society, whether to create change peacefully or violently, reviewers questioned the film's pat philosophy that violence was the answer, or at least the logical and irrepressible result of slavery and racism.[7] Released after the riots in Watts and Detroit, the film was a biting reminder of the justifiable anger still seething in the black community.

By the 1970s then, the films utilizing an antebellum setting had not yet become critically accepted, but they were making money. *Slaves* never earned what was expected, but in re-release in early 1980, it continued to draw. The "R" ratings, the violence, and the sexual promiscuity in films such as *The Quadroon* (1971) even drew white audiences interested if not in the interpretive aspects at least in the visual ones. *The Quadroon* promised the thrill of "one quarter black, three quarters white, all woman."[8] Productions like Warner Brothers' picaresque comedy of the slave South, *The Skin Game* (1971), with James Garner and Lou Gossett hardly stood a chance against such competition; it was perhaps too understated.

Though many whites still avoided the new cinematic interpretations of the antebellum South, the excitement if not the politics of the scripts made considerable inroads. In the mid-seventies, the producer Dino DeLaurentis followed the highly profitable *Mandingo* (1975) with *Drum* (1976). Other films, like *Passion Plantation* (1978) "where your real roots are," sought to keep up with the demand. Laced generously with sex and violence, *Mandingo* had earned $8.6 million, and placed 18th of the 104 most profitable films of 1975; *Drum* ranked 71st of 116 for the following year.[9] However, as black audiences cheered while the slaves burned the plantation in *Slaves* and cried

"Go Mandingo" as the incensed fieldhands murdered the whites in *Drum*, there was reason to believe there were still two distinct audiences. One watched the long-awaited films of revenge and another viewed the 1972 re-release of *Song of the South* and the previous year's re-issue of *Gone with the Wind* or the new musicals set in the South, the profitable *Tom Sawyer* (1973) and its sequel *Huckleberry Finn* (1974), both financed by *Reader's Digest*.

The competition in the face of rising prices, decreasing audiences, and the demands for enticing, exciting entertainment seemingly favored such new films as *Mandingo* over the tired formula remakes or reissues. Advertising and publicity definitely reflected the trend towards films of rape, mayhem, murder, and assorted other ingredients necessary to new films about the slave South.

The publicists for *Mandingo* exhorted the public to "expect the savage, the sensual, the shocking," to be prepared for "all that the motion picture screen has never dared to show before—expect the truth." The hyperbole for *Drum* rivalled even that; it "out-Mandingoes *Mandingo*" in a film that "scalds, shocks, whips, bleeds." *Passion Plantation* held out the chance that "anything could happen."

Despite the obvious attempts to titillate, the films did contain much that was revealing. As reinterpretation—or for most, as initial introduction—the several movies commendably exposed much of a system long presented in popular culture as simple and benign. For that accomplishment alone, the films long relegated to the "blaxploitation" genre deserve scrutiny. The horrors of the Middle Passage and slave seasoning stations in *Drum*, the miscegenation in *The Quadroon*, the brutal beatings in *Passion Plantation*, and the slave breeding practices in *Mandingo* are just a few examples of the surprising revelations to those accustomed to films of the old mythology produced as recently as the early sixties.

The attempts to rectify the former romanticism were in earnest. Producers, directors, and actors threw themselves into exploring racial themes with obvious commitment. What Babb and Biberman had preached in the 1960s, others continued. Dino DeLaurentis felt his productions *Mandingo* and *Drum* were to "reach beyond the sentimentalized South of other films with uncompromising honesty and realism to show the true brutalizing nature of slavery."

A new look at the old South, *Drum:* Drum (Ken Norton) attempts to protect Augusta (Fiona Lewis) from rape during a slave revolt.

But critics responded unfavorably time after time. *Slaves* was perceived as only a "mawkish, cliched piece of drivel" which was all the more disappointing for the many who realized its initial potential. As one writer remarked, too often it was only a "cinematic carpetbagging project in which some contemporary moviemakers have . . . attempted to impose . . . their own attitudes that will explain 1969 black militancy."[10]

*Mandingo*, though a considerable moneymaker, did no better with the critics. It was universally perceived as a racist "conspiracy of depraved minds" who fashioned "the most salacious miscegenation-inspired sex fantasies." The interracial sex, nudity, and violence of *Drum* supposedly exposed a film "less interested in information than titillation, which, in turn, reflects contemporary obsessions rather than historical truths."

Amidst the overwhelmingly enthusiastic black response at the box office and the constant harping of the critics, it has constantly been overlooked that both the escapist traditional and the revealing revisionist cinematic views of the Old South suffer from oversimplifications apparent from the first film adaptations of *Uncle Tom's Cabin* in 1903 to the most recent in 1969. As *Gone with the Wind* was in its view of the region a story only of whites happening to be among blacks, so too are the newest films like *Passion Plantation* not an examination of black-white relations, but the reverse—a tale of blacks among whites.

In the haste to reinterpret a body of film admittedly entertaining but finally recognized as racist and paternalistic, the complexities of slavery have been ignored. Understandably, it is time the slave character is at last afforded his due measure of attention in cinema, but the productions have gone too far in creating another character just as unbelievable as in earlier films. Henry Walthall in *Birth of a Nation*, George Brent in *Jezebel*, or Bing Crosby in *Mississippi*, all gallant gentlemen in ruffled shirts, as surely fail to capture the essence of white Southern manhood as do Perry King in *Mandingo* or Warren Oates and John Colicos in *Drum*, portraying sadists, degenerates and fops. The same is also true of black characterizations. All antebellum blacks are not adequately characterized by the roles played by Clarence Muse in *So Red the Rose*, Bill Robinson in *The Little Colonel*, Eddie Anderson in *Gone with the Wind*, or Stepin Fetchit in *Hearts in Dixie*; nor do they conform conveniently to the rebellious stud portrayal given by Ken Norton in *Mandingo* or Yaphet Kotto in *Drum*.

The reversals of stereotypes, for all their considerable worth as a step in the right direction for reinterpretation still carry a danger. In particular, the slave character still labors under a mythology, although a newer one. Negroes are never condemned in the new films. Thus their blemishes of character, if any, are accepted simply as the result of white injustice, and therefore their virtues are not a product of free choice but of a personality awarded them by liberal cinema. Conservatives like D. W. Griffith had once shaped a similar perfect character for the white planter. There is the distinct danger of disenchantment with yet another stereotypical characterization, at the expense of the considerable progress of the last twenty years, in a reassessment of the plantation South and the Afro-American experience.

## NOTES

[1]For an overview of the government's influence in Hollywood during World War II, see Clayton R. Koppes and Gregory D. Black, "What to Show the World: The Office of War Information and Hollywood, 1942–1945," *Journal of American History*, 44 (June, 1979), 87–105; and Allan M. Winkler, *The Politics of Propaganda: The Office of War Information, 1942–1945* (New Haven: Yale Univ. Press, 1978), especially pp. 57–60.

[2]For a broad examination of the impact of political and social changes on the general image of blacks in film, see Thomas J. Cripps, *Slow Fade to Black: The Negro in American Film, 1900–1942* (New York: Oxford Univ. Press, 1977); Donald Bogle, *Toms, Coons, Mulattoes, Mammies, and Bucks: An Interpretive History of Blacks in American Film* (New York: Viking, 1973); and Jim Pines, *Blacks in Film: A Survey of Racial Themes and Images in the American Film* (London: Studio Vista, 1975).

[3]*Variety*, 19 June 1965.

[4]For representative reviews, see *Milwaukee Journal*, 22 July 1969, and *Variety*, 19 June 1965.

[5]Baltimore *Sun*, 1 June 1969; see also *Pictures*, 11 June 1969; *New York Times*, 19 Jan., 3 Jul. 1969; *Washington Post*, 21 May 1969; and *Hartford* (Conn.) *Times*, 10 July 1969.

[6]For adverse critical response, see *Pictures*, 11 June 1969; *Denver Post*, 16 June 1969; Wilmington (Del.) *Evening Journal*, 5 July 1969; *Atlanta Constitution*, 24 June 1969; *Chicago Tribune*, 1 July 1969; *Christian Science Monitor*, 28 July 1969; *Hartford* (Conn.) *Times*, 10 July 1969; Louisville *Courier-Journal*, 9 Aug. 1969; *Boston Globe*, 17 July 1969; *Detroit Free Press*, 4 July 1969; Charlotte *Observor*, 22 Aug. 1969; *New York Times*, 3 July 1969; *Film Daily*, 27 June 1969. Among the few complimentary reviews were *Cleveland Plain Dealer*, 14 May 1969; and *Variety*, 7 May 1969.

[7]*Film Daily*, 27 June 1969; *Atlanta Constitution*, 24 June 1969; *Chicago Tribune*, 1 July 1969; *Detroit Free Press*, 4 July 1969; and *Cleveland Plain Dealer*, 11 May 1969.

[8]*Atlanta Constitution*, 22 Oct. 1971; see also *Variety*, 31 May 1972.

[9]*Variety*, 7 Jan. 1976; 5 Jan. 1977.

[10]*Denver Post*, 13 June 1969; *New York Times*, 3 July 1969.

# The Human Landscape of John Ford's South

J. P. TELOTTE

In the minds of practically all moviegoers, John Ford's name is inextricably linked with the Western. And apparently he relished that identification, for at a Screen Director's Guild meeting he supposedly introduced himself as follows: "My name's John Ford. I make Westerns."[1] During a fifty-year career as America's foremost filmmaker, however, he frequently turned his attention to other genres and themes. Because of Ford's outstanding work in the Western genre, though, many of his other film interests have been relatively neglected.[2]

If Ford had any consistent concern, it was probably with the integral, almost self-contained cultures which he located not only in the American West, but also in his Irish heritage, in the professional military fraternity, and elsewhere. One of Ford's interests was in Southern culture and its traditions, upon which a major body of his work focused, despite the fact that he lacked a personal familiarity with the region. While his Southern films do not, as a group, match the complex, epic sweep so often achieved in the Westerns, their number implies that Ford consistently found something in Southern culture which encouraged him to pursue his typical concerns. His approach to Southern settings, however, is in marked contrast to his treatment of the West, a fact which suggests that a proper appreciation of Ford's work should incorporate an understanding of his distinctive Southern vision.

Unfortunately, no accurate assessment can be made of the exact number of Ford's Southern films, nor of their percentage in his total canon, due to the haphazard records of early film history and the singular problems presented by film preservation, thanks to which

117

many of his early films no longer even exist. Extant information indicates at least eleven films which we might, because of principal characters or settings, safely characterize as Southern.[3] Significantly, the majority of these were made prior to Ford's landmark Western, *Stagecoach*—the movie which firmly established him as the foremost interpreter of our national experience—and therefore also prior to his discovery of that archetypal Western setting, Monument Valley. A tentative list of Ford's Southern films includes four silent features— *The Scarlet Drop* (1918), *Hitchin' Posts* (1920), *Cameo Kirby* (1923), and *Kentucky Pride* (1925)—four films from the middle period of his work—*The World Moves On* (1934), *Judge Priest* (1934), *Steamboat 'Round the Bend* (1935), and *Tobacco Road* (1940)—but only three projects undertaken during the height of his career—*The Sun Shines Bright* (1953), *The Horse Soldiers* (1959), and the "Civil War" sequence of *How the West Was Won* (1962). Of these last films, the first is basically a remake, although far less romanticized, of *Judge Priest*, while the latter two seem much more reminiscent of Ford's Westerns of the same period. To gain a perspective on Ford's depiction of the South, then, we might focus our attention on several of his films made prior to the bellwether *Stagecoach* and the justly celebrated Westerns which followed it. Particularly, two of Ford's most successful and accessible films, *Judge Priest* and *Steamboat 'Round the Bend*, both starring Will Rogers, seem characteristic of his perception of the South. Both investigate the interrelationship between the locale or community, which provides the formal conditions of life, and the individual inhabitants who are shown to be the real source of its vitality.

## II

Numerous critics have noted Ford's almost iconic use of landscape, especially his tendency to develop "the relationship of characters to their physical environment in related formal ways."[4] This evocative use of locale, especially the famous Monument Valley setting which formed the backdrop for seven of his films following *Stagecoach*, is easily the most distinctive feature of Ford's Westerns. As Todd McCarthy suggests, by continually returning to this stark setting for his films, Ford effectively transformed a "unique spot" in the Utah desert into a national icon, emblematic of the American West for native movie-goers and enthusiasts of the genre world wide.[5] The valley's stark, flat floor and suddenly up-thrusting sandstone buttes offered more than simply a picturesque backdrop for these films, however. Throughout his career Ford was equally celebrated for "his mastery of character type,"[6] and a major factor in the success of his Westerns was probably their full integration of these concerns with character and setting. In the broad contrasts provided by Monument Valley Ford found a ready-made, almost symbolic statement on the Westerner's relationship to his environment. Through his lingering long shots and open compositions, therefore, Ford was able to transform that land-scape into a framework for viewing and evaluating human achieve-ment; the valley's sharply rising "monuments," standing out against the horizon, became a measure of the men riding across that heedless terrain.

In Ford's Southern films, however, this emphasis on setting, the almost reverential treatment he so often accorded the environment, is noticeably lacking. Despite its title, Ford's *Tobacco Road* is preemi-nently concerned with investigating character quirks. The main ac-tion in Ford's contribution to *How the West Was Won* occurs at night and was shot on a sound stage, the result being an indistinct locale, more an anonymous backdrop against which characters might con-verse and reveal their motivations. With *The Horse Soldiers* Ford evokes the South more by *fiat* than by imagery. A series of titles *tells* us where various actions in the film occur: "Lagrange, Tennessee," "Newton Station," "Jefferson Military Academy." By a few long shots of Greenbriar, an archetypal Southern plantation, Ford seems to reach for an atmospheric setting such as he so easily attained in his West-erns,[7] but John Wayne, portraying Colonel John Marlowe, head of a raiding Yankee cavalry unit, looks distinctly out of place in that gen-teel plantation setting, as if the definitive Western hero could not help but evoke his similar role in Ford's famous cavalry trilogy—*Fort Apache, She Wore a Yellow Ribbon*, and *Rio Grande*—made a few years before.

Certainly the South does not lack such evocative settings, as classic films like *Birth of a Nation, Gone with the Wind, The Southerner*, and even the recent *Stay Hungry* attest. Many students of Southern writing have pointed out that a distinctive sense of place has always seemed a hallmark of this region's artistic productions. These estimations probably derive in great part from statements on Southern culture made by the "Agrarians," who in their famous protest against the modern disintegration of Southern values espoused a return to a traditional "culture of the soil," whereby one could "identify himself with a spot of ground," which would, in turn, impart "a good deal of meaning."[8] The land and the traditions associated with it were thus thought to offer a stable influence, a tested set of values to which the Southerner might turn in a troubled and transitional time.

These elements, however, could hardly be expected to evoke the same resonances for the outsider as for the native. Since Ford did not have a personal experience of the South to draw upon, he turned to the prevalent myths and stereotypes of the region, which popular literature fostered. Of course, historians have suggested that "the South is in many ways the product of an overactive imagination, both regional and national," and that because of the numerous distortions of its history, "the distinction between a *historical* and a *fictitious* South becomes a particularly difficult one."[9] Even if Ford had been more intimately acquainted with the region or been able to shoot on location there, the product might therefore still have been quite singular.

In any case, in conjuring up his own South, Ford seems to have placed little weight on that sense of "place" which he elsewhere uses to denote a community of common interests, of inherent and shared meanings. Instead, he focuses primarily on character, perhaps because the truths of human nature are constant, but also because Ford was always on home territory when it came to character development. Here too, though, Ford wrought subtle changes in his Southern characters.

Well into the twentieth century the South was still basically an agrarian society firmly attached to the land and committed to that community which shared this heritage. At the same time, however, the Southern character evidenced a staunchly individualistic impulse, one which, according to W. J. Cash, derives from a basic similarity between the conditions of the old South and those prevailing on the Western frontier.[10] In this respect, Ford's Southerners are very much like his Western heroes, clearly individualists; at the same time, though, they seem uprooted from the land, almost alienated from the world they continue to inhabit and the community of which they are supposedly a part. Certainly we expect that outsider's stance with Colonel Marlowe of *The Horse Soldiers*, for he is at war with the South, bent upon wreaking havoc in that world. A similar displacement, though, afflicts his opposite number, the protagonist of *Judge Priest*, who is himself a former Confederate officer. He lives alone in a house haunted by the memory of his dead wife and son, and in a small but telling action, one which intimates his growing alienation from the mainstream of his community, he responds to an ungentlemanly remark from his barber about a local girl by removing his shaving mug from a wall of other cups in the barbershop. The judge is firm in his values, even though they decree that he withdraw from a traditional center of local society.

That staunchly individualist character and the sense of immersion in the flow of time are constants in Ford's work. In his Southern films they give rise to an interesting dialectic between the forces of stability and change. Ford places his steadfast characters in a world of rapid change which threatens their old-fashioned ways and ideals, and he consistently associates that sense of change with man's divorce from a prior, almost edenic relation to his environment and his fellow men. Again, *The Horse Soldiers* offers a prime example, for in that film Ford focuses on the Civil War to depict the devastation wrought upon the South by the Union invaders, and specifically to suggest the monumental destruction carried out by Sherman in his march to the sea. As momentous as that devastation, though, is the near mortal blow which this conflict apparently dealt to the way of life, the system of values which the South had produced. Ford dramatizes the death of that romantic, antebellum world of genteel manners and Southern cavaliers in the suicidal charge through the streets of Newton Station which the one-armed Confederate colonel Jonathan Miles leads against the carefully dug-in Yankee raiders. However admirable they appear, such old-fashioned heroics are clearly futile, even foolhardy gestures in the face of Yankee pragmatism and rapid-fire weapons. Throughout his Southern films, and even in many of his Westerns, Ford used the Civil War as a recurring image for what might be termed the "fall" of Southern man, with its backlash felt by all of his Southern characters, even those in a more contemporary film like *Tobacco Road*. For him that conflict apparently suggested a cause for both the pervasive sense of displacement experienced by his characters and an attendant deterioration of basic values.

As Ford clearly recognized, though, the human memory and those values which it clings to often remain unvanquished by the passage of time or sense of displacement. Common to all of his films, then, is a deep sympathy for the dispossessed and an enoblement of those who have suffered some great loss, yet have managed to tenaciously hold to a strong set of values and thus impart some stability and continuity to their world. What stands out about Ford's Southern films, however, is his tendency to isolate this concern, to create a sense almost of man in a vacuum. He does not use setting iconically to evoke this human situation; in fact, when the setting becomes noticeable at all, it seems nearly alien to Ford's protagonists. Instead, he concentrates attention on the persons of his heroes, those who recognize yet continue to inhabit that world of flux. These characters are aware of the inevitability of change and of its end result—making them increasingly outsiders in their own world. Still, they manage to draw from within themselves a steadfastness, which enables them to endure and offer a measure of stability to the culture of which they continue, almost anachronistically, to be a part. Aware of just how fragile any external support, including an "agrarian" ideal, must ultimately be, Ford apparently sought to lay bare the human spirit—particularly that Southern spirit—which persists in clinging to and fashioning something of worth.

### III

Both *Judge Priest* and *Steamboat 'Round the Bend* are set in the early 1890s, when the Civil War was still a vivid memory for many of their characters, continuing to color their thoughts and actions. A rolling title opens *Judge Priest* and formally announces this relation, stating that "The War Between the States was over, but its tragedies and comedies haunted every growing man's mind." The South Ford wishes to evoke, then, is very much a "haunted" world, less an actual physical setting than a mental or even spiritual one, colored by one specific event; and its inhabitants must contend with these ghosts of their past, even as they face a new and ever-changing situation. Judge Billy Priest, a Civil War veteran, is being challenged for his Circuit Court seat by the new breed of Southern politician, the pompous Senator Horace Maydew, who believes Priest's "hankering for the spirit of the law, if not the letter" is both impractical and anachronistic. The judge almost seems to live with the spirits of his wife and son who, like the South of his youth, have passed away, while he tries to uphold his legal duties and help along his nephew 'Rome, a beginning attorney "about the same age" as his own son would have been. Similarly, Dr. John Pearly of *Steamboat* has lost most of his family, for his beloved sister is dead and her son Duke is to be hanged for murder. At times he reminisces about his past—for instance, how during the war he "sure used to make them Yanks run"—and about the former glories of his now dilapidated steamboat *The Claremore Queen*, winner of the annual race down the Mississippi to Baton Rouge "back in '84." Now, however, all Dr. John desires is to live free and easy on his boat, fishing all day while Duke pilots it along the river.

To emphasize the general feeling of isolation that besets these characters, Ford removes much of the sense of place from *Judge Priest* and repeatedly undercuts it in *Steamboat*. In the former film he furnishes all the superficial trappings and clichés often associated with the South; there is drinking of mint juleps, reference to the smell of honeysuckle, moss hanging from a few trees, and even stereotyped "darkies" singing "My Old Kentucky Home." In short, it is less a realistic world than a cliché, conceived by someone lacking personal familiarity with the region, though sure of the personal vision which he brought to it. *Judge Priest* was obviously shot primarily on a sound stage, which accounts for its emphasis on interiors and that lack of a real sense of place that location shooting normally imparts. Superficial elements thus function as compensation for what might otherwise seem a glaring absence of an identifiable locale and atmosphere. In *Steamboat* most of the exterior scenes appropriately focus on the old sternwheelers, steaming along the river. In the main, this is stock footage, though. Moreover, the river here is almost a non-place, a complex image suggesting both man's inevitable *immersion* in the flow of time and that longed-for freedom from the world along its banks—a world which, incidentally, is hardly shown at all. When the river is pictured, it is in extreme long shots, with the steamboats and their occupants standing out against the tangled horizon afforded by the riverbanks, just as Ford's cowboys appear all the more impressive when posed against the expanse of Western skyline. A careful examination, though, reveals how much less Ford was concerned with this setting—and hence with whatever values it might potentially have evoked—than with his distinctive characters. The on-board shots of *The Claremore Queen*, for instance, are obviously faked through a combination of skimpy sets and rear-projected footage of the river, while the staging of these shots emphasizes Dr. John's character at the expense of a realistic concern for the location and for what we usually term "screen logic." One example occurs when the boat approaches a river landing and Dr. John hails the dockworkers. As the scene begins, a long-shot shows that the landing and workers are on the port side of the ship; the medium and close shots of Dr. John trading quips with the dockmen, though, place him at the starboard window of his pilothouse, talking to what should be, according to the geography created by the camera, nothing but open river! Such errors recur throughout the movie, but we might read them less as errors than as indicators that Ford's priority lay elsewhere than in an evocative use of setting.[11] Essentially, his tendency in these films, unlike in his Westerns, is to consistently subordinate setting to characterization, place to the *irreplaceable* individual.

In Will Rogers, of course, Ford had found an actor whose strong but quiet persona almost dictated this subordination. Moreover, Rogers provided Ford with a previously established persona that could easily evoke those values which audiences of the period would associate with the South (see accompanying illustration). By the mid-1930s Rogers had become installed in the national consciousness as a figure who spoke for and embodied the best aspects of the regional character. Through a number of films, as well as a national radio program, syndicated newspaper column, and personal appearances, Rogers presented the image of a wise, down-to-earth type, mindful and respectful of the past, yet aware of and involved in the present. He combined a general human sympathy and affection with a strong sense of integrity to suggest a dependable value system, one which Peter Rollins finds "seemed miraculously unaffected"[12] by the rapid disappearance of these same qualities in the world around him. Simply by starring Rogers, then, Ford opted for an emphasis on character, specifically one which would convey an established and valuable set of principles to the movie audience. How well he understood this can be seen in Ford's admission that he often allowed Rogers to improvise many of his lines and scenes[13]—a freedom the notoriously tyrannical Ford permitted few others.

Predictably, the heroes of both *Judge Priest* and *Steamboat* are essentially extensions of the Rogers persona placed within Ford's larger humanistic framework. As the titles of these characters suggest, they both hold positions of authority in their communities, even if Dr. John's rank seems more a comic adjunct of his patent medicine line than an earned title. Ford's real interest, in any case, is in the character behind the title, the worth of the man holding the position. While Horace Maydew, who seeks Judge Priest's circuit court seat, already holds the title of Senator, he is clearly nothing more than a pompous blowhard, the archetype of the bombastic, self-aggrandizing Southern politician. Such types mainly serve as foils for Ford's heroes who, in

The Will Rogers persona: as Dr. John conning the public in *Steamboat 'Round the Bend.*

contrast, shine forth all the brighter. Through long experience, especially the test administered by the Civil War and reconstruction
period, they have learned how to balance their idealism with an
element of practicality, an innately sentimental nature with the plea-
sures of a harmless chicanery, the needs of the community with those
of the self. The values of both Priest and Dr. John, however, are in the
process of being tested once more, for both men stand poised against a
world fast changing, a new South whose modern order of politicians
and legalities seems just as much a threat to the old as does Captain
Eli's *Pride of Paducah*, the new boat which has already rendered Dr.
John's *Claremore Queen* obsolete.

## IV

To dramatize this conflict between the old and the new, between
individuals and their changing world, Ford has suffused these two
films, like so many of his others, with ceremonies.[14] *Judge Priest*, for
example, is framed in ritual, for it opens on one trial and ends with
another, which finally dissolves into a parade honoring Confederate
Memorial Day. *Steamboat* likewise abounds in such rites—revival
meetings, baptisms, a wedding, and a public hanging—which again
frame the main action. A major reason for these ceremonies is apparently to create a communal or cultural environment which might
throw the characters of Judge Priest and Dr. John into greater relief.
Therefore Ford does not allow any ritual to stand without comment,
though the critique provided may seem somewhat disconcerting.
Each ceremony is in some way undercut, its real worth subtly called
into question. *Steamboat*, for instance, begins with the paralleling of
two similar "con jobs," first the New Moses' temperance/revival meeting, and second Dr. John's pitch for his patent elixir, delivered to the
same crowd and with manifestly better results. Ford's sympathies are
clearly with the latter, who is able to tell his listeners the lies they
really want to hear—such as how drinking his Pocahontas Remedy
excuses one from "doing a lick of work"—without losing sight of his
own rascality in the bargain. In the same vein, both films contain
formal legal trials which, in turn, are shown to be little better than
farces, their outcomes determined less by the letter of the law than by
either sentiment or prejudice.

In fact, these repeated trial scenes are rather deceptive, for even as they focus our attention on a minor character's plight and the community's general indifference, they also point obliquely to a more complex trial underway in each film.[15] Ford is ultimately less concerned with the often spurious rites of a particular region, than he is with the personal trials which his protagonists undergo—Judge Priest to see if his home-spun notions of justice still apply in his world, and Dr. John to determine if that free life of the river remains accessible. No simple verdict of guilt or innocence is sought; rather, *validity* is the central issue: can a person's ideals hold up when put to the test? In the literal trials in which they are involved, Judge Priest and Dr. John lead the way in acquitting the accused. In those personal tests which accompany these trials, they vindicate their own characters, as well as those values by which they have lived their lives and to which their communities continue to pay lip service. What Ford thereby reveals is how much the community or region owes to the individual and his standards, and how those common ceremonies that infuse both films take their real worth from those greater personal trials which so often go unnoticed and unlauded in everyday life.

In *Judge Priest* the smaller rituals of courtship, a taffy pull, the trial of a chicken thief, and the judicial election offer opportunities for a superficial demonstration of communal values. They also provide a contrast for that more significant display of individual character, as the judge tries once again to affirm a moral order which seems increasingly out of place in the modern South. Having been rebuffed by Ellie May, Flem Talley, the local barber, revenges himself by making malicious comments about her character to everyone who enters his shop. Bob Gillis who, because of his past prison record, has never revealed that he is Ellie's father, punches Flem for the remarks and is later vengefully attacked by the barber and his friends. When Gillis knifes Flem in self-defense, his attackers accuse him of starting the fight and bring charges against him of attempted murder; and Gillis, whom everyone believes to be a Yankee, is generally presumed guilty by the community. By depicting this small-minded community with its mean and prejudiced characters, Ford is thus able to explode one myth, that of a common Southern gentility, gallantry, and honesty.

While these values are not manifest in the community at large, they may still exist, Ford then demonstrates, within certain individuals, notably Judge Priest. Since his nephew 'Rome is defending Gillis, the judge excuses himself from hearing the trial, though he does join in his defense. The argument he musters for the defense, however, seems less concerned with the facts of the case than with establishing the character or personal worth of the accused. Priest rightly intuits that the details of the incident have been twisted to create a false view, and he recognizes that he cannot *logically* prove Gillis's innocence. Drawing on his personal estimation of the jury's leanings and of the defendant's character—that is, on his ability to *judge* human nature—Priest therefore sets about manipulating the jury into a similar faith in his client. Through the Reverend Brand's impassioned testimony about Gillis's Civil War heroics and unselfish concern for his daughter's reputation, together with a coordinated rendition of "Dixie" from outside the courthouse window, Priest sways the feelings of the jury—which is, naturally, composed of war veterans—and wins acquittal for his client. While "justice" is, after a manner, accomplished here, Ford reveals that the community or locale is itself no guarantor of truth or right; its passions are too easily swayed in one direction or another. Rather, such values depend on a few individuals who, through their determination and right thinking, can point the community in the proper direction or save it from its own worst instincts.[16] Judge Priest clearly understands his community's foundation on the myth of a past glory, and he plays off of it to win his case. More importantly, though, he seeks to bolster the legend of a genteel, harmonious South, not because it is true, but primarily because he sees how valuable, indeed necessary, its maintenance is for his community's survival. As the newspaper editor in Ford's *The Man Who Shot Liberty Valence* avows, "When legend becomes fact, print the legend"; Judge Priest affirms the legends of his culture, but only because it ultimately depends on these illusions, kept alive by a few individuals, to maintain its stability.

In *Steamboat* we never see the actual trial scene, only the empty courthouse following the conviction of Dr. John's nephew Duke for killing a man—here, too, in self-defense and after insulting remarks were made about his girl Fleety Belle. In this instance Ford more clearly emphasizes the fact that it is Dr. John who is really being put to the test. He is, as the opening demonstrates, a familiar American figure, a direct descendant of Melville's "confidence man," but with a benevolent turn. Apparently his one desire is to retire to his old steamboat and fish while Duke pilots it along the Mississippi. In fact, once aboard his crumbling but once-proud ship, Dr. John seems most reminiscent of some Fisher King, waiting for a young knight—in this case, Duke—to come and restore life to his domain.

From the time of Duke's arrival with Fleety Belle, chased by both her folks and the law, Dr. John is himself forced into action. First, he convinces Duke to surrender himself to the sheriff and "straighten things out"; and Duke agrees, telling Fleety Belle that "you and me gotta be free to get married and live on this boat." They recognize, in other words, that any real freedom must come from the individual and his personal commitment to a code of justice. Dr. John's task, then, is to validate this code of ethics, to prove his nephew innocent in the eyes of the law and thereby win his liberty. Since the New Moses, the only witness to that fatal incident, is off "doing the Lord's work," Dr. John and Fleety begin cruising up and down the river, searching the backwaters for the "prophet" and seeking to raise money for a "big city lawyer" to handle Duke's appeal. When their efforts apparently fail, Dr. John takes *The Claremore Queen* down river to see Duke one last time before he is hanged; however, he can do so only by joining the annual steamboat race to Baton Rouge, risking his boat against its modern nemesis, *The Pride of Paducah*—in a sense, staking his way of life against creeping modernism. In the course of the race Fleety spots the New Moses, Dr. John ropes and drags him aboard, and despite his protest that "I got souls to save," they convince him to help stoke the boilers and win the race, because he also has "a life to save, and the Lord don't care which of your jobs you do first." The concluding race down the Mississippi becomes, then, not simply a contest between two boats, but Dr. John's race against time to bring in new evidence and so save Duke from the gallows. In order to work up a final head of steam and reach Baton Rouge in time, even the patent medicine is sacrificed to the ship's furnaces, Dr. John's "confidence game" forfeited so that truth might win out.

To pass such trials, both Judge Priest and Dr. John must manifest a more complex vision than seems characteristic of other members of their society. They understand that they must rely less on the reputed values of their Southern culture than on personal strength and resourcefulness—universal attributes which Ford celebrated in his other films as well. In *Judge Priest* the small-town Southern society receives a humorous send-up, especially with the comic Confederate Memorial Day parade with which the film ends; and that humorous view derives mainly from the sort of reflexive vision which Priest is able to maintain. He clearly respects the myths which inform his culture—and he has a real fondness for mint juleps—but at the same time he understands what weak props they finally are for human action, that ultimate value must spring from the individual himself. It is precisely this dualistic vision, a simultaneous awareness of the demands of past and present, of myth and reality, that enables the judge to manipulate the feelings of the townsfolk in the service of truth and justice. At the same time, it is this vision which raises both *Judge Priest* and *Steamboat* above the level of the simple stereotype.

In *Steamboat* Ford fashions a world where flux is clearly the natural order of things, almost demanding such a dualistic perspective from its inhabitants. As the opening suggests, here the evangelist and the con man have become nearly mirror images of each other, and as we later see when Dr. John mistakes the New Elijah for the New Moses, even the prophets of this land look pretty much alike. In order to raise the fee for Duke's lawyer, Dr. John takes a wax museum aboard his boat, noting that "if we get right down to earth and . . . change these people into people that these folks on the river want to see, we can make a lot of money." Hence, the wax figures of two Old Testament prophets are converted, simply by changing their clothes, into outlaws—the James brothers; a "virgin queen" receives a husband; King George III becomes his old nemesis George Washington; and Ulysses S. Grant, minus his cigar, naturally turns into his Confederate counterpart, Robert E. Lee. Even Dr. John's assistant receives another identity. Baptized David Begat Solomon, he changed his name to George Lincoln Washington, only to be rechristened Jonah when found sleeping inside a wax whale. Not only, then, does every image implicitly contain its opposite, but it easily, almost naturally undergoes such transformation, hardly suggesting thereby a world of permanence or stability.

Despite the trappings of a traditional culture, therefore, Ford evokes a world of mutability where one must learn not to depend so heavily on things or external support. Instead, it is man who must impart stability by influencing his culture toward a truly human end. With Duke's life on the line and *The Claremore Queen* out of fuel, Dr. John demonstrates this commitment; he sacrifices his steamboat, the major image of the Southern culture, so that Duke might live. First the deck and cabins of the boat are ripped up to provide the needed firewood. The figures of the wax museum are next to go, as the New Moses, as if in practice for some future heavenly chore, tosses them "into the fiery furnace." Finally, Dr. John feeds his patent medicine into the flames to get his boat in on time. Essentially, everything which suggests an attachment to the culture which bounds the river, to "place," is eagerly sacrificed for that last dash downstream which saves Duke from the gallows.

Both of these films end on a triumphant note. Judge Priest stands at the head of a parade with the acquitted Bob Gillis in arm, and Dr. John fishes from his new boat, *The Pride of Paducah*, won in the race and now piloted by his freed nephew. Their characters have been put to the test, and by their capable response to these challenges Judge Priest and Dr. John have reaffirmed their own values, despite the generally callous attitudes taken by their communities. *Judge Priest* opens on a tight medium shot of Will Rogers at the bench, announcing that "the court is now in session," and this statement effectively serves as a *coda* for both films. In *Judge Priest* and *Steamboat 'Round the Bend* John Ford conducted a much larger trial to be sure, more precisely, an investigation of that Southern culture which so fascinated him throughout his career.[17] As in many of his other films, he actually ended up investigating a mythic region instead of a totally realistic world; hence, the South he conjured little resembled that which anyone had ever actually seen. However, that locale itself seems less important to Ford than the characters with which he populated it, for it is in them that he lodged his values. His abiding interest in human nature—indeed, his *hopes* for man—led him to discover in that South of the imagination an especially strong and uncommonly sympathetic character, one who could cling to his ideals despite their general disintegration amid the changes in his surround-

ing culture. Equally important was the capacity of people like Judge
Priest, Dr. John Pearly and others to see themselves and the world
they inhabited clearly, and to understand the true relationship between the two. In this human respect, at least, Ford's reel world more
nearly corresponded to that real South which was indeed losing its
distinctive coloring, but whose people, like those in so many other
cultures, continued to impart a measure of stability and value. While
the region never quite provided him the distinctive picturesque setting which became the hallmark of his great Westerns, the South
inspired a viable substitute: a vital human landscape which had been
long nurtured by that region and which—as even an outsider could
recognize—remained its greatest resource.

## NOTES

[1]Related in Peter Bogdanovich's *John Ford* (Berkeley: Univ. of California Press, 1978), p. 19.

[2]J. A. Place's recent study, *The Non-Western Films of John Ford* (Secaucus, N. J.: Citadel Press, 1979), is a notable exception.

[3]In these determinations I have relied extensively on Bogdanovich's comprehen-sive filmography (*John Ford*, pp. 113–49), and to a lesser extent on that included in Andrew Sinclair's critical biography, *John Ford* (New York: Dial, 1979).

[4]Peter Lehman, *Authorship and Narrative in the Cinema*, with William Luhr (New York: Capricorn, 1977), p. 157.

[5]"John Ford and Monument Valley," *American Film*, May 1978, p. 12.

[6]Stuart Kaminsky, *American Film Genres* (New York: Dell, 1977), p. 254. Kaminsky further suggests that throughout his Westerns Ford sought to juxtapose characters with a striking setting to show how "men and the artifacts of civilization are vulnera-ble, weak in the face of nature" (p. 258). In his Southern films, I would suggest, that adversary relationship is filled not by images of nature or locale, but by an abiding sense of time.

[7]In fact, Ford introduces Greenbriar with the theme music from one of his most mythic Westerns *The Searchers*, a film shot almost entirely in Monument Valley.

[8]*I'll Take My Stand* (New York: Harper and Brothers, 1930), p. 19.

[9]*Myth and Southern History*, eds. Patrick Gerster and Nicholas Cords (Chicago: Rand McNally, 1974), p. 307.

[10]*The Mind of the South* (New York: Random House, 1941), p. 39.

[11]Ford similarly broke the basic rule of "stage line" in *Stagecoach* when he shot the Indians chasing the stagecoach from two opposite directions, thus giving the impres-sion of a complete change of direction in the midst of the chase. When questioned about this apparent lapse by Bogdanovich, Ford indicated that the light had necessi-tated the shift in perspective in this case, but also that "I usually break the conven-tional rules—sometimes deliberately" (p. 72).

[12]Peter C. Rollins, "Will Rogers: Symbolic Man and Film Image," *Journal of Popular Film*, 2 (1973), 343.

[13]Bogdanovich, p. 57.

[14]Lehman calls special attention to the conflict or paradox which these recurring ceremonies so often suggest. He sees them as images of the inherent contradictions in the society which Ford depicts. Apparently, it is by means of these ceremonies that

Ford's characters are able to overlook or—if only for the moment—overcome the fundamental contradictions which continually threaten their culture.

[15]See also Sam Rhodie's essay, "Who Shot Liberty Valence? Notes on Structures of Fabrication in Realist Film," *Salmagundi*, No. 29 (Spring 1975), pp. 159–71, for an analysis of the levels of deception woven into several of Ford's films.

[16]In the remake of *Judge Priest*, *The Sun Shines Bright*, Ford is even more explicit on this point. The judge prevents his community from lynching an innocent man, and when the truth is discovered, the townsfolk parade through the streets, bearing a banner which reads, "He Saved Us from Ourselves."

[17]In his recent biography of Ford, Andrew Sinclair makes note of the director's "pride in his wife's southern ancestry" and his predilection for books about "the Confederate generals, particularly about Robert E. Lee" (p. 34). This latter point throws another light on Ford's recurring interest in the South. Apparently through the South's Civil War heritage, Ford was able to consistently touch on another of his favorite subjects, the military life and that fraternity which it seems to foster.

# The South in the Films of Robert Altman

GERARD PLECKI

The South represents a cross section of American attitudes and lifestyles in the films of Robert Altman. His Southerners embody some of the best and worst traits of the American public. They are typically proud, resilient, and forceful, but they are also prone to racial and regional biases, to stubborness and greed. Complacency appears to be the dominant trait of the Southerner. It is in this that the Southerner most resembles the majority of the population of the United States—a population which, according to Altman, implicitly accepts corrupt political and economic institutions as natural parts of the American way of life. The South is depicted as the locus of conservatism in the United States. Altman seems to argue that the tendency to ignore or reject platforms for social change often results in the denial of individual freedom. This perspective is suggested in Altman's early films *M\*A\*S\*H* (1969) and *Brewster McCloud* (1970), and is more clearly developed in the later films *Thieves Like Us* (1974) and *Nashville* (1975).

Captain Duke Forrest in *M\*A\*S\*H* is a good example of Altman's view of the Southerner as a witty, resourceful, and likable man. Forrest quickly befriends the young Korean servant Ho-Jon, who has been forced by Major Burns to read the Bible aloud. He gives him a magazine featuring naked women because "it's easier to read when you have pictures." He is the instigator of the shower scene with Major Houlihan (Sally Kellerman). After Major Burns is carried away in a straitjacket, it is Forrest who points out the irony of the situation, asking Colonel Blake (Roger Bowen), "If I nail Hot Lips and punch Hawkeye can I go home?"

However honest and amiable Forrest is, he is nonetheless a

134

character whose personality is flawed by racial prejudice. Forrest's irrationality becomes apparent when Hawkeye Pierce (Donald Sutherland) suggests that, in order to win their football game with the "regular Army" team, they must requisition a ringer, a Captain Oliver Wendell "Spearchucker" Jones (Fred Williamson). Forrest concedes that Jones is an excellent football player and neurosurgeon. When Pierce and McIntyre (Elliott Gould) mention that Jones will reside in the officers' tent with them, Forrest strenuously objects. He states that Jones is black—that it is bad enough living with two yanks like Pierce and McIntyre, but that living with Jones in the Swamp would be pushing camaraderie much too far. When Forrest voices this sentiment, the viewer's perception of him changes drastically and immediately. Forrest's attitude towards Jones alienates him from the uncompromising and irascible anarchists of the mobile army hospital, Hawkeye and Trapper. They push him aside when he objects to the personal contact that their new relationship with Jones would necessitate. In this incident from M*A*S*H the Southerner alone subscribes to racial biases, but in other Altman films it is apparent that the South is not unique in fostering this type of intolerance. In *Buffalo Bill and the Indians* (1976), for example, Buffalo Bill and his Wild West entourage hold similarly outlandish beliefs. During a rehearsal of the Wild West Show, Buffalo Bill remarks to Sitting Bull, "Chief, we got a colored standin' in for you, cuz he's the closest thing on my staff to an injun." The beliefs of Forrest in *M*A*S*H* represent the prejudices that unfortunately have always been a part of the American national character.

Robert Altman's next film, *Brewster McCloud,* was set in Houston, Texas, where police and city officials headed by Captain Crandall (G. Wood) and Haskall Weeks (William Windom) try to stop a series of murders committed by Brewster (Bud Cort). Despite Crandall's thorough and systematic use of "good old fashioned police work," he cannot solve the case. Weeks, therefore, hires a California detective named Frank Shaft (Michael Murphy) to assist them, but they do not really trust this outsider. When investigating the scene of a murder, Shaft asks Crandall if the corpse was in its present condition when it was first discovered. Crandall is irritated by what he perceives to be the negative connotations of Shaft's question. He angrily replies, "Of course that's the way we found him. What do you think we are down here? Stupid?" Crandall's emotional outburst at the innocent query reveals his extreme regional pride. The defensive stance he adopts to counter the Northern slurs against his homeland is similar to the opinions voiced by Barbara Jean (Ronee Blakley) in her song "My Idaho Home" in *Nashville*.

Other characters in *Brewster McCloud*, especially law enforcement agents, all seem to suffer from some laughable mental or physical incompetence. Officer Johnson (John Schuck) reads a Captain America comic book while he is supposed to be watching for Brewster's stolen car; Officer Breen (Bert Remsen) attempts to extort a Nikon camera from Brewster; Officer Leadberry fails on several occasions to capture Brewster, who is seemingly trapped in the Astrodome. A Texas senator is interested in the series of murders only because his girlfriend wants to meet Frank Shaft. Haskall Weeks is involved in the case for the publicity it may yield. Too stubborn to inform the police of the whereabouts of Brewster and too deluded to recognize his own imminent danger, he confronts Brewster alone, at which point the investigation of the murders ends rather abruptly for Weeks. An overweight hoodlum named Billy Joe Goodwill who attacks Brewster is seen wearing a Porky Pig T-shirt. A police alert includes the phrase "Approach with caution, y'all." With these caricatures Altman humorously reiterates several Northern stereotypes of the nature and quality of Southern city life. Southerners are not alone, however, in their obsessions, greed, and hypocrisy. The belief that all Americans share these traits is obvious from the words and actions of the non-Southerner Frank Shaft, whose egomania and compulsiveness force him to shoot himself when he fails to capture Brewster. In *Brewster McCloud* Houston is the perfect setting for a satiric attack on the dreams, ambitions, and foibles of middle America.

*Thieves Like Us* is Altman's first serious investigation of life in the South. The film is based on the Edward Anderson novel, *Thieves Like Us*, which had been filmed in 1948 by Nicholas Ray as *They Live By Night*. In Anderson's novel, three convicts named Bowie, T-Dub, and Chicamaw escape from prison. They reunite on occasions to rob banks throughout the South. T-Dub is shot while attempting to rob a bank with Chicamaw, who is recaptured. Bowie, who lives with his girlfriend Keechie, decides to attempt to rescue Chicamaw. He helps Chicamaw escape, but abandons him on a country road. Bowie and Keechie are later killed in a police ambush.

The producer of *Thieves*, Jerry Bick, commissioned Calder Willingham to write a screenplay. Willingham's treatment of the story concentrated heavily on chases and on the mechanics of the robberies, and it was rejected by Altman, who hired Joan Tewkesbury to write a new script. Her treatment was, for the most part, faithful to the novel, and upon its completion Altman began forty-three days of location shooting in the South. The $1.25 million budget for the film would not, however, permit extensive set construction or period adjustment with or without the heavy rains that plagued the production. Altman was therefore forced to move from town to town until he found locations that could be used as they stood. Apparently the director felt that the 40-year time differential—the difference between the 1930 setting of the film and the conditions of the present settings—would not detract from the realism for which he was striving. The changes in the small towns and highways were believed to be minimal, and to Altman the people must have appeared unchanged.

The realities that the characters in the film face are indeed grim. In *Thieves Like Us*, the criminals and the rural dwellers of the South have striking similarities. Their lives are economically depressed; they feel downtrodden, bitter, and vengeful. All the people that Bowie (Keith Carradine) and Keechie (Shelley Duvall) encounter in *Thieves Like Us* are greedy, corrupt, and untrustworthy. For Bowie and his two associates T-Dub (Bert Remsen) and Chicamaw (John Schuck), bankers, lawyers, and police officers are "thieves." None of the characters in the film possesses any real freedom, and the three men live in the midst of an actively hostile environment. Their existence is claustrophobic. They are defeated by laws they neither understand nor embrace: by the betrayals of their friends, and often by their own superstitions. It is from this landscape that Altman draws some bleak generalizations about our culture.

Bowie, T-Dub, and Chicamaw have little regard for social norms. The only unpleasant aspect of robbing banks, stealing cars, and killing people is that one can be apprehended and will thus have to return to prison. As the mastermind of the gang, T-Dub is more concerned with

*Thieves Like Us*—John Schuck, Bert Remsen and Keith
Carradine connive.

enumerating the exact number of banks he has robbed than with
counting the stolen money. Chicamaw's reason for involvement with
the gang is publicity: he envies the headlines and newspaper descriptions of Bowie and T-Dub. Bowie is the naive member of the gang. In
many ways he is a "team player." His motivation for robbing banks
derives in part from his desire to maintain a friendship he feels for
T-Dub and Chicamaw. Despite their illegal activities and unusual
lifestyles, Bowie believes that they are no different from anyone else.
Once again, Altman does not suggest that Bowie's method of rationali-
zation, or the moral insalubrity of the three men, is unique to the
South. The setting is merely another good example of the casual
disregard for the lives of others common throughout the United States.
For example, Bowie justifies the murder he committed by explaining
to Keechie that it could be considered self-defense. He believes that
he alone can judge the appropriateness of his actions. In *The Long
Goodbye* (1973) Philip Marlowe (Elliott Gould) restates this belief.
Terry Lennox (Jim Bouton) objects that Marlowe is "breaking the
law" when Marlowe points a gun at him. Marlowe then tells Terry,

"Believe me, that's the last thing I'm breaking." Both Marlowe and Bowie feel that social norms are inapplicable to them, and that they alone should determine right or wrong by their own rigid standards.

   *Nashville* is a more ambiguous and perhaps more optimistic film than *Thieves Like Us*, but it still defines a disheartening national mood by depicting life in the South, this time in a present-day large city. The film does not propose a particular remedy, nor does it advocate one explicit ideological perspective. The film does suggest the desperate need for a moral reawakening of the United States.

Country artists Barbara Jean and Haven Hamilton (Renee Blakely and Henry Gibson) sing at a rally at the Parthenon in *Nashville*.

   The film opens with the Athens of the South commencing its Grand Ole Opry celebration. In following scenes the director explicates the shallow and parasitic nature of character interactions of a group of Southerners, including waitresses and singing stars, lawyers and farmers, reporters and salesmen. The film also describes the activities of John Triplette (Michael Murphy), the public relations man for a presidential candidate named Hal Philip Walker. Triplette infiltrates the country western music scene, influencing the upper echelons of the music industry. The film ends with the assassination of Barbara Jean (Renee Blakely) at a concert sponsored by Triplette. The crowd then begins to sing "It Don't Worry Me," the lyrics suggest both the resilience and the apathy that those Southerners who witnessed the assassination seem to possess. (A happier moment early in the concert at Nashville's Parthenon is shown in accompanying still.)

Politics and business are inseparable in *Nashville*. Both institutions are corrupt and overwhelmingly powerful. The political manipulation of the Nashville constituency relies for its success on the same absurd credos, tactics, and slogans espoused by that city's music industry. The traditional Grand Ole Opry concert at Opryland is used to sell Goo-Goo candy bars, which are named with the acronym of Grand Ole Opry. Stockcars at the raceway, promoting the names of favorite singing stars, and the campaign van of Hal Philip Walker, which broadcasts his name through the streets of Nashville, accomplish similar ends. The calculated sales pitches of the Walker campaign and of the country western industry appeal to the lowest common denominator—the gullibility of the average citizen. The political commentary is therefore disparaging, but not singularly Southern.

The complacent acceptance of violence in *Nashville* also provides a striking index of the decadence of society within this Southern city. One representative incident in the film involves a multiple car crash on an expressway. The collisions sanction a free-for-all atmosphere. Those people caught in the bumper-to-bumper traffic quickly abandon their cars en masse and join the fracas. Their favorite activities include autograph seeking, ambulance chasing, and fist fighting. Speaking over the blaring horns and sirens, a reporter sums up the frustration prevalent in the crowd behavior. But she does not state, "It's typically Southern." Instead she remarks, "It's America—all those mangled bodies." When Barbara Jean is shot at the concert, Haven Hamilton (Henry Gibson), another singer, shouts to the crowd, "They can't do this to us here in Nashville." Earlier in the film, Triplette complimented Haven for a witty remark he made, stating, "That's very fast." Haven replies "Yeah, we have to be." His outlook echoes the philosophy of Captain Crandall in *Brewster McCloud*.

Both men are proud of being Southerners, and they react identically when they feel that their region is being maligned. Haven commits a faux pas, reminiscent of Captain Forrest's remark in *M*A*S*H*, when Haven offers a piece of watermelon to black country western singer Tommy Brown (Timothy Brown). Brown is well liked and respected by Haven and Barbara Jean, but their racial slurs make his social connection to them appear tentative. In these cases Altman is not proposing that Southerners have monopolies on pride or racism. The characters of Nashville are no more than examples of the intolerance which the whole country manifests.

The songs in the film depict a divided and irresolute America. They also illustrate the conflicting extremes of optimism and frustration apparently felt by citizens throughout the country. Haven Hamilton's "200 Years" and "Keep A-Goin' " prescribe patriotism, faith, and perseverance as simple solutions to the problems of everyday life. Haven may indeed feel "we must be doing something right to last 200 years," but a contrary opinion is expressed by Tommy Brown in "Bluebird." Life for him is "that long lonesome road" filled with economic and professional pressures. Since freedom is impossible amidst these social constraints, Brown finds himself futilely looking for "the rainbow in my dreams." Along his "lonesome road" one finds failure. Together, the songs in *Nashville*, from "My Idaho Home" to "Rolling Stone," describe an individual who hopes for a better life but is disillusioned by what he sees around him, who would like to shape his own destiny to a greater extent but does not know how to undertake such a risky venture, and who is vaguely aware of his diminishing freedom, but is unable and unwilling to challenge traditional social norms. In short, they depict the potentially strong and uncompromising American who has capitulated to superior and corrupt forces, basing his surrender on terms that enhance his material surroundings.

Thus in *M*A*S*H*, *Brewster McCloud*, and especially in *Thieves Like Us* and *Nashville*, Robert Altman uses settings, characters, and interactions based in the urban and rural South to present a composite picture of America—his sobering vision of complacency and hypocrisy in American life. Altman points out the deadly effects of racism, unrestrained regional ethnocentrism, and apathy towards reform. He apparently argues in his films that these social, political, and economic values are corrupt, and that they may very well lead to the loss of individual freedom in America unless they are first recognized as abusive conditions, and then corrected.

# "How Come Everybody Down Here Has Three Names?": Martin Ritt's Southern Films

## MICHAEL ADAMS

In recent years no major director has made as many films with Southern settings as has Martin Ritt. A New York Jew born in 1914 who briefly attended Elon College in North Carolina in the 1930s, Ritt began his acting career in the late thirties and directed plays while in the army during World War II. He acted in and directed plays and television programs (he was blacklisted from television in 1951) for several years before directing the first of his twenty-two films, *Edge of the City*, in 1957. Nearly a third of these films have been set in the South: *The Long, Hot Summer* (1958), *The Sound and the Fury* (1959), *Sounder* (1972), *Conrack* (1974), *Casey's Shadow* (1978), *Norma Rae* (1979), and *Back Roads*, to be released in 1981.[1] This group of films exemplifies the way the South has been treated by Hollywood over the past twenty-five years, revealing a mixture of suspicion and affection, amusement and outrage. Ritt's attitudes toward the South have changed surprisingly little over the years. He seems genuinely fond of the region and the character of its people but is too often condescending. Among the most frequent themes in these films are the relationships among family members, the effects of outsiders on close-knit communities, the isolation of the community, family, or individual, and the place of blacks in the South.

*The Long, Hot Summer*, like all but one of Ritt's Southern films, was made on location, this time in and around Clinton, Louisiana. Ritt said at this time, "I prefer to do as much of my pictures as I can on location. The sense of atmosphere, the feeling of contact with the real thing, helps the actors in their roles—and helps me too."[2] Loosely based on William Faulkner's *The Hamlet* and "Barn Burning," *The Long, Hot Summer* was written by Irving Ravetch and Harriet Frank, Jr. This

143

husband-wife screenwriting team from New York, who had written mostly B-Westerns before beginning a longtime collaboration with Ritt, also wrote the scripts for *The Sound and the Fury, Hud, Conrack*, and *Norma Rae*.[3] *The Long, Hot Summer* bears little resemblance to its sources with many of the characters' names changed and their personalities drastically altered. Faulkner's slimy toad of a villain Flem Snopes becomes the blue-eyed, redneck prince Ben Quick, and all conflicts are hastily resolved in an epitome of the contrived Hollywood ending. According to Bruce Kawin, the filmmakers "deliberately reversed the value structure" of *The Hamlet*, "turning Faulkner's anti-capitalist black comedy into a Horatio Alger bedtime story. . . . *The Long, Hot Summer* is just the kind of success story *The Hamlet* parodies."[4] With a very heavy Orson Welles as Will Varner, wanting more than anything heirs to inherit his kingdom, it is closer to *Cat on a Hot Tin Roof* than to Faulkner. According to the Ravetches, they chose to emphasize the "glimpses of robust health and zest for life" they found in *The Hamlet*.[5]

The lust-under-the-magnolias cliches aside, *The Long, Hot Summer,* which is Ritt's most entertaining movie *because* of its excesses, introduces many of the elements the director is to elaborate in later

Orson Welles and Paul Newman provide a glimpse of "robust health and zest for life" in *The Long Hot Summer.*

films. One is the outsider who appears out of nowhere to affect the lives of all those around him, a motif which implies that the South is susceptible to change when given a little push. Ben Quick arrives penniless in Frenchman's Bend and soon progresses from sharecropper to general-store clerk to heir apparent to the town's most powerful citizen while dispersing the malaise which has settled over the entire Varner clan, especially the icy facade Miss Clara has built to protect herself from life. She secretly longs, however, for the touch of a real man in dirty work clothes. A second motif is the fluctuating relationships between family members. Clara and her brother Jody hate their father at various times but finally respect him grudgingly; the family threatened with disruption becomes healthy and whole as it does in varying degrees in *The Sound and the Fury, Sounder, Casey's Shadow,* and *Norma Rae.* This film presents the first of many unconventional family relationships which are present in Ritt's Southern films but absent from most of his non-Southern films, the Italian-Americans in *The Black Orchid* and *The Brotherhood* being notable exceptions. This unconventionality is epitomized in *The Long, Hot Summer* by Clara's sharp-tongued exchanges with her father, exchanges which profess her hate but imply her love, and by Jody's locking Will in a barn and setting it on fire only to rescue and embrace him. A final element is the isolation of the Southern community. Frenchman's Bend seems miles from any other town, totally cut off from the rest of the world and in a world of its—and Will Varner's— own creation. The characters have little awareness of anything beyond Frenchman's Bend, and nothing seems to happen there except what involves the protagonists. The life in Ritt's rural South is usually limited by its provinciality.

While doing pre-production work for *The Sound and the Fury,* Ritt said, "We've now made it a conventional story but preserved the basic quality."[6] Unfortunately, Ritt, the Ravetches, and producer Wald did not apparently understand what this "basic quality" is, for their adaptation of Faulkner's masterpiece is one of the most ineffective movies based on a serious literary work.[7] The novel is about time, responsibility, suicide, madness, incest, greed, and the disintegration of a family and a culture. The film is only about the problems the second Quentin Compson has while growing up. The novel's villain becomes the movie's hero as Jason Compson tries to raise his stepniece Quentin as well as he can while keeping her away from the influence of Caddy, the sluttish mother who abandoned her. As played by Margaret Leighton, Caddy seems more like Blanche DuBois than Faulkner's creation; Ritt and the Ravetches once again try to turn Yoknapatawpha, Mississippi, into Williams, Tennessee. The most drastic changes are to eliminate the first Quentin Compson's story completely while turning this vivid symbol of alienation into dull, alcoholic Uncle Howard and to make Jason a Compson by adoption, the son of Mr. Compson's Cajun second wife. The latter change is necessary to explain the casting of the exotic Yul Brynner and the romantic involvement of Jason and his stepniece at the end of the movie. The film is not bad because of these changes but, as Bruce Kawin points out, because the changes are not "dramatically interesting."[8] The film also lacks any of the humor and vulgar vitality of *The Long, Hot Summer;* it just lies there on the screen, hardening into a monument to ineptitude.

Ritt seems handicapped not only by the changes and the casting, but by the lack of the inspiration he claims to need from shooting on location. Filming on a Hollywood backlot to avoid weather problems which hampered the making of *The Long, Hot Summer,* Ritt made *The Sound and the Fury* into the dullest, most plodding of his movies. Even evidence of his specialty, directing actors, is missing; only Jack Warden as Benjy seems to have any conviction about what he is doing.[9]

As for Ritt's usual motifs, we have unusual family relationships with an adopted stepson ruling over his aging mother, drunken stepbrother, retarded stepbrother, wandering stepsister, and rebellious stepniece, and finally becoming both father, mother, and, apparently, husband to the latter. Jason's exact connection to each of these characters is so imprecise it can easily be misunderstood. Jason is also a modified version of Ritt's outsider in charge of straightening things out. Another outsider, carnival roustabout Charles Busch, unintentionally helps bring matters to their conclusion by trying to run away with Quentin. The sense of the town's isolation helps to underscore Jason's sense of responsibility. One final element of note is Ethel Waters' performance as Dilsey, the loyal retainer. This characterization foreshadows the moralizing of *Hud's* Homer Bannon and the too-good-to-be-true blacks of *Sounder*. The filmmakers may be trying to invest her with some dignity, but she comes off as a clichéd all-wise mammy.

Faulkner praises Dilsey of *The Sound and the Fury* and blacks like her for their endurance, and Ritt's *Sounder* is a paean to the dignity, loyalty, love, and patience of poor Southern Negroes. Partially because it is a quiet, charming, yet moving film released at a time when most screen depictions of blacks emphasized sex and violence, *Sounder* received the highest critical praise of any of Ritt's films. Pauline Kael called it "the first movie about black experiences in America which can stir people of all colors," and Vincent Canby, who did not like the film, said it "has been endorsed by everybody with the exception of God, but God doesn't have an outlet."[10] Because of the crossover appeal and the critics' enthusiasm, *Sounder* has been the most financially successful Ritt film.[11] The praise for *Sounder* was not, however, as universal as Canby claimed. Many blacks and white liberals saw it as patronizing and dishonest. Because of the characters' passive acceptance of injustice, some critics charged that Ritt was presenting a racial stereotype. Edward Mapp writes, "Negative attitudes about 'happy darkies' are reinforced each time Rebecca [the mother of the film's family] meets misfortune with a healthy display of dentures. . . . Neither by rage nor rebellion possessed, she is a good nigger, patient and acquiescent. It is unlikely that white movie audiences, unfamiliar with the code of living forced upon blacks in the South during the 1930s, will recognize the historical context of this story. They are more likely to see Rebecca as a black woman who knows her place."[12]

A more accurate appraisal of *Sounder* lies somewhere between the extreme responses the film elicited. Ritt had treated racial material earlier in *Edge of the City, Paris Blues, Hombre,* and *The Great White Hope.* With *Sounder* his liberal views about racial matters merge with his material to produce his most effective statement about race and about the family. *Sounder* is his most successfully realized film, approaching sentimentality at times but never going too far in its sweetness or didacticism.

Based on William H. Armstrong's Newberry Medal-winning 1969 novella, *Sounder* is one Ritt adaptation which adds more to its source than it takes away. Screenwriter Lonne Elder III, the black playwright best known for *Ceremonies in Dark Old Men,* takes a fairly slight story about a boy's affection for his imprisoned father and for their hunting dog and changes it into a powerful tale about the bonds which hold a family of sharecroppers together during the hard times of the Depression in Louisiana. About the only arguable change Elder makes is the rather peaceful arrest of the father; Armstrong's version is violent. Because the movie was produced by Robert Radnitz, a maker of children's films, and financed by the Mattel toy company, it had to be tame enough to receive a "G" rating.

*Sounder* shows what life was like for a black family in the rural South during the 1930s: hoeing the fields, hunting for game, surviving as a unit, continuing to survive when the father is arrested for stealing meat, a theft justified by circumstances. *Sounder* is much subtler than the usual Ritt movie, depicting the family's hardships without melodrama. The love of the family members is also understated, coming across in the way they exchange glances and do things for each other. According to black film historian Donald Bogle, *Sounder* "picked up many of the things toyed with before [in American movies] and amalgamated them to create a rich and fully realized portrait of the black family in America."[13]

One would expect Ritt to emphasize the injustice depicted in the story since the family has to suffer the deprivation of the father just because he is trying to feed them. But Ritt and Elder are more interested in downplaying their moral indignation to portray the son's growth into maturity as he assumes the burden of being the man of the family while also maintaining his desire to be educated, and the mother's strength in helping the family survive. Ellen Holly has praised this character as "a role that at long last gives a certain kind of black woman her decent due," and Pauline Kael called her the "first great black heroine on the screen."[14] The emotional depth of *Sounder* comes across in several scenes: the family's pride in the father's baseball pitching, the return of the father, limping from a prison accident (a scene patterned after a similar one in King Vidor's 1929 *Hallelujah*), and the father's urging the son to seek the world beyond their farm.

Ritt underscores the isolation of his characters at the beginning of

*Sounder,* but a sense of the outside world evolves as the son travels about trying to learn what prison camp his father is in. Ritt wants to show that the boy—and all black Southerners—is not limited by his immediate environment. These scenes and the rest were filmed in Louisiana's East Feliciana and St. Helena parishes, the same location as that of *The Long, Hot Summer.* They give an even better sense of place than Ritt usually does because of the variety of locales and the beauty of John Alonzo's cinematography. (He also photographed *Conrack, Casey's Shadow,* and *Norma Rae.*)

*Conrack,* again written by the Ravetches, is based on *The Water is Wide* (1972), white Southerner Pat Conroy's account of the months in 1969 he spent teaching black children on Daufuskie Island, South Carolina, near his home town of Beaufort. (The movie was filmed mostly on St. Simons Island, Georgia.) Because the island community is poor, black, completely insulated from the rest of the world, and primarily because no one seems to care about them, the students do not know anything, even the name of the ocean a few yards from their homes. Conroy, whose name is pronounced *Conrack* by the children, tries to overcome this backwardness through unconventional teaching methods, pouring a mass of unrelated facts into the children's minds, trying to make them care more about themselves and what will happen to them. In doing so he encounters the wrath of an ignorant black principal who wants him to be a strict disciplinarian (he tells her, "We're off the plantation, Mrs. Scott, and I'll be goddamned if you're going to turn me into an overseer") and a reactionary white superintendent ("I never in my heart accepted Appomattox") and loses his job, leaving the children, the film says, with no prospects for the future.

*Conrack* exemplifies some of Ritt's worst failures as a liberal filmmaker. He says that he wants the viewer to come away saying, " 'Ok, it's nice to feel that the human race is still several steps above the other species. And it's nice to feel that a man will commit himself for what he believes even if it seems likely he will suffer for it.' "[15] But does Conroy suffer? Since he is not part of this community, has no permanent commitment to it, he can go back to his relatively comfortable white-middle-class world, write a book about his experience, sell it to the movies, and continue his career as a writer.[16] The real-life

Conroy says, "If I'd stood on my head for them for ten years, basically there wasn't much that could have changed, except maybe for the next generation."[17] But the movie implies otherwise in his accomplishment of so much to motivate the children in a few months.

*Conrack* is filled with contradictions and omissions. Conroy wants to combat the attitudes of the principal who calls the students "babies," yet he cradles a ten-year-old in his arms while playing a recording of Brahms' "Lullaby." He claims to have once been a racist who threw watermelons at blacks, but we get no indication of what has caused him to change. More seriously, Ritt shows nothing of what life is like for the islanders. Except for one young moonshiner and a pimp we never see anyone but the students and a few old people. Where are the children's parents, brothers, and sisters? What do the islanders do to support themselves? How big is the island? Such questions bother the viewer because the omission of details is so glaring. Conroy is admirable for teaching his students about Picasso and Jackie Robinson; but he does not seem at all interested in *their* lives, in the possibility of anything of interest *on* the island. Ritt and the Ravetches apparently love their protagonist so much that they lose sight of everything else. We admire the strength of their feelings and share them to some extent, but that is not enough to make the film successful.

The outsider motif is important in *Conrack,* but the family is less evident than in Ritt's other Southern films although Conroy and his students develop into a family of sorts with their seeing him as a benevolent older brother. Isolation, however, receives its biggest emphasis here. Not only do the children live on an island, but they have never been off it because of the islanders' ignorant fear of the water. (None of the students can swim until Conroy throws them into the ocean.) When he takes them to Beaufort for Halloween, their faces on the boat display pure terror. Ritt makes an interesting observation here about change in the South, noting that opposition to it does not result just from conservatism, racism, or greed, but from ignorance, fear, and innocence.

*Casey's Shadow,* Ritt's next Southern film, differs greatly from *Conrack* for he uses the South only as the background for its first half. The main emphasis is on quarter-horse racing in southwestern Louisiana and Ruidoso, New Mexico, and on the relationship between block horse trainer Lloyd Bourdelle and his three sons. The film, with a script by Carol Sobieski based on John McPhee's *New Yorker* article "Ruidoso" (29 April 1974), has only a few Southern details, such as Bourdelle's exchanging Cajun French pleasantries in a cafe. The isolation motif is less important than usual. The Bourdelles live on a solitary, run-down ranch, but their isolation is not important.

Ritt does, however, present another unusual family relationship. Bourdelle's wife has run away years earlier, leaving him to raise his sons, now around ten, eighteen, and twenty-five. Because of Bourdelle's gruff manner and lack of success, his sons view him with a mixture of affection and exasperation. Like good Southern sons, they obey him but not without arguing first. The family threatens to be split over Casey's Shadow, a potentially great race horse. Bourdelle's lack of money has not bothered him until this horse offers him a chance finally to become someone. He is even willing to risk losing his sons' regard by deciding to race the horse, although it has an injury, in the All-American Futurity, the world's richest race, at Ruidoso Downs. The horse wins but is severely injured and is to be destroyed. The sons have fought Bourdelle about the horse's treatment, reversing the conflict Ritt depicted in *Hud* by having the young make moral judgments about the old. When the horse is unexpectedly saved, all is well again, and the family has a new sense of closeness. Ritt shows some maturity by accepting that his protagonist is imperfect; the man who made *Hud* would not have been so forgiving of Bourdelle's selfishness. *Casey's Shadow* also displays some awareness about how the South has changed for the better; the fact that the horse's owner is black is presented matter-of-factly.

The black-white relations in *Norma Rae* are also natural and friendly—about the only indication that this is the New South. Otherwise, the film, set in 1978, could be taking place in 1958 or even 1938. The subject matter, the difficulty of starting a labor union in a textile mill, seems anachronistic but accurately reflects management-employee relationships that still exist in some areas of the South. *Norma Rae* is based on a *New York Times Magazine* article by Henry P. Leifermann about the inability of workers to start a union at a J. P. Stevens mill in Roanoke Rapids, North Carolina, focusing on one worker, Crystal Lee Jordan, the model for Ritt's heroine.[18] (The film, set in a place called Henleyville, was made in Opelika, Alabama.) The effort to start a union, however, is not what most concerns Ritt and the Ravetches. (For some reason, we never see the owners or executives who run the mill. The film implies that the foremen are in charge.) They are interested in presenting a lovable portrait of their protagonist.

Norma Rae is uneducated and promiscuous yet honest, hardworking, inquisitive, sensitive, loving, and funny. Like the blacks in *Sounder*, she is almost too good. We are supposed to love her for the strength of her character, her determination to see that right is done, her lack of pretentiousness, and her take-me-as-I-am-or-to-hell-with-you brand of individualism. Another sign of Ritt's maturity is that the promiscuity he so hated in Hud is tolerated in Norma Rae. The most revolutionary aspect of the film is the heroine's relationship with Reuben Marshasky, the New York Jew who comes to Henleyville to organize the union. Norma Rae and Reuben help, respect, and learn from each other without the slightest hint of potential romance, a remarkably contemporary treatment of a male-female friendship.

Sally Field in her Academy-award winning performance as a defiant *Norma Rae*.

Reuben, like Conroy, is another variation on Ritt's great white liberal who hits town to correct all its problems before riding off into the sunset in his rented car. The director's idealism allows his outsider to succeed here even though the real-life model did not.

The isolation of Henleyville is not emphasized, though it is apparently miles from anywhere and its citizens inbred, giving no thought to moving elsewhere for higher pay or better working conditions. (Their complacency makes their pro-union vote less credible.) Ritt builds such a sense of a dead-end hick town that we are shocked when Norma Rae shows up with a Dylan Thomas paperback she has just purchased; obviously it did not come from Woolworth's. *Norma Rae's* family relationships are underdeveloped. Norma Rae has only one scene of any consequence with her children (though they are silent), her husband virtually disappears after they are married, and her parents hardly talk to each other. The father's overprotective, you're-still-my-little-girl, almost incestuous attitude toward the thirtyish Norma Rae is, however, quite believable.

What is most distressing about *Norma Rae* is that after all these years Ritt (and the Ravetches) is still occasionally inaccurate about and condescending toward the South. Many little details are irritatingly false. Norma Rae says "five-and-dime" when most Southerners like her would probably say "ten-cent store," and a millworker (Ritt in a one-word cameo) hurls the decidedly non-Southern epithet "Fink." Reuben asks, "How come everybody down here has three names?" because most of the characters are called by such names as Jimmy Jerome or Billy Joe. But one is more likely to find this habit of naming in the Southwest than in the deep South. One of the most embarrassingly inept scenes in movie history occurs when Norma Rae and Reuben are out recruiting support for the union and encounter six old men (one a token black) loafing on a grocery-store porch, and the director, in the apparent interest of "action," has all six whittling. Rarely has patronizing Hollywood clubbed the South with such a clumsy cliché.

Ritt says, "I like the South. The essence of drama is change, and the section of the country that is most in flux appears to me to be the South; therefore, I go there to make films."[19] Yet he deals with this flux only superficially in his films, being attracted again and again to the region's backwardness. He does have something to say about isolation, prejudice, injustice, greed, and the forces which disrupt and the love which holds together the family. This would be enough if he was not so often self-congratulatory about his love for the "little people." Ritt claims to be a professional and a craftsman, not an artist,[20] and perhaps what is wrong with these films is that he does not give us the insights about the South that an artist would.

## NOTES

[1]*Back Roads*, about the relationship between a prostitute and an ex-boxer, was filmed from Gary DeVore's script in the Mobile area in May and June, 1980. The film was released in March 1981 and had a mixed reception. Andrew Sarris wrote in *The Village Voice*: "Sally Field and Tommy Lee Jones are about as ideally cast as knockabout-lovers-on-the-run in *Back Roads* as one could wish. . . . The only problem they have is that director Martin Ritt and scenarist Gary DeVore lack the breathtaking talent it would take to bring off this *It Happened One Night* of the lower depths" (11–17 March 1981, p. 47).

[2]Quoted by Arthur Knight, "Filming Faulknerland," *Saturday Review*, 7 Dec. 1957, p. 53.

[3]The Ravetches wrote one of Ritt's non-Southern films, *Hombre,* and also adapted Faulkner's *The Reivers* (1969), directed by Mark Rydell.

[4]*Faulkner and Film* (New York: Ungar, 1977), p. 53.

[5]Irving Ravetch and Harriet Frank, Jr., "On Putting Faulkner on the Screen," unpublished memo quoted in its entirety in George Sidney, "Faulkner in Hollywood: A Study of His Career as a Scenarist," Diss. Univ. of New Mexico 1959, p. 244.

[6]Quoted by Howard Thompson, "Ritt for the Record on Direction," *New York Times*, 1 June 1958, Sec. 2, p. 5.

[7]Jerry Wald tries to justify the changes in "From Faulkner to Film," *Saturday Review*, 7 March 1959, pp. 16, 47.

[8]*Faulkner and Film*, p. 23.

[9]Ten performers in Ritt films have been nominated for Oscars with three winning the awards: Patricia Neal and Melvyn Douglas for *Hud*, Sally Field for *Norma Rae*. These and other actors have won other awards for Ritt films.

[10]*Reeling* (New York: Warner, 1976), p. 21; "All But 'Super Fly' Fall Down," *New York Times*, 15 Nov. 1972, Sec. 2, p. 1.

[11]According to *Variety*, 9 Jan. 1980, pp. 24, 44–54, 74, Sounder's American and Canadian rentals totalled $8,726,000, almost a million more than any other of his films.

[12]"Black Women in Films: A Mixed Bag of Tricks," in *Black Films and Film-Makers: A Comprehensive Anthology From Stereotype to Superhero*, ed. Lindsay Patterson (New York: Dodd, Mead, 1975), p. 199. Patterson's own "*Sounder*—A Hollywood Fantasy?" pp. 106–08, is a harsh attack on the historical accuracy of the film.

[13]*Toms, Coons, Mulattoes, Mammies, and Bucks: An Interpretive History of Blacks in American Films* (New York: Viking, 1973), p. 240.

[14]"At Long Last, the Super Sound of 'Sounder,' "*New York Times*, 15 Oct. 1972, Sec. 2, p. 15; *Reeling*, p. 24.

[15]Quoted by Betty Jeffries Demby, "The Making of *Conrack*: An Interview with Martin Ritt," *Filmmakers Newsletter*, April 1974, p. 30.

[16]Conroy used the proceeds of his book to set aside $1,000 for each of his students when they reached eighteen (Demby, p. 27 ).

[17]Quoted by Kael, *Reeling*, p. 401.

[18]"The Unions Are Coming," *New York Times Magazine*, 5 Aug. 1973, pp. 10–11, 25–26.

[19]Quoted by Donald Chase, "Martin Ritt and the Making of *Norma Rae*," *Millimeter*, 7 (June 1979), 45.

[20]Demby, p. 31.

# The Southern Woman as Time-Binder in Film*

VICTORIA O'DONNELL

Southern women have been richly signified in films, especially in the 1940s and 1950s when the plays and novels of Tennessee Williams and William Faulkner were brought to the screen. Many famous actresses have portrayed Southern heroines, thus passing on certain characteristics, often stereotypical ones, which audiences have come to associate with the women of the South. As with most stereotypes, the exaggerated qualities are recognized, but they still influence people's perceptions and expectations of people they think will fulfill the stereotypical views. The people in the audiences for the films about the South have included not only the general public but also the real Southern women who observe and sometimes absorb the qualities which have been dramatized and passed on to them.

Through the visual and aural symbols of film, as in other symbolic art forms, knowledge is transmitted from generation to generation. Our ability to span time through the use of symbols was labeled "time-binding" by Alfred Korzybski. Korsybski saw the time-binding capacity as a peculiar and characteristic feature of human beings: "Man improves, animals do not; man progresses, animals do not; man invents more and more complicated tools, animals do not; man is a creator of material and spiritual wealth, animals are not; man is a builder of civilization, animals are not."[1]

The time-binding capacity of the human race is a mark of our ability to use symbols to stand for the ideas which are passed on to future generations. Harry Weinberg, another general semanticist, called our symbol-using capacity to time-bind our "most powerful tool and

*This paper was presented in a slightly different form at the Southern Speech Communication Association convention in April 1979.

156

weapon, both useful and dangerous to ourselves and others."[2] Weinberg warned us to be wary of the transmission of false information which could be received and treated as truth.

Information is transmitted in many symbolic forms. Since film is primarily visual, time-binding information is mainly embodied in the visual sign accompanied, of course, by dialogue and narration. A complete visual sign is made up of a signifier and a signified. These terms are adapted from Ferdinand de Saussure's typology in "On the Nature of Language."[3] Sign designates the unity or the whole of a sound-image and its concept. The signifier is the sound-image; the signified, the concept. The signifier includes symbols which, when recepted by an audience, produce meaning in a process of signification. The visual coders determine what is signified; the visual critics open up the sign to decode what is signified by the signifiers. Using the concept of time-binding through filmic signification, the image of the Southern woman can be analyzed according to the signification process.

The Southern woman in film has been signified by certain actresses as *icons* as well as by the types of women they portray. Icons are defined as conventional configurations which recur often enough to be recognized as conveyers of meaning. Since the meaning usually goes beyond the presence of an icon in a single film, film icons can be considered as time-binders. Hattie McDaniels and Ethel Waters were typecast as mammies. Vivien Leigh came to signify the Southern belle, first as Scarlett O'Hara and later as the aging Blanche DuBois. Elizabeth Taylor, Joanne Woodward, and Geraldine Page have appeared frequently in screen adaptations of Williams and Faulkner.

Iconography was at one time necessary to cinema. Erwin Panofsky explained in "Style and Medium in the Motion Pictures" (1934): "Audiences had difficulty deciphering what appeared on the screen. Fixed iconography was used by Hollywood filmmakers to aid understanding and provide the audience with basic facts with which to comprehend the narrative."[4] Panofsky classified women, for example, as straight girls and vamps, one of the earliest categorizations of women in film. Certain actresses who could visually represent such icons were chosen to play those roles over and over again. Under these circumstances, iconography operated as a cluster of signs based on certain conventions within the Hollywood genres and has been responsible, in part, for the stereotyping of women in cinema.

The picture of Hattie McDaniels, who won an Oscar for her portrayal of Mammy in *Gone with the Wind* (1939), is an icon (see accompanying illustration). One has only to look at her to see that she is a slave by the way she is uniformed in her wrapped head and kerchief. Her ample body and open, honest expression tell us that she is maternal and reliable. She has become the Southern archetype of the earth mother.

Molly Haskell claims in *From Reverence to Rape: The Treatment of Women in the Movies* that the Southern heroine, because of her conditioning and background, is a natural superfemale. Like the European woman, she is treated by men and her society with something close to veneration, a position she is not entirely willing to abandon for the barricades. Rather than rebel and lose her status, she plays on her assets, becomes a self-exploiter, and uses her sex without ever surrendering it to gain power over men.[5] Southern stereotypes are not, however, unchanging. Southern women characters in films before 1950 generally signify something different from those in more recent films.

The Old South has had the following kinds of women as its signifiers:

*The Feminine Woman.* She is beautiful but more artificial than natural. She wears corsets for a tiny waist, crinolines for a doll-like appearance, and her skin is very pale. She is vain, coy, proud, and uppity. She is, of course, Scarlett O'Hara of *Gone with the Wind*, who possesses tremendous endurance and determination despite her frail body and appearance (see frontispiece of this issue). She does not use her strength to make progress for herself but rather to preserve her father's plantation and to entice the weak and traditional Southern gentleman, Ashley Wilkes (Leslie Howard), a remnant of the Old South like Tara the plantation. Haskell says that Scarlett "is a diabolically strong woman—deceptively so, in the manner of the southern belle—and she fears the loss of her strength and selfhood that a total, 'animal' relationship with Rhett (Clark Gable) would entail."[6] She is left desolate and still self-centered in the end, a figure of self-deception.

*The Female Woman.* She is an earth mother, nurturing and natural. She is large, has a strong, loud voice, and is very religious. She is capable, loyal, generous, and wise. She is the Mammy figure, "mother" to the white plantation family which relies on her as a mainstay. Donald Bogle, who classified the dominant images of blacks in film in his book, *Toms, Coons, Mulattoes, Mammies, and Bucks*, said that the mammy is a "desexed, overweight, dowdy, *dark* black woman" (emphasis Bogle's).[7]

*The Real Lady.* She is lovely without being artificial. She is pure and genteel, the soul of honor. She is kind and long-suffering, a woman of courage but not necessarily strength. She is Melanie (Olivia DeHavilland), the woman who marries Ashley Wilkes, thus becoming the envy of the feminine woman who wants him so. Perhaps because she is so chaste and good, she is often dull and uninteresting. Because she is soft and genuinely frail, she may not survive.

*The Fallen Woman.* Once she was the feminine woman, the belle. She longs for and is trapped in her past; indeed, she herself is a remnant of the past. When placed in an alien environment, she is harshly revealed. She is, of course, Blanche DuBois in *A Streetcar Named Desire* (1951). When her gentleman caller Mitch (Karl Malden) rips off the paper lampshade she has hung over a bare bulb in her sister's apartment, the harsh light shows him the tattered reality of Blanche's age and shabby clothing. She says of herself, "I don't want realism; I want magic." She tries very hard to maintain her masquerade. Even when threatened with rape by her brother-in-law, Stanley Kowalski (Marlon Brando), Blanche keeps her coquettish mask to conceal her fear. After she is raped, she collapses and has a mental breakdown, yet it is she who bears the guilt and suffering. Esther Merle Jackson, in *The Broken World of Tennessee Williams*, sees Blanche as an "anti-heroic Orestes, in flight from her own transgressions."[8] She travels downward and realizes that she, not her ancestors, is responsible for her sufferings. Like Orestes, she has made a guilty choice which has involved her in the sufferings of others. She knows it, but she cannot stop herself. She replays the feminine Southern belle, but never with vulgarity. Her name, Blanche, seems not to signify the white of purity but the whiteness of death and ghosts, a South of the past which exists only in her mind.

(Ona Munson also played a more conventional "fallen woman" as Belle Watling in *Gone with the Wind*.)

Scarlett, Mammy, Melanie, and Blanche are embedded in archaic soil, time-binders for the old South. The New South is earthier, gaudier, signifying fresher though not necessarily finer clay. The woman as signifier for the new South embodies carnal qualities, for she has lost her purity and chastity and is glad of it.

*The Sexual Woman.* She is beautiful, voluptuous, only partially clothed, and openly erotic. She is able to give sexual fulfillment, but she does so in order to impart strength to her man. Her sexuality is a key to helping the weaker male find his manliness. Bonnie (Faye Dunaway), in *Bonnie and Clyde* (1967), signifies the modern South, poor but striving for recognition, writing poetry on one hand while robbing banks on the other, and, above all, reassuring her man Clyde (Warren Beatty) that he is virile. Maggie the Cat (Elizabeth Taylor), in *Cat on a Hot Tin Roof* (1958), goes sexually unfulfilled even though she is remarkably desirable. She is a foil to a weak and impotent husband (Paul Newman). The husband Brick is sexually ambivalent and not up to snuff. Maggie, at least, is able to articulate her frustration to her husband. "I want to live," she cries, not willing to give up easily.

*The Unfulfilled Sexual Woman.* She wants to be sexually attractive, but she has little to offer in terms of physical beauty. She is trying to break away from dominating parents and traditional ways. She is searching for her own femaleness and longs to bear children. Joanne Woodward's Rachel in *Rachel, Rachel* (1969) is a plain and very ordinary woman who is getting stronger everyday. She learns that a sexual affair with Nick (James Olson) is not the romance that she yearns for, and, indeed, is far from liberating. She knows that she must make a new life on her own, first breaking away from the chains of the old life, a nagging mother, the ghost of her dead father. Most of all, she is able to accept herself as ordinary and not be defeated by the recognition of it. She has hope and moves in a positive direction.

*The Rich, Spoiled Woman.* She has everything—beauty, money, men, and friends. She is spoiled and wild. Her wealth is new money and she flaunts it. As portrayed by Cybill Shepherd in *The Last Picture Show* (1971), she is a flirt and a tease like the Southern belle of the Old South, but she can cast a man aside if she wants. She is shallow and cynical. She may seek sexual fulfillment, but is not willing to give it like the sexual woman does for the sake of a man.

*The New Female Woman.* She is the new black Mammy, an earth mother but no longer the mainstay of a white family. She is the support for her own family. Cicely Tyson's Rebecca in *Sounder* (1972) is a strong, tough, enduring, religious, dark black woman. Unlike Mammy in *Gone with the Wind*, she is slender, soft-spoken, and beautiful. She is also sexually fulfilled and fulfilling to her husband, a man whose only threat to his manhood is white bigotry and discrimination. She bolsters her family in the time of need and is fairly successful.

Rachel and Rebecca as time-binders signify new qualities of the Southern woman, qualities which have been important in the development and growth of both the South and the modern woman as well. Rachel is determined to make it on her own despite her ordinariness. She has optimism and a dream that includes both a career and motherhood. She goes away to Oregon, far from the South to find her dream. That she is unable to find it at home may be significant. Perhaps there will soon be a film in which the white Southern woman stays in the South with Rachel's determination to be strong and successful. Rebecca, in a sense, is trapped in the South by poverty, family, and loyalty to her husband and friends, yet it does not occur to her to leave. She works ceaselessly, and she is successful. Perhaps she and her husband will not make much progress, but there is hope for the next generation, her children in whom she has instilled her admirable qualities.

These fictional characters, women as time-binders, impart information through the filmic medium, about the Southern woman with lightly veiled references to the South itself. There is no doubt that many of the characteristics of these women and the South they seem to represent are overblown and generalized, but they also stand as evidence of recurring qualities passed on from one generation to another (indeed, four generations have seen *Gone with the Wind*) that perpetuate the myth of the Southern woman. She is a stereotype but not a single type. She can be categorized into several types, types which seem to represent both cultural and historical attitudes about the South. At one point in *Gone with the Wind*, Rhett Butler contemplates leaving Scarlett but wants to stay with his child. He says to Mammy,

"I'd like to see what my own child looks like." Mammy, sarcastically referring to the immature Scarlett, answers, "You've been seeing her for a long time." We have been seeing the Southern woman on the screen for a long time too, and it has no doubt influenced our attitudes toward her.

## NOTES

[1]*Manhood of Humanity* (New York: Dutton, 1921), p. 186.
[2]*Levels of Knowing and Existence* (New York: Harper and Row, 1959), pp. 156–57.
[3]In *Introduction to Structuralism*, ed. Michael Lane (New York: Basic Books, 1970), pp. 43–56.
[4]Quoted in Claire Johnson, "Myths of Women in the Cinema," in *Women and the Cinema*, ed. Karyn Kay and Gerald Peary (New York: Dutton, 1977), pp. 407–08.
[5](New York: Holt, Rinehart, and Winston, 1974), p. 167.
[6]Haskell, p. 167.
[7](New York: Viking, 1973), p. 17.
[8](New York: Doubleday, 1965), pp. 43–44.

Hattie McDaniels as the familiar stereotype of Mammy in *Gone with the Wind*.

# Black Women in Film

LENORA CLODFELTER STEPHENS

The early MGM Hollywood films *Hallelujah* (1929) and *Cabin in the Sky* (1943) contain images, values and views which have defined the position of the black female, not only in films, but in her relationship with men and with society. The films feature a good Southern colored boy led astray by the sensuous, light-skinned tragic mulatto who introduces him to the evils of the urbanized lifestyle. The predictable end is death and destruction, with the young male returning to the bosom of the long-suffering, dark-skinned mammy and the salvation of the pastoral environment. The Southern rural black family is depicted as a tightly knit, cohesive, virtually indestructible unit,[1] under the matriarchal rule of the mammy.

The two basic female stereotypes in the films—the seductress and the mammy—were introduced at the birth of filmmaking. Exotically seductive West Indian dancers provided the subject matter for Thomas Edison's experiments with kinetoscope vignettes in the 1890s. The mammy appeared as a hearty blackfaced maid in Biograph's *A Bucket of Ale* (1904).[2] D. W. Griffith was the first major movie director to set the pattern of color distinction between the seductress and the mammy. In Griffith's *The Birth of A Nation* (1915) the seductress was played by a white actress in blackface, as a passionate and anguishing female. The mammy, also played by a white actress, was much darker in complexion, overweight and sexless.[3] The MGM films employed Griffith's character distinctions to advance other images and themes, which have been repeated so often in films that they have become symbolic of the black experience.

Complacent Southern environments were disrupted by fast-paced, urbanized, "high-yeller" strumpets who led the pastoral folk hero from the rural bliss to the wicked city. *Hallelujah* featured Nina Mae McKinney as the seductress Chick, Hollywood's first black love goddess. Her sensual swagger and hands-on-hips arrogance were imitated by such "bad girls" as Lena Horne in *Cabin in the Sky* and Dorothy Dandridge in *Carmen Jones* and *Porgy and Bess*.

These light-skinned black queens epitomized the tragedy of mulattoes who were doomed to death and self-destruction because their one drop of black blood made them inherently evil. Despite the reform efforts of the good colored boys, the bad girls would inevitably yield to temptation, dragging the good colored boys after them. The preacher Zeke converts Chick in *Hallelujah*, but she runs off with Hot Shot, the gambling man. Despite the fervent prayers of his mammy-type wife, Little Joe Jackson succumbs to the temptation of Sweet Georgia Brown in *Cabin in the Sky*. In *Carmen Jones*, the honorable soldier, Joe, goes AWOL for Carmen, who runs off with Husky Miller, a prize fighter. Bess leaves her good man in *Porgy and Bess* to run away, North to Harlem with Sportin' Life, a flashy con man.

The good colored boys in *Hallelujah* and *Carmen Jones* pursue and kill the objects of their wasted affection. The scene of Chick dying in the arms of Zeke is repeated twenty-two years later with Carmen's death in Joe's arms. Bess dies in the urban squalor in *Porgy and Bess* and everyone dies in Little Joe Jackson's dream in *Cabin in the Sky*. The audience does not sympathize with any of the villainous heroines who are overcome by their own evil.

The tragic mulatto has, typically, been played by white performers when the filmmaker sought audience identification and sympathy. White actresses played the suffering heroines in all three film versions of *Showboat* (1929, 1936, 1951), in *Lost Boundaries* and *Pinky* in 1949 and in the up-dated version of *Imitation of Life* in 1959. Likewise for black males, the tragic hero was played by white actor James Whitmore in the serious role of a white man turned black in *Black Like Me* (1964), while the comedy version starred black actor, Godfrey Cambridge, in *Watermelon Man* (1970).

"Crying At The Movies," by Willette Coleman, explains the distinction between white and black tragic film characters. Coleman observes that there is always a tear-jerking story behind the suffering that eventually leads a white woman to prostitute herself, "but because it is generally understood that black women do this as standard practice, the need for a reason for forgiving is barely touched upon, if considered at all."[4]

The black actresses who portrayed the tragic mulattoes soon realized that Hollywood had little more to offer than a one-shot opportunity to star in a major film. Nina Mae McKinney, the first recognized black film actress and the first in the tradition of light-skinned black leading ladies, was also the first to discover that there were no more leading roles. Barely five years after her stellar performance in *Hallelujah*, McKinney was forgotten in America, having secured only minor film roles and appearances in little known short films. She found European audiences more receptive, and toured as the Black Garbo, singing in cafés and nightclubs. She returned to America, where she played what Donald Bogle describes as McKinney's last important role as a "razor-totin', high strung, high-yeller girl" in *Pinky* (1949). Bleary-eyed she hardly resembled the carefree, bright-eyed girl who had played Chick at 16 years old.[5]

In *Green Pastures*, the next all-black Hollywood musical to follow *Hallelujah*, Edna Mae Harris played the high-yeller strumpet as if it was her last role—and it was.[6] Dorothy Dandridge died at the age of forty-one from an overdose of anti-depression pills. The star of *Carmen Jones* and *Porgy and Bess* had lived out the life of the tragic mulatto, trapped because of her color, bankrupt with no film opportunities, few club offers and occasional television appearances.[7]

Lena Horne, the seductress in *Cabin in the Sky*, recognized early in her career that it is easier to be a singer because black singers are more readily accepted than black actresses.[8] Diahann Carroll attests to the fact that the situation still exists for the sensuous black leading lady. Carroll, nominated for an Academy Award for her role in *Claudine* (1974), says the money that she has made in motion pictures would not pay the rent for one room of her house. The majority of her yearly earnings come from her singing engagements. She does admit that she is looking for a challenging film role.[9]

The black female stars who played *Coffy* and *Cleopatra Jones* in 1973, as composite seductress and strong mammy-type, are also seeking roles of some depth. A spokesman for Coffy, Pam Grier, indicates that she is concerned about her image and has turned down a number of things that have been offered to her. Cleopatra Jones, Tamara Dobson, says that she has been trying for a long time to find a film that would allow her to be an actress.[10]

One reason for the dearth of film opportunities may be the lack of depth and meaning with which roles for blacks are conceived. According to black actresses Paula Kelly and Denise Nichols, Hollywood fails to recognize distinctions in the talents and qualities of black performers. The producers summon blacks of all ages, types, and physical appearances for a single role, which Nichols says " 'speaks to that invisibility we still have.' "[11]

The effects of the images presented in *Hallelujah* and *Cabin in the Sky* go beyond the personal tragedies of black performers. The stereotype film images of the high-yeller seductress and the stoic, sexless mammy pervade the relationships between black males and females in this society. Hollywood films promote a one-dimensional definition of beauty for women, based on a white standard of beauty as a soft, gentle, petite, fair-skinned, blue-eyed blonde. The leading ladies in black films have traditionally been mulattoes who have come as close as possible to that ideal.

As a woman who married an African and left America to live in Nigeria, Ye Ye Akilimali Funua Olade has observed the effects of such views and values. Young black males, in their quest for Hollywood's love of the "beautiful" body, face, hair and skin tone, have rejected the big, tall, strong, dark women. These women often misinterpret their own desire for love as sex-love and engage in homosexual relationships. Black female homosexuality also exists among light-skinned women who realize that "almost white" beauty does not bring happiness, but instead leads to exploitation by black males who only love them for their physical appearance.[12]

The sexy black male, unlike his female counterpart, was carefully censored in the early Hollywood films. Handsome stars like James Edwards and Harry Belafonte had to be sexually antiseptic in roles as nice, decent colored boys. Joe Adams, who played Belafonte's rival as the prize fighter in *Carmen Jones*, never went far in films because he was such an overtly sexual performer.[13] The new style black male sexuality was allowed in the 1964 films *Nothing But A Man* with Ivan Dixon and *One Potato, Two Potato* with Berne Hamilton; but neither actor worked steadily in Hollywood films.[14]

The image of the sexy black male was never popular with white audiences because he was seen as a threat to white male power. Historically, black men accused of raping white women have had their bodies dismembered by crazed lynch mobs. This pathological attitude toward sex and race is an outgrowth of the white male's paranoid reaction to his view of black male virility and sexual power.[15]

The public reaction to interracial love in *Island in the Sun* (1957) is, therefore, not surprising. Belafonte received hate mail, protesting his romance with Joan Fontaine in the film and the Ku Klux Klan staged numerous picketings. Before the film was released, theater owners, mostly in the South, threatened to boycott it. The South Carolina legislature even threatened to pass a bill to levy a fine of $5000 on any movie house showing the film.[16]

The agressive black male superstud only became popular in Hollywood's search for an audience to bail the film industry out of a financial recession in the 1970s. The one-dimensional black brute images of the blaxploitation films grossed huge profits and attracted urban black audiences who were starving for heroes.[17] The rural pastoral hero, who simply endured his plight, was too close to the Uncle Tom image. The new urban outlaw superheroes did not merely endure, they prevailed in the urban milieu. Unfortunately, the limitless power that Hollywood paraded across the screen was only available to the young black males in the audience through black-on-black violence and sexism, an artificial personal power over women as a substitute for real social power over one's destiny and daily life.[18]

Black-on-black violence and sexual abuse are not difficult to understand in view of the film industry's portrayal of black life as meaningless. Blacks who kill other blacks go unpunished in such early Hollywood films as *Hallelujah* and *Porgy and Bess*, where black men escape their responsibility for murder. The situation remained the same in the 1970s, as observed by Dr. Roland Jefferson, a black Los Angeles psychiatrist: "Films such as *Hell Up in Harlem, Across 110th Street, Trouble Man, Coffy,* and *Black Caesar,* typify the central underlying message: the life of a black man or woman has absolutely

no value in our society and serves to reinforce already existing negative and worthless self-images . . ."[19]

Dr. Maulana Karenga calls the ensuing situation a cultural crisis.[20]
The images, values and views presented in the films have become
symbolic of the black experience, repeatedly reflected in plays, literature and television programs and reinforced by theories on inherent
black inferiority, the superiority of the plantation society, and the
matriarchal black family.

The cultural crisis may be effectively combated with a change in the
images, values and views that have become symbols. These must be
redefined and a new set of symbols developed to provide new defini-
tions of black men and women and their relationships. Realistic,
sensitive films about blacks can serve as one vehicle to promote this
change, by shaping images, values and views in the best interests of
black people.

*Sounder* (1972) was successful in sensitizing even the youthful
black audiences to the realities of rural Southern existence. Such
Hollywood productions are rare because they require a skilled
filmmaker who can treat sensitive subjects without excessive romanticism and who can sell the product to a white market that often may
not even be able to recognize a good film about blacks.[21]

The "little movie" movement that Loren Miller promoted in 1934[22]
has a greater chance for success today with black organizations and
groups of individuals increasingly able and willing to invest in films.[23]
The distribution of films will become easier with the advent of vid-
eocassette libraries and cable television technology enlarging public
access to channels of communication. The new filmmakers must be
prepared, however, for a lengthy battle to reverse the images, values
and views which have saturated movie audiences for almost a century,
beginning with Edison's kinetoscope vignettes in the 1890s.

## NOTES

[1]Donald Bogle, *Toms, Coons, Mulattoes, Mammies and Bucks: An Interpretive
History of Blacks in American Films* (New York: Viking, 1973), p. 339.

[2]Thomas Cripps, *Black Film as Genre* (Bloomington: Indiana Univ. Press, 1979), p.
13.

[3]Bogle, pp. 18–19.

[4]Willette Coleman, "Crying at the Movies," *Black Collegian*, Jan./Feb. 1975, p. 32.

[5]Bogle, p. 44.

[6]Bogle, p. 95.

[7]Bogle, p. 248.

[8]Gary Null, *Black Hollywood: The Negro in Motion Pictures* (Secaucus, N.J.: Citadel Press, 1977), p. 70.

[9]Louie Robinson, "Have Blacks Really Made It in Hollywood?" *Ebony*, June 1975, pp. 36, 38.

[10]"How to Survive in Hollywood Between Gigs," *Ebony*, Oct. 1978, pp. 36, 40.

[11]Robinson, pp. 40, 42.

[12]Ye Ye Akilimali Funua Olade, "Many A Lost Tomorrow: A Sister Speaks from Africa," *Black Male/Female Relationships*, 2, No. 1 (1980), 19. Olade has found that in most African religions, such as the Yoruba religion, a woman may be "Oya," tough, masculine, raging or "Oshun," sexy, soft, melting, lovely and there is a man for both/all types of women. She attributes this to the distinction between multi-view African religion and Europeanized Christianity, Islam and Judaism, which stress one type, including one "god."

[13]Bogle, p. 287.

[14]Bogle, p. 239.

[15]"BBB Interviews Dr. Frances Welsing," *Black Books Bulletin*, 6, No. 4 (1980), 61; "The Resurrection of the Black Male: The $1 Trillion Misunderstanding," *Black Male/Female Relationships*, 2, No. 1 (1980), 34.

[16]Bogle, p. 243; "Belafonte Sours on Films, Disco Music, TV Racism, Backsliding Blacks," *Jet*, 26 April 1979, p. 31.

[17]Renée Ward, "Black Films, White Profits," *The Black Scholar*, 8 (May 1976), 16.

[18]Maulana Karenga, "The Black Male/Female Connection," *Black Male/Female Relationships*, 2, No. 1 (1980), 23.

[19]Ward, p. 23.

[20]Karenga, pp. 25–26.

[21]Sidney Poitier, "Walking the Hollywood Color Line," *American Film*, April 1980, p. 29.

[22]Loren Miller, "Uncle Tom in Hollywood," *Crisis* reprint, Nov. 1970, p. 348.

[23]"Countdown at Kusini," *Ebony*, April 1976, pp. 90–94.

# William Faulkner and the Silent Film

JEFFREY J. FOLKS

Much of the research concerning William Faulkner's relationship to film focuses on the writer's experience as a scriptwriter during the 1930s and 1940s, perhaps assuming that Faulkner's serious interest in film began only with his arrival in Hollywood in 1932.[1] As a result, students of Faulkner have been confronted with the puzzling conclusion that "the pre-Hollywood *The Sound and the Fury* and *Light in August* are more cinematic than *A Fable* (1950), which was originally intended as a scenario."[2] Indeed, in the period preceding his arrival in Hollywood, Faulkner had already produced novels which, to many readers, appear to reflect the techniques of the cinema. While we cannot know precisely what attitudes he embraced toward film, Faulkner's comments scattered throughout the first three novels and early short stories reveal a writer knowledgeable and interested, at times clearly fascinated, by the products of the young American film industry.[3]

Silent film comprised a significant part of available popular entertainment in Oxford during Faulkner's youth. During his childhood and adolescence Faulkner attended silent films regularly, as often as twice a week according to Murray Falkner, who remembered seeing "mostly Westerns."[4] Examination of the Oxford *Eagle* from 1910 (the date of the first commercial film showing) through 1915 reveals the types of film which Faulkner undoubtedly viewed regularly during his youth. Since the earliest films shown in Oxford were not advertised by title, it is not possible to determine exactly what films Faulkner might have seen in the first years of film showings, but the standard features certainly consisted to a large extent of Westerns, melodramas, and comedies. By 1915 the typical weekly fare at the

171

Lyric Theatre included: Monday nights, Hearst-Selig News Pictorial, a comedy, and *Perils of Pauline*, a serial; Tuesday nights, six reels; Wednesday nights, four reels plus University Orchestra accompaniment; Thursday through Saturday, four reels. Some of the titles listed in the Oxford *Eagle* were *The Pit* (from the Frank Norris novel), *Mrs. Wiggs of the Cabbage Patch*, *The Road of Strife*, *Exploits of Elaine*, *Hazards of Helen*, and *Across the Border*. One may assume that among performers featured were Mary Pickford, Lillian Gish, Charles Chaplin, Buster Keaton, Harry Langdon and Fatty Arbuckle. The many Westerns which Murray Falkner recalled having seen with his brother may well have featured Tom Mix, William S. Hart, and Broncho Billy (G. M. Anderson), as well as many lesser known performers. In the summer of 1915 the Lyric changed from exhibiting films of the General Film Company to those of Universal Service, which distributed the comedies of Hank Mann, Max Asher, Eddie Lyons, Lee Morgan, Billy Ritchie, and Harry Gibbon.

Faulkner possessed an extensive knowledge of the silent film of the teens, as is clearly demonstrated by the many references to film in his fiction. In his first three novels alone, a large number of passages depend upon references to film, and undoubtedly this reliance on film as the basis for literary comparisons carries into the major fiction as well.

Faulkner's early novels contain some shrewd film criticism, much of it centering on the story treatments of contemporary film. In *Mosquitoes* Jenny makes a wry comment which likens the rich, idle passengers of the *Nausikaa* to the characters in a film: "This is kind of funny, ain't it? They are not going anywhere, and they don't do anything . . . kind of like a movie or something."[5] This comment indicates Faulkner's awareness of film as a narrative medium, but also reveals his consistent practice of comparing film to literary methods and standards. This practice of examining film for narrative structures did, in fact, leave its mark on his fiction.

The distinctive characteristics of several individuals in *Mosquitoes* almost certainly derive from particular traits popularized by film comics. In fact, the very mode of comedy which Faulkner attempts in his second novel owes much to the structure of silent film, as Jenny suggested in the above comment.

During the early and middle twenties, Faulkner frequently spoke of his characters and of himself as "the little man" or "the tramp," a reference to the persona made famous in Chaplin's films. In *Mosquitoes* the aesthetic discussion criticizes art which is "too engrossed in trying to create great living characters ... and overlooked the possibilities of the little man."[6] Earlier, in "Out of Nazareth" Faulkner had used the word "tramp" to refer to his character David, a young vagabond whom Faulkner and Spratling admire.[7] Furthermore, Dorothy Oldham recalls that, predicting his future success, Faulkner told her around 1920: "Who knows, someday you may see a headline in the newspapers, 'Tramp Becomes Famous.' "[8] Faulkner also referred to himself as a "tramp" in the semi-autobiographical essay "Mississippi," which he wrote in the early fifties, describing "the young man's attitude of mind" in April 1917 as adopting "the avocation he was coming more and more to know would be forever his true one: to be a tramp, a harmless possessionless vagabond."[9]

In *Mosquitoes*, Pete seems also to refer to Buster Keaton. Pete wears a stiff straw hat with which he refuses to part. Julius and Fairchild remark the appropriateness of the hat to Pete's face. Fairchild says: "Pete has a kind of humorless reckless face that a stiff straw hat just suits. A man with a humourous face should never wear a stiff straw hat. But then, only a humorless man would dare buy one."[10] Likewise, Buster Keaton wore a stiff straw hat as a mark of identification in his films, and Keaton's humorless, nearly expressionless attitude earned him the name "the Great Stone Face." The word "reckless" could also be identified with Keaton's acting, as the numerous injuries he suffered in performing would attest.

That Faulkner made use of reference to silent film from an early point in his apprenticeship as a writer is indicated by further examples. Not only were prominent film stars the object of his writing, but more general conventions of plot and action were repeated. One convention of this type—the working into the plot of the starchy, snobbish Englishman—is suggested in Faulkner's early story "Love." Joseph Blotner states that "Love," an unpublished fragment from around 1921, "combined different materials. The elaborate and melodramatic romantic triangle was quite common both in motion pictures and magazine fiction. Though the Major may have been

American, his elegant appearance and clipped speech suggested a certain British stereotype. The batman-valet and the house-party situation both reinforced this effect."[11] In film versions, the snobbish Englishman acted as a foil to the democratic American hero, usually competing in a love triangle. Lord Rockingham in *Fast and Loose* (1930) is a later example of this type. The suave, socially conscious Englishman or European was a highly familiar stock character, always presented as obnoxious or foolish and always defeated by the hometown American male. In the films of the thirties the suave aristocrat emerged as often from American backgrounds as from European, as did Dick Boulton in *Night After Night* (Paramount, 1932) and Tod Newman in *Dancing Lady* (MGM, 1933). Whether the product of American new wealth or European aristocracy, the social snob was presented so as to satisfy the democratic emotions of the mass film audience.

As several critics of Faulkner's apprenticeship fiction have demonstrated, the meaningfulness of the very language which one employs to conduct social and family relationships is subjected to scrutiny, a skepticism toward language which is suggested by the technique of the silent film. Michael Millgate interprets *Mosquitoes* as a treatment of this important theme: "The whole book becomes, in a sense, a demonstration of the futility of talk, of words, and we have already seen that this may be related to Faulkner's growing awareness of his own needs as a writer—an awareness also reflected in the statements on art and literature made at various points in the book."[12] Similarly, Olga Vickery believes that the theme of abstract as opposed to concrete meaning underlies *Mosquitoes*: "Thus, Gordon, who is the only genuine artist in the group, has the least to do with talk. Talliaferro, on the other hand, verbalizes all possible approaches to action, and for that very reason is incapable of performing any act."[13] Silent film, as a graphic, pictorial medium chiefly concerned with gesture and visual detail, represented a contemporary form of narrative which subordinated language to physical action and gesture.

From the beginning of his career Faulkner created crucial scenes that are often enacted in silence. Regardless of the extent to which he consciously resorted to the technique of silent film to convey his meaning, the aesthetic convergence of narrative methods in fiction and film is a significant phenomenon. At times mute characters in the fiction appear to pantomime their meaning in much the same way silent film actors and actresses learned to do. Dialogue is perfunctory and often meaningless, while characters who speak easily are suspect, as are the socially accomplished Mrs. Maurier in *Mosquitoes* and the "erudite" Januarius Jones in *Soldiers' Pay*. Rather, the emphasis is on communication through intuition, pantomime, and action. At one point in *Soldiers' Pay* George Farr and Januarius Jones, in an attempt to elude one another and join Cecily Saunders, spend an entire night in the game of silent hide-and-seek. The sense of pantomime in the following passage suggests the same reliance on gesture as the mutely enacted chase scenes of silent film comedy:

> He stood near a tree at the corner of the lawn and after a short time he saw something moving shapeless and slow across the faint grass, along a hedge. He strode out boldly and the other saw him and paused, then that one, too, stood erect and came boldly to meet him. Jones joined him, murmuring, "Oh, hell," and they stood in static dejection, side by side.[14]

The effect of this sort of visual emphasis on the major fiction is equally significant. Passages of interior monologue from *The Sound and the Fury* reveal a silent world in which gesture and movement are burdened with meaning. Within the final section of the novel, one notices Benjy's sensitivity to physical change (the effect of a broken narcissus; Luster's driving the carriage the wrong way around the square). Early in the novel Benjy's vulnerability to change is enacted in his silent world of exaggerated motion, in which images rush chaotically across the limited screen of vision:

> I wasn't crying, but I couldn't stop. I wasn't crying, but the ground wasn't still, and then I was crying. The ground kept sloping up and the cows ran up the hill. T.P. tried to get up. He fell down again and the cows ran down the hill. Quentin held my arm and we went toward the barn. Then the barn wasn't there and we had to wait until it came back. I didn't see it come back. It came behind us and Quentin set me down in the trough where the cows ate. I held on to it. It was going away too, and I held to it. The cows ran down the hill across the door. I couldn't stop. Quentin and T.P. came up the hill, fighting. T.P. was falling down the hill and Quentin dragged him up the hill. Quentin hit T.P. I couldn't stop.[15]

The disorienting effect of alcohol merges with the psychological loss that Benjy feels at Caddy's wedding; the instability of the entire

Compson household as the idiot intuitively grasps it underscores the sense that the entire landscape and the people who inhabit it have in fact gone mad. Resembling the point of view shot in cinema, Benjy's perception is treated as if the reader were looking through a camera, with Faulkner in effect having scripted a complex scene involving a mixture of pans, tilts, dollies, and point of view shots.

The silent film also furthered a new consciousness of the individual and human aspects of all levels of society. Recording the growing diversity of American life, the cameras balanced this vision with their photographic evidence of the essential sameness of humanity. In Faulkner's early fiction the same impulse toward inclusiveness shapes the selection of characters, as illiterate and socially excluded persons occupy central positions while more conventional and "respectable" individuals take on peripheral roles. The idiot, the amnesiac, the confused adolescent, the rural peasant, and the immigrant receive important and psychologically convincing treatments, just as they are the central concern for more sensitive filmmakers of the teens and early twenties.

Even the extent to which Faulkner turned to the portrayal of grotesques may well have been influenced by the contemporary growth of popular taste for the horror and fantasy film. The qrotesque had been popularized in such Lon Chaney vehicles of the twenties as *The Phantom of the Opera, The Hunchback of Notre Dame, The Monster*, and *London at Midnight*. The same period saw several versions of *Dr. Jekyll and Mr. Hyde* and culminated in the Tod Browning production of *Freaks* (1932), a disturbing and controversial depiction of real-life freaks of the circus world. The impetus toward artistic depiction of grotesque material was also furthered by such German horror films as F. W. Murnau's *Nosferatu* (1922), Paul Wegener's *The Golem* (1923), and Fritz Lang's *Dr. Mabuse* (1922) and *Metropolis* (1926). The most widely admired of the German silent fantasies, Robert Wiene's *The Cabinet of Dr. Caligari* (1919), combined an acclaimed artistic production with a chilling murder story told, as one learns at the end of the film, by a madman confined in a mental institution. The popular demand for grotesque tales of violence closely parallels Faulkner's apprenticeship period, in which he experimented with a wide range of fictional subjects and techniques. It seems likely that his publication of *Sanctuary* in 1931 reflects both an awareness of the public's taste for the grotesque and a fairly extensive knowledge of the horror film as a genre.

That Faulkner's sensibility tended to explore the boundaries of conventional society is evident from the early sketches which he contributed to the New Orleans *Times-Picayune* in 1925, as it is in the list of psychological grotesques in his first novel, *Soldiers' Pay*. In the creation of such characters as Donald Mahon, Margaret Powers, Cecily Saunders, and Januarius Jones, Faulkner was participating in the cultural rebellion of the twenties against arbitrary restraints on artistic subject matter. Within the same period of cultural exploration, D. W. Griffith filmed *Broken Blossoms* as well as *Intolerance*, Mary Pickford acted the part of an orphan struggling for her freedom in *Swallows*, Von Stroheim filmed *Greed* from Frank Norris's novel *McTeague*, and Fritz Lang participated in German Expressionism's revelation of aberrant psychology and behavior.

In filming such treatments of the illiterate and dispossessed, silent filmmakers worked from a position of artistic strength, relying on photographic detail rather than language and dialogue. Furthermore, their techniques of cross-cutting and parallel editing were suited to the task of documenting sharp contrasts in social conditions. The historical imagination of Griffith had employed such editing techniques to juxtapose conflicting groups in *Birth of a Nation* and to alternate between four historical periods in *Intolerance*. Similarly, the radical contrasts developed in *The Sound and the Fury* rely on the cinematic techniques of pantomime, visual juxtaposition, and rapid movement exclusive of language. In this respect the scene in which Quentin befriends Julio's sister illustrates the similarity of aesthetic approaches employed by Faulkner's literary art and the popular medium of silent film. Despite his indisputable facility with language, Quentin communicates with women as poorly as either of his brothers. The meeting with the Italian girl dramatizes Quentin's alienation through his exaggerated attempts to pantomime meanings:

> "Does that look like your house?" I said. She looked at me over the bun.
> "This one?" I said, pointing. She just chewed, but it seemed to me that I

discerned something affirmative, acquiescent even if it wasn't eager, in her air. "This one?" I said. "Come on, then." I entered the broken gate. I looked back at her. "Here?" I said. "This look like your house?"[16]

As Quentin's urgency to locate the girl's parents increases, he repeats the fundamental gesture of friendship in his offers of food, though such bestowals of kindness have only the ironic effect of enticing the child further from home. Quentin's discomfort in this situation precipitates a sequence of events characteristic of popular literature and film—a chase scene in which the Italian girl relentlessly pursues Quentin until the appearance of her brother Julio. Several of the conventions of silent comedy which D. M. Murray has noted in Faulkner's writing appear in the scene: frantic action, comic distortion of character, and sudden appearance of a character. Here Faulkner employs cinematic technique to great advantage, for Quentin clearly mimes his own psychological orientation toward Caddy, a little sister whom he can never escape nor address through language.

The antithetical presentation of women in film has, in fact, been examined by critics who note the tendency to stereotype women by setting the roles of all-American girl and mother against the femme fatale, vamp, and prostitute. Unlike male actors who retained a creditable position as the kind-hearted, ordinary Joe, women were typed as entirely virginal and pure-hearted or immensely evil and corrupt. The public's adulation of Mary Pickford in the role of ingenue alongside the simultaneous popularity of Theda Bara's vamp in *A Fool There Was* and *Camille* in the mid-teens attests to the cultural polarization in the presentation of women in film.

The sentimentality connected with the role of motherhood is also rampant in melodramas and westerns of the silent film period, as Griffith and Mayer have noted: "What deep vein of sentimentality and repressed guilt she touched in the American soul it is hard now to say, but Mother was a figure of supreme importance in the silent drama, symbolizing not only self-sacrifice but rectitude, authority, and an apron-strings world to which many perhaps longed to return."[17] Yet underlying such emphasis on polar roles of women is the fact of growing cultural change. The reverence accorded the maternal role is matched by the repetition of the *East Lynne* motif in early silent film, the drama of a mother deserting her family and returning much later to be reunited with her grown children.

The artistic tension resulting from such cultural ambivalence toward women comprises an interesting element in Faulkner's depiction of women. It is the underlying cultural motif behind the drama, often the melodrama, of several of his major novels. While no specific silent film "source" should be assigned as the "influence," the significance of early films in defining the dramatic situation of women seems incontestable, since it could scarcely have arisen from the highly traditional culture of provincial Mississippi. Similar to the attitude toward women in the silent film, Faulkner's portrayal is neither traditional nor radically modern. Rather, it is dramatic. Change is viewed as inevitable, but change is painful as well. Women in traditional roles—Miss Jenny in *Sartoris*, Rosa Millard in *The Unvanquished*, Dilsey in *The Sound and the Fury*—inspire respect and warmth, yet they act primarily as observers of the emerging future, into which they are incapable of projecting their stable sense of order and value. Faulkner's modern heroines also inspire admiration and warmth, yet they are equally doomed by motion and time: Caddy Compson is fearless and yet reckless as she climbs defiantly up the pear tree to peer into the parlor window. Thus, in the same passage she is nostalgically described by Benjy as "smelling like trees," and addressed by Dilsey as "You, Satan."

Typically, the tension evoked by such ambivalent treatments of women was resolved in the endings of silent film through the imposition of one form or another of "happy ending," whether a conventional romantic pairing or a transformation in which ugliness is transformed into beauty, hatred into love. As Charles Higham rightly observes, "Hollywood was, as late as 1919, a largely rural community" and, consequently, "the cinema sustained the attitudes of nineteenth-century comedy, melodrama, and rural romance."[18] Hollywood's foremost director of the teens, D. W. Griffith, produced films such as *A Romance of Happy Valley* within this mode. As Edward Wagenknecht states, Griffith's film demonstrates an unusual "knowledge of the rural American temperament."[19]

To a greater extent than one might at first realize, Faulkner evokes the mood of popular romance in many of his works, yet it is romance overshadowed by realism and time. From the beginning of his writing career, he constructed stories which rely to a considerable extent on popular romantic motifs. In his first novel *Soldiers' Pay* the romantic couple of Margaret Powers and Joe Gilligan suggest characters from magazine fiction and the cinema as well as models from high literature. Despite an early passage comparing Margaret to a Beardsley drawing, she is more the product of the Jazz Age than the Nineties. Paired with Joe Gilligan, a hard-drinking private with a background in crap games and casual sex, at the beginning of the novel Margaret appears the typical heroine of urban popular culture—the hardened, unsentimental, disillusioned companion of the latest in a series of men. It is the meeting with the wounded Donald Mahon that softens both Margaret and Joe into compassionate, responsible protectors of the dying pilot. The novel's subtext consists of the transformation of its romantic couple from modern urban culture to the mode of rural romance. Yet the story's resolution is overwhelmingly ironic, for the small Southern town of Charlestown, Georgia, the locale for the novel, has abandoned the pastoral mode as one community member after another is unmasked as flapper, social climber, gossip, or lecher. The tone of the novel comes to resemble a sophisticated film comedy of the sort popularized by Ernst Lubitsch, who satirized the artificial and selfish lives of America's wealthy. In the sense that *Soldiers' Pay* is also structured largely as a satire, it is perhaps less difficult than has been supposed to explain Faulkner's experiment with an even more satiric mode of writing in his second novel, *Mosquitoes*.

The inception of many of Faulkner's attitudes and fictional motifs can be traced to his early viewing of silent films that reflected the conventions of popular literature. The popular stories of Faulkner's childhood and youth were adapted readily from one medium to another, appearing in popular fiction, stage performances, film versions, and from there made their way through hands like his into serious experimental literature. The emphasis on conflict and pursuit in the countless Westerns which the Falkner children viewed eventually emerged as a feature of the popular consciousness with which the mature William Faulkner had to deal as an author. The ambivalent roles of women in the silent cinema certainly contributed to the view

of women which is reflected and, to some extent, modified in Faulkner's fiction. Clearly, Faulkner was well acquainted with the subjects,
characters, and techniques of the silent film. Many years before his
own arrival in Hollywood, Faulkner had studied its products in the
early Westerns, melodramas and comedies which had appeared in
Oxford. It was out of this prior association with the cinema that he was
led to consider, adapt, and revise in his own imagination the popular
vision of the silent film. The Lyric Theatre brought a vision of a larger
world into remote and isolated Oxford, Mississippi.

## NOTES

[1]See Bruce Kawin, *Faulkner and Film* (New York: Ungar, 1977); Edward Murray,
*The Cinematic Imagination: Writers and the Motion Pictures* (New York: Ungar,
1972); and D. M. Murray, "Faulkner, the Silent Comedies, and the Animated Car-
toon," *Southern Humanities Review*, 9 (Summer 1975), 241–57.

[2]Murray, pp. 154–55.

[3]Such statements include the comparison of a courthouse in *Flags in the Dust* to a
"theatre drop, flamboyant and cheap and shoddy; obviously built without any definite
plan by men without honesty or taste" (New York: Random, 1974), p. 400. In the story
"Cheest" the narrator had described a motion picture: "Well, they was showing a
racing fillum. Cheest, it was terrible. They was one horse looked like a winner, with a
decent jock he could of walked away. But this bird done everything he could, setting
too far back and letting hisself be dragged along by the reins, letting another skate take
the rail on him and break his stride," *New Orleans Sketches* (New York: Random,
1958), pp. 42–43. Faulkner's later story "Two Soldiers" relies on a similar confusion
concerning the distinction between the photographic image and reality.

[4]*The Falkners of Mississippi* (Baton Rouge: Louisiana State Univ. Press, 1967), pp.
49–52. Murray Falkner comments further that movies "provided a vast new field of
incredibly attractive entertainment. This was especially true in such a small town as
Oxford," p. 52.

[5](New York: Boni and Liveright, 1927), p. 75.

[6]Kenneth W. Hepburn, "Faulkner's *Mosquitoes*: A Poetic Turning Point," *Twentieth Century Literature*, 17 (1971), 22.

[7]*New Orleans Sketches*, ed. Carvel Collins (New York: Random, 1958), p. 101 ff.

[8]Joseph L. Blotner, *Faulkner: A Biography* (New York: Random, 1974), I, 292.

[9]William Faulkner, *Essays, Speeches and Public Letters*, ed. James B. Meriwether
(New York: Random, 1965), p. 21.

[10]*Mosquitoes*, p. 253.

[11]Blotner, p. 323.

[12]*The Achievement of William Faulkner* (New York: Random, 1966), p. 72.

[13]*The Novels of William Faulkner: A Critical Interpretation* (Baton Rouge:
Louisiana State Univ. Press, 1959), p. 9.

[14]*Soldiers' Pay* (1926; rpt. New York: Signet, 1968), p. 160.

[15]*The Sound and the Fury* (New York: Random, 1946), p. 24. Like Benjy, Pete's
mother in *Mosquitoes* is partially mute. "She didn't hardly talk at all any more: only
made sounds, wet sounds of satisfaction and alarm; and she saw her older son's face
and she made these sounds now, looking from one to the other but not offering to touch
them," p. 248. While Benjy does not have the ability to speak, the Italian woman does,
and it is interesting that the cause of her failure to speak is the rapid social change of

her family. From a modest family restaurant to a slick bootlegging operation her family has prospered and become Americanized, but the mother has not adapted to change. Instead, her alarm at the negative effects of this "progress" (the deterioration of family and community ties, the replacement of traditional roles by meaningless materialism) is voiced by her inarticulate sounds.

[16]*The Sound and the Fury*, p. 163.

[17]Richard Griffith and Arthur Mayer, *The Movies*, rev. ed. (New York: Simon and Schuster, 1970), p. 16.

[18]*The Art of the American Film* (Garden City, New York: Anchor, 1973), p. 4.

[19]*The Movies in the Age of Innocence* (Norman: Univ. of Oklahoma Press, 1962), p. 118. A further example of Faulkner's involvement with the popular culture of the teens is his interest in the romantic fiction of Henrik Sienkiewicz, an author whose *Quo Vadis?* enjoyed considerable popularity during the period of Faulkner's youth. An Italian film version of the novel received widespread attention in America in 1912. In his "Foreword" to *The Faulkner Reader* (New York: Random, 1954) Faulkner dated his reading of the novel to 1915 and 1916, and to some extent the popularity of the novel must surely be attributed to the enormous success of the film version. Sienkiewicz's importance to Faulkner is attested by the fact that his work is echoed in Faulkner's Nobel Prize Acceptance Speech.

# Tomorrow and Tomorrow and *Tomorrow*

JACK BARBERA

When *Tomorrow* opened in New York in 1972, many reviewers were enthusiastic. On WNBC Gene Shalit, certainly aware it was only April, proclaimed *Tomorrow* one of the year's ten best films, and in *New York* magazine Judith Crist praised the acting of Olga Bellin and Robert Duvall for providing "an offering of such subtlety that it will glow—and grow—in the retrospect" (10 April 1972, p. 61). Sad to say, there has not been much retrospect, as the film is little known. But should *Tomorrow* eventually receive proper attention, it would not be the first instance of artistic integrity delaying consequent enduring recognition.

While *Tomorrow* was being shot, Joseph Anthony, its director, noted two aspects of its integrity. The first had to do with a decision of the producers about the film's distribution: "Artistically, I am very confident of this movie, but commercially, nobody knows. The producers are so determined to protect the character and quality of this story they have made no distribution deal, and won't until it is finished so that there can be no distribution pressures involved." Unfortunately, the film has yet to find a major distributor and is still available only through the producers' New York company, Filmgroup Productions. Until recently there was not even available a 16mm print because of the concern of the producers, Gilbert Pearlman and Paul Roebling, that reduction to 16mm would result in a loss of visual quality. Anthony mentioned, as a second aspect of the film's aesthetic integrity, its black and white cinematography: "the producers and author are convinced that black and white is most suited to Faulkner and particularly this work. This is in defiance of contemporary work where most use color, but color today is not true enough for a work of

183

this nature. I personally prefer not to use it, not for a movie about a poor dirt farmer."[1] The non-commercial decision to shoot *Tomorrow* in black and white was in line with Roebling's insistence that it be patterned after Walker Evans's celebrated photographs of sharecroppers. As Bruce Kawin notes, the result is that "one can practically chart the grain in each plank of the sawmill's walls."[2]

A third aspect of *Tomorrow*'s integrity, one probably *not* contributing to its small audience, is that it was shot on location in Northeast Mississippi—not a light undertaking for a New York company filming a Faulkner story in 1970! Olga Bellin recalls that many people in the Tupelo area read the script: "the South has been so maligned in movies, they wanted to know what it was all about."[3] And Norma Fields, in her Tupelo newspaper article on the filming of *Tomorrow*, observed that members of the film company were sometimes greeted with distrust and suspicion. She suggested this happened because some Mississippians believed Faulkner portrayed only what is bad about the state. An anecdote by Richard McConnell, who plays Isham in the movie, suggests another reason for the distrust and suspicion: "Some guy came up to me here and asked, 'Are you with that movie bunch?' I told him yes, and he said, 'Is this another one of those integration things?' I said, 'Hey, man, no! It's a love story' " (Fields).

The incongruity of *Tomorrow*'s production company shooting in the Tupelo area is suggested by Fields's account of how she came to write her story. She had been covering the City Hall beat on an ordinary day. Then:

> A somewhat grubby, curly-haired young man needing a haircut brushed brashly into the mayor's office during the routine, but usually uninterrupted, interview. In a startling New York accent, he said something about getting things unloaded at the Community Center. On introduction, Mike Haley said, "Oh, hi. Nice tumeetcha," and disappeared as quickly as he came.
>
> This picture of the sometimes obstinate, always well-tailored, barbered mayor of the City of Tupelo and his easy rapport with the young unkempt movie-maker from New York kept haunting.

"By and large," Fields reported, the rapport held. In fact, the eventual cooperation and friendliness of the community became an enormous help to the film company.

One form of that help, and a reason for shooting on location, was the availability of authentic sets. Tupelo was chosen because a local woman who knew Faulkner and learned of the plans to make *Tomorrow* wrote the producers suggesting the area. Electricity and phones were relatively new to some of the country people, and poor dirt farming and sawmilling, elements of Faulkner's story, were common to the region some decades earlier. For a film in which "one can practically chart the grain in each plank," the use of actual structures was a boon. Exteriors were shot at T. C. Russell's sawmill north of Tremont, and interiors of the shack at the sawmill were taken inside its walls, but at the Tupelo Community Center. Permission was obtained to dismantle the shack, move it, and re-assemble it inside the Center. The town of Tupelo provided the Center, according to Horton Foote, so shooting could proceed "in case of rain."[4] Mrs. Chamblee, who with her husband owned and operated a general store in Itawamba County that had been closed for some decades, reopened it so a short scene could be filmed inside. Other scenes were shot at the Old Jacinto Courthouse.

Besides permission to use and tamper with buildings, local good will manifested itself in other ways. Residents provided antiques and searched out clothes stored for years, to be used for period detail. James Franks, a car collector from Prentiss County and the man who plays Preacher Whitehead in *Tomorrow*, supplied the 1920s auto used in the film. And he scouted up harmonica players for the soundtrack. A lot of excitement was stirred up not only by the fascination of a film crew—a circus come to town—but also by the use of local people in bit parts. Residents began to take pride in the production.

Filming on location also gave the New York actors and actresses a chance to develop and perfect local speech. Duvall and Bellin have different accents in the film—Duvall's backwoods and Bellin's Delta—and the difference reflects the rich variety of Southern accent which can exist even in the same area. On one occasion Duvall traveled to a nearby county, posed as a farmer from Alabama and was taken for the real thing by the local people. In fact, when *Tomorrow* was shown in Faulkner's home town of Oxford, the reviewer for the University of Mississippi newspaper praised Duvall's accent as "excellent, slow and tinged with uncertainty—we all know people who talk as he does."[5]

We have considered three aspects of *Tomorrow*'s integrity: distribution pressures did not influence artistic decisions; the film was shot in less commercial but arguably more appropriate black and white; and it was shot on location. A fourth aspect, its integrity as an adaptation, introduces a dilemma. In a recent book, Morris Beja contrasts the theories of André Bazin and Béla Belázs to indicate "two basic approaches to the whole question of adaptation":

> The first approach asks that the integrity of the original work—the novel, say—be preserved, and therefore that it should not be tampered with and should in fact be uppermost in the adapter's mind. The second approach feels it proper and in fact necessary to adapt the original work freely, in order to create—in the different medium that is now being employed—a new, different work of art with its own integrity.[6]

So, do we go with Bazin, saying integrity resides in fidelity to the literary text, or with Belázs, stressing the artistic requirements of film? I suggest we avoid an a priori approach: particular filmed adaptations should test the theories, rather than be tested by them. Formulating and refining theories do help clarify thought, but theory becomes pernicious when it substitutes for thought, cuts off experience, makes us think we need not see a film but need only know how closely it parallels a text—or how filmic it is—to judge whether it is good. An adaptation taking the approach recommended by Bazin, or that recommended by Belázs, might be good *or* bad. Only viewing the film will let us know.

In any event, integrity in a movie based on a literary work does not mean, cannot mean, that there are no changes. Going from one medium to another *is* change. In the case of *Tomorrow* we have three media to consider. Faulkner wrote the short story, "Tomorrow," which Horton Foote used as the basis for his play of the same name. The film was the result of the screenplay Foote adapted from his play, altered by the contributions of the director, actors, and others—sometimes even by the accidents of filming. One such "accident," for example, was the dialogue of the boy raised by Duvall in the movie. According to Foote, "he was not a trained actor and was very shy" (p. 162). In an interview Duvall commented: "We got him from Possum Trot, Mississippi, he'd been an incubator baby, small for his age. I whispered things to him. A lot of guys in the South, when they want affection, they say to their dogs, or to their kids, 'love muh neck.' So I'd just whisper that, 'love muh neck,' and he'd give me a big kiss in the neck.'[7] By winning the boy's confidence, Duvall was able to improvise scenes with him, "using whatever the boy said spontaneously" (Foote, p. 162). Whatever the mix of contribution, the end result of any successful adaptation is, in Beja's words, "an artistic achievement that is in some mysterious way the 'same' as the book but also something other: perhaps something less but perhaps something more as well" (p. 88). The rest of this essay has to do with the less and more of the three versions of *Tomorrow*. My title refers to these versions and echoes the phrase repeated in each, which Faulkner got from the famous soliloquy in *Macbeth*. That soliloquy, of course, provided Faulkner the title not only for this story, but also for his novel *The Sound and the Fury*.

However, before we consider some of the changes from version to version, focusing on those between the story and the film, a short plot summary is in order. When Stonewall Jackson Fentry was about twenty-five, he left his father's poor cotton farm to earn a little extra money working thirty miles away at a sawmill owned by Mr. Ben Quick. One day Fentry met a pregnant woman. She died after giving birth, and Fentry returned to the farm to raise her baby. Although the woman had been abandoned by her husband and family, her family showed up a few years later to take her son from Fentry. Still later Buck Thorpe, the grown man and scoundrel the boy had become, was murdered in self-defense by a Mr. Bookwright. At the subsequent trial, Fentry happened to be on the jury, and it was hung eleven to one for acquittal. Fentry would not vote to acquit because there remained for him, somewhere in Buck Thorpe, the memory of the little boy Fentry had loved.

Central in Faulkner's story is the theme which shines through the play and movie as well. It is also the theme of Faulkner's Nobel Prize speech, in which he said man not only would "endure," but would "prevail." Faulkner found in men like Fentry the strength which justified his optimism. Such men are, as Gavin Stevens (Bookwright's lawyer) says, "the lowly and invincible of the earth," who "endure and endure and then endure, tomorrow and tomorrow and tomorrow."[8] What endures is not the human shell, but the capacity for love, even

Robert Duvall in *Tomorrow:* (top) with the woman Olga
Bellin; (bottom) with the boy, Johnny Mask. (Courtesy of
Pearlman/Row, Inc.)

when love is denied and remains only a dream or a memory. Such endurance is a magnificent mystery, and the wonder of it is put well by Isham Quick, the sawmill owner's son:

> What I seem to have underestimated was his capacity for love. I reckon I figured that, coming from where he come from, he never had none a-tall, . . . that even the comprehension of love had done been lost out of him back down the generations where the first one of them had had to take his final choice between the pursuit of love and the pursuit of keeping on breathing (Faulkner, p. 98).

It is characteristic of Faulkner that his story is universal but also Southern, and critics have not been insensitive to this. Not only is Fentry named after a famous Confederate general, but he names the boy he raises "Jackson and Longstreet Fentry," because "Pa fit under both of them." A tradition of pride and courage and dignity, qualities Fentry himself has, is evoked here; for one must respect Fentry's father and the men like him who fought under generals such as Jackson and Longstreet, whatever one's opinion of the Confederate cause. The tradition evoked, as M. E. Bradford expressed it, is one of fierce "brigades who stood firm in the face of grapeshot at Manassas and made endless forced marches . . .—the slaveless men to whom 'the war' had been an invasion and whose self-respect had demanded they . . . repel the invader."[9] Had the boy, Jackson and Longstreet, not been taken from Fentry and become Buck Thorpe, indications are he would have grown up a proper heir to the tradition evoked by his name. And an heir, also, to Fentry. As Bradford notes, the boy was Fentry's hope for a "tomorrow," a posterity to give full meaning to his endurance: "Faulkner understands well what sons mean to a man," *especially* "to the land-loving traditional Southerner" (p. 236). And especially to Stonewall Jackson Fentry. As his neighbor puts it, although Fentry's land is poor, "his pa and his grandpa worked it, made a living for themselves and raised families and paid their taxes and owed no man" (Faulkner, p. 92). The Fentry pride, and endurance, and land, are intertwined.

Although all three versions of *Tomorrow* celebrate Fentry's capacity for love, differences among them are not hard to find. Some of the differences are slight, and it is difficult to see how they could be significant to an esthetic judgment of the versions. Name changes provide one example. Stonewall Jackson Fentry and Jackson and Longstreet Fentry are historically resonant, but the names of minor characters do not vibrate with such meaning. So it matters little that in the play and movie Gavin Stevens is changed to Thornton Douglas "for legal reasons" (Foote, p. 159). The name of the sawmill owner's son, Isham Quick, is retained in both Foote's play and the first draft of his screenplay; but in the movie the name becomes Isham Russell—a change probably related to the production company's permission to use Russell's sawmill and shack for their shooting.[10] I had no idea why Preacher Whitfield becomes Preacher Whitehead in the play and movie, but again it doesn't matter. Another kind of change, which at first might seem significant, concerns a phrase used by Isham Quick. He calls the mother of Jackson and Longstreet "black-complected" (Faulkner, p. 100). Horton Foote has commented that "both actresses, Kim Stanley and Olga Bellin, who have played Sarah are blonde, but they did understand the fierce pride of the woman" (p. 153). Foote did not *intend* the change in complexion: in the first draft of his screenplay he even has the woman remark, before she dies, that her son is like her in being "black-complected." It is important to know that blonde actresses were not employed to avoid an "integration thing," for "black-complected"—in the time and place of Faulkner's story—did not mean "Negro."[11] If Faulkner *had* intended us to understand that the mother of Jackson and Longstreet was of Negro ancestry, then of course the use of blonde actresses to portray her would have been a significant and compromising change.

The *significant* changes in the adaptations of Faulkner's story have little effect on what it celebrates. The changes involve the way plot is treated: what is retained and what is left out, how it is ordered, the point of view from which it is told. Let us begin our analysis by considering a dramatic moment in the story. Isham Quick is telling about a day when Buck Thorpe was drinking and fighting at a general store, and Jackson Fentry rode up on a mule: "I don't know how long he had been there, not saying nothing, just setting there and looking at Thorpe; then he turned the mule and rid back up the road toward them hills he hadn't ought to never have left" (Faulkner, p. 104). Foote's remarks about the treatment of this moment in the adaptations raises an interesting question:

I think it was most effective in the theater. There was something immediate and quite wonderful about the meeting of the two in the scene that we found in the play version. In the screen version, the scene was shot and I understand that it was very difficult for Bob Duvall, that it was not in the final cut of the screenplay, because he felt so strongly that in some ways, it was his best work, and the producer and the director told me that they did indeed agree that it was (p. 158).

The question is, if the producer and director of *Tomorrow* agreed that Duvall's acting was most powerful in this dramatic scene, why was it cut? I am not sure who had the ultimate say, or on what basis the decision was made, but it is defensible on artistic grounds. [12] If a filmmaker is not willing to discard some of his best footage when it does not work in the whole film he is making, his film cannot succeed. To understand why the filmmakers' decision to cut the encounter between Buck Thorpe and Jackson Fentry was wise, we must consider the vast difference between the approach to "Tomorrow" taken by Faulkner and the approach taken by the filmmakers. This difference in approach can also explain the fact that, while Fentry's father is alive at the end of Faulkner's "Tomorrow," we learn of his death at the end of the film.

Faulkner tells "Tomorrow" as a detective story. It is one of six stories in the collection *Knight's Gambit*, all of which involve the detective figure Gavin Stevens. Stevens's nephew, Chick Mallison, is the narrator of "Tomorrow." Chick begins by telling us that his lawyer uncle had only one case before he became Yoknapatawpha County Attorney more than twenty years ago. It was the Buck Thorpe murder case, and Stevens served as counsel for the defense. When a mistrial was declared, Chick accompanied his uncle into the countryside. Stevens had to find out why Fentry, who never met Bookwright and who didn't deny Stevens's arguments, refused to vote acquittal. After being driven off the Fentry farm at gunpoint by Fentry's father, Stevens stops at the Pruitt house a mile away. He gets information from the Pruitts which, combined with the information he later gets from Isham Quick, reveals that Buck Thorpe had once been Jackson and Longstreet Fentry. Thus Stevens has unraveled the mystery of Fentry's conduct on the jury. When Chick declares he would have voted to free Bookwright, if he were Fentry, his uncle grips him on the knee and explains why Chick "wouldn't have freed him either. Don't ever

forget that. Never" (Faulkner, p. 105). Chick's naiveté serves as a foil
to his uncle's wisdom. Presumably Chick never did forget; twenty
years later he tells us of his experience and of his uncle's understanding of Jackson Fentry's heart. Thus, in the form of a detective story,
piecing together the puzzle of Fentry's vote, Faulkner introduces us to
a deeper mystery of enduring love.

The use of a complex time sequence and several narrators suits
Faulkner's artistic purposes. We learn we are going to get background
on Gavin Stevens, the lawyer who figures in the other stories in our
collection. Then we move back over twenty years, to the trial, and
have our mystery posed. After the trial, the Pruitts tell of Fentry's
leaving for the sawmill, years before, and of his returning with and
raising a boy. One day Fentry and the boy disappear, and when Fentry
returns he is without the boy. The Pruitts have provided information
but more questions as well, and no answers. Finally Isham Quick
solves the mystery, filling us in on Fentry's meeting with the pregnant
woman, of the time a few years later when the Thorpes took the boy
from Fentry, and of the time still later when Fentry encountered Buck
Thorpe at the store. The last is probably on Chick's mind when,
driving home with his uncle, he says he would have freed Bookwright
because Thorpe was a bad man.

The three paragraphs in which Isham Quick told about Fentry's
time with the pregnant woman (Faulkner, pp. 99–100) first made
Norton Foote agree to adapt the story for Playhouse 90:

> I began somehow in the most obsessive, vivid kind of way to want to
> discover for myself, as a writer, what went on between Jackson Fentry and
> this black-complected woman. . . . I called this woman Sarah, although
> Faulkner never names her and I had her married to a man named Eubanks.
> And so . . . I began to dramatize what I felt was the story of Jackson Fentry
> and Sarah Eubanks. . . . I realized that what I had written was monstrously
> out of proportion to the rest of the story. I wanted to retain this, and I wanted
> to see it used so I began to construct the rest of the play around the story of
> these two people. (pp. 153–54)

Foote did construct his play, and then his screenplay, around the story
of Jackson Fentry and Sarah Eubanks. He had to invent what went on
between them, and his expansion of their encounter is the most
significant change between Faulkner's story and the play and movie

adaptations. Because Foote concentrates on the bond of love which slowly develops between Jackson and Sarah, he has no need for the several narrators and complex time sequence employed by Faulkner. Foote's decision to simplify the sequence and manner of telling is not only in the interest of dramatic clarity, it is perfectly consistent with his shift in focus from detective story to love story.

Detective story conventions Faulkner used are not completely abandoned, however. In both the stage and film adaptations they remain as a narrative frame. The play opens with the Pruitts on their porch as lawyer Thornton Douglas and his nephew drive up to learn what they can about the Pruitts' neighbor, Jackson Fentry. Ed Pruitt tells the whole story, in order, starting with the night Fentry left for the sawmill. Or, rather, the story is acted out, with Pruitt used from time to time as a voice-over to make scene transitions and provide important facts. Then we are back on the Pruitt porch, the mystery solved. Douglas and his nephew have the exchange about voting Bookwright free, and the play ends with Douglas as voice-over, commenting on "the lowly and invincible of the earth" while we see Fentry working in the fields. In the movie the narrative frame is set at the courthouse. Douglas as voice-over is addressing the jury, as we see the fatal shooting of Thorpe. There are some outdoor scenes of the courthouse as the title and credits roll by, and then we are inside watching Douglas's summation. In the jury room we see Fentry refusing to acquit. Douglas, as voice-over, explains that he had to find out why. He tells of his discovery that many years ago Fentry left home for a job. There is a montage of Fentry leaving, church singing as he walks down country roads, guitar music as he settles in at the sawmill, a high angle shot of him asleep in the boiler shed while the last of the credits rolls by. After these first approximately ten minutes, the narrative frame ends and the story proper begins. Much later, when the Thorpes take Jackson and Longstreet away, lawyer Douglas returns as a voice-over, tells us of the death of Fentry's father, and for about the last five minutes of the film we are back at the courthouse and Douglas' summation. In a series of dissolves we see a close-up of Fentry's face, shots of his joy with Jackson and Longstreet, footage of the fatal shooting and, again, Fentry's refusal to acquit. Douglas continues as voice-over, and as Fentry rides from the courthouse on a mule, Douglas combines the speech Faulkner gave Isham, about Fentry's capacity for love, with the "lowly and invincible" speech.

The differences between the play and movie adaptations can be accounted for by the differences in media and, I think, by a fuller understanding on the part of the filmmakers of the simplicity befitting *Tomorrow* when told as a love story. An advantage of the stage is dramatic immediacy—recall Foote's words about the special effectiveness on the stage of the encounter between Buck Thorpe and Jackson Fentry. The play also retains the dramatic words of the lawyer to the nephew, about the nephew not voting Bookwright free. The nephew, the Pruitts, and the scene in which Fentry encounters Buck Thorpe are eliminated in the film. Buck Thorpe's cruelty, underlined in the Fentry encounter sequence, suggests the justice of freeing Bookwright and complicates our response to Fentry's vote. We understand the nephew's protest. With the film's elimination of this complication of feeling, we experience more powerfully the heroism of Fentry's vote. Returning to the other question we raised—about Fentry's father—we can now see why he is alive at the end of the story and dead at the end of the film. At the end of Faulkner's story, Gavin Stevens goes to Fentry's father in an attempt to solve the mystery of the hung jury. The attempt doesn't work, but it is part of Stevens's effort at detection. However, the attempts at detection do not shape the unfolding of the film. When Thornton Douglas tells us at the end of the film that Fentry's father died and Fentry worked the land alone, we are left with thoughts of Fentry's even more heroic endurance, because of the vastness of his solitude.

Although plays can be more dramatic than films, presenting people in the flesh rather than motion pictures of people, films have their advantages. As Foote commented, "there's always the notion of having enormous visual and physical freedom with the camera, which was not allowed to me in theater or television." So, in the film, "we took Fentry and Sarah outside the cabin as much as possible, dramatizing the moment when he shows where he hopes to build her house" (p. 161). Another delight of the film is the montage of Fentry's rearing the boy, for which many new scenes were created. The soundtrack comes alive with music and, among other vignettes, we have

Fentry carrying the boy like a papoose, picking cotton with him, hugging him in bed, playing with him in tall grass, and catching fish with him. One critic praised the film's lighting and composition "for being rigorous, formal, and tender—studies in the eloquence of the simple" (Kawin, p. 65). Consider one particular shot. As the narrative frame ends, and before Fentry meets Sarah, there is a sequence which visually establishes his solitude. In a long take from a fixed position some distance from Fentry, we see him sitting alone, eating. Isham goes by the window, enters the shed, and wishes Fentry a Merry Christmas. Fentry continues eating and Isham asks if he doesn't ever get lonesome. Finally there are some close-ups of their faces as Isham suggests that they go hunting together some time. Finding nothing else to say, he leaves. The camera has returned to its position some distance from Fentry, in effect, returning him to solitude after the momentary intimacy of the friendly offer. We get a visual echo of this shot—Fentry in the same chair, the camera fixed some distance from him—after Sarah's death and before the baby's cry rouses him. The simplicity of this visual style—no zooms, nothing fancy—continues throughout. It is effective and appropriate and consistent with the decision to film in black and white.

It is a shame that *Tomorrow* is not better known. Along with praise, it received some bad reviews, and they were enough to scare off the distributors. Thus the perils of an independent production in contemporary America. One of the bad reviews came from Andrew Sarris, the influential critic of the *Village Voice*. He complained about many things: the "Philco Playhouse School of Drama"; the implausibility of Faulkner's plots; the "artificially fragmented speech patterns" of the characters in the film. At one point he wrote: "what is it that Father Faulkner is preaching on this occasion, but merely that the poorest, the humblest, the most despised, the most forgotten among us may be capable of the most extraordinary love and devotion. If Faulkner's tone were any less awkwardly didactic than it is, it would be infinitely more condescending" (8 June 1972, p. 61). Let us ignore the logical problem Sarris poses of an awkwardly didactic tone's saving Faulkner or anyone from condescension. Sarris implies we should not be impressed that Jackson Fentry remained capable of fierce love. But grinding loneliness often kills human spirit. In complaining about the *film,* Sarris does attribute *esthetic* wisdom to Faulkner: "The beauty of the Faulkner story rests in the respectful distance the author keeps from beings of a different order." Who is condescending now?

Don't let Sarris discourage you. Bruce Kawin says *"Tomorrow* is simply one of the best independent productions in the recent history of American narrative film" (p. 65). See it, if you ever get a chance.

NOTES

I thank Jan Willis for guiding me through the files of the Lee County Library in Tupelo, Mississippi. In addition to clippings about the filming of *Tomorrow,* the library owns a copy of the screenplay's first draft, dated 10 August 1969, donated by Horton Foote.

[1] Norma Fields, " 'Tomorrow' Crew Trying to Make Faulkner Story Show True," *Daily Journal* [Tupelo, Mississippi], 20 March 1970, p. 20. This article appears on only one page. All further references to it omit the page number and appear in the text cited as Fields.

[2] *Faulkner and Film* (New York: Ungar, 1977), p. 65. All further references to this work appear in the text cited as Kawin.

[3] William T. Miles, "Tomorrow Comes to Tupelo June 1," *See Tupelo,* 9 (May/June 1972), p. 6. Many details in my essay, about local people and places used in *Tomorrow,* are drawn from this article. The quotation cited here is taken by Miles from an interview published elsewhere.

[4] Horton Foote, *"Tomorrow:* The Genesis of a Screenplay," in *Faulkner, Modernism, and Film: Faulkner and Yoknapatawpha, 1978,* ed., Evans Harrington and Ann Abadie (Jackson: Univ. Press of Mississippi, 1979), p. 162. All further references to this essay appear in the text cited as Foote.

[5] Jody Neblett, "Tupelo-made 'Tomorrow' opens," *Daily Mississippian,* 18 September 1972, p. 9. In her article, cited above, Norma Fields also mentions the authenticity of Duvall's "back-country Mississippi accent."

[6] *Film & Literature: An Introduction* (New York: Longman, 1979), p. 82. All further references to this work appear in the text cited as Beja.

[7] Chris Chase, "Quick—What's This Man's Name?," *New York Times,* 23 April 1972, Sec. 2, p. 16. All further references to this article are cited as Chase.

[8] William Faulkner, "Tomorrow," *Knight's Gambit* (New York: Random, 1949), p. 104. All further references to Faulkner's story appear in the text cited as Faulkner.

[9] "Faulkner's 'Tomorrow' and the Plain People," *Studies in Short Fiction,* 2 (1965), 237. All further references to this essay appear in the text cited as Bradford. For another essay on the Southern significance of "Tomorrow" see Elmo Howell, "Faulkner's Enveloping Sense of History: A Note on 'Tomorrow,' " *Notes on Contemporary Literature,* 3 (March 1973), 5–6.

[10] As indicated, I have consulted the Lee County Library for the screenplay. Foote's stage play version was written for the CBS Playhouse 90 television program. It was published, with certain cuts restored, in a volume by Foote titled *Three Plays* (New York: Harvest-Harcourt, 1962), pp. 49–93.

[11] See Calvin S. Brown, *A Glossary of Faulkner's South* (New Haven: Yale Univ. Press, 1976), p. 31, for the definition of black-complected—"having a dark complexion." We must remember that in the South the use of "black" to mean "Negro" is relatively recent.

[12] A convenient fiction of film criticism is that the director is the "author" of the final product, in that he "controls" the whole—and sometimes this fiction comes close to

the truth. Editing can greatly affect any film, and Foote has noted the joint effort in *Tomorrow*, the producers and director working "many hours with Reva Schlesinger, the cutter" (Foote, p. 161). Duvall observed that attempts were made to keep him from the cutting room. Even in an independent production, he complained, "the power still lies with the producer and the cutter" (Chase, p. 16).

Stan Woodward filming *It's Grits* in Frank's Hot Dogs, Columbia, South Carolina (by Harry Gandy, courtesy of Nan Robinson and the South Carolina Arts Commission).

# Southern Exposure:
# Kudzu *and* It's Grits

GORHAM KINDEM

Kudzu (Pueraria lobata), an Oriental weed that is consuming the South, and grits, that delectable portion of the corn plant that the South consumes, are the subjects of two recent documentary films, *Kudzu* (1976) and *It's Grits* (1978). Filmmakers Marjie Short and Stan Woodward inform and entertain us with facts and opinions about this notoriously prolific plant and extremely popular ethnic food.

They interview a cross-section of Southerners and ask them to respond to such questions as "is grits singular or plural?" "how would you describe grits to someone who has never tasted them before?" and "is kudzu beautiful or ugly, beneficial or harmful?" The responses they receive to these questions are sometimes surprising, often funny, and always revealing. *Kudzu* and *It's Grits* differ somewhat stylistically, but they share a common purpose: to probe beneath the Southern surface and expose some of the sources of the region's inner vitality, rich cultural traditions, and irrepressible ethnic pride.

One of the purposes of documentary films is to inform audiences about specific topics. *Kudzu* and *It's Grits* fulfill this function by providing a storehouse of information about the origins, uses, abuses, values, and meanings of kudzu and grits. Both filmmakers rely upon experts to convey historical background information. Botanist Dr. Tetsuo Kyama describes kuzu's (kudzu's name in the Orient) Japanese heritage prior to its introduction to America in the 1870s. U.S. government soil conservationist W. Crawford Young explains the pervasive use of kudzu in the 1930s to stop the erosion of Southern soil. In *It's Grits* a black farmer explains the age old process of extracting grits from the corn plant. The ears are shucked, shelled, stone ground, sifted, and separated into corn meal, grits, and bran at a water-driven

199

grist mill. Mississippi native and *New York Times* food editor Craig Claiborne demonstrates the proper preparation of grits that even Yankees love. Both films clearly and authoritatively document the origins of their respective topics with graphic demonstrations and expert commentaries.

The uses and abuses of kudzu and grits are also graphically portrayed by Short and Woodward. Kudzu has a beautiful reddish-purple flower, hides garbage, provides exterior decoration, stops erosion, carpets the ground, regenerates the soil, and is used in the production of paper products in Japan. But it also withers and turns to an ugly brown tangle of vines and dead leaves at the slightest onset of cold temperatures, hides snakes, engulfs productive crops and property, and is extremely difficult to kill and control. Grits fed the South when Yankee soldiers walked off with many cows, pigs, and chickens during and after the Civil War. Today it remains a plentiful, nutritious, and inexpensive source of food that few Yankees have ever learned to

Kudzu: overruns road; (facing page) engulfs abandoned automobile. (frame enlargements courtesy of Marjie Short)

appreciate. But it is also regularly abused by fanatics and fools who freeze it (gritsicles), undercook it, or mix it with hot sauce and peanut butter.

Marjie Short examines the aesthetic value and meaning of kudzu through the poetry of James Dickey, whose poem "Kudzu" (portions of which he recites during the film) extracts symbolic meaning from "this vegetable form of cancer."

> Japan invades. Far Eastern vines
> Run from the clay banks they are
>
> Supposed to keep from eroding,
> Up telephone poles,
> Which rear, half out of leafage,
> As though they would shriek,
> Like things smothered by their own
> Green, mindless, unkillable ghosts.
> In Georgia, the legend says
> That you must close your windows

At night to keep it out of the house.
The glass is tinged with green, even so . . .

                    (*Poems 1957–1967*, c. 1967, p. 140)

Kudzu symbolizes foreign invasion and domination, government intervention, scientific incompetence, unspeakable hidden horrors, fecundity, and "the tremendous power of life to go on maybe senselessly, maybe divinely, beautifully, uselessly." Regardless of whether or not kudzu has practical value, it clearly has cultural meaning and value for the entire South. Through the verbal and visual poetry of James Dickey and Marjie Short, it acquires aesthetic value as well.

Taken as a whole, *It's Grits* reflects the tremendous cultural value inherent in this ridiculous sounding, rather bland tasting food. Its universal popularity in the South may simply reflect its ability to be all things to all people. Each individual can combine it with his or her favorite food, whose flavor grits readily adapts to and absorbs. Its popularity, as Senator Strom Thurmond suggests, may also be related to the popularity of corn products in general. But by far the most telling indication of the cultural meaning and value of grits emerges from the Civil War stories of families that have owned and operated grist mills for over a century in the South. Grits is the South. It represents an acquired Southern taste that has never been widely shared by Yankees. It is a source of sustenance and strength that has helped the South to survive a multitude of difficulties and radical changes which have come from within and been imposed upon it from outside. It is a constant reminder of the South's ethnic identity, cultural heritage, and regional pride.

All of these probing themes might lead one to the erroneous conclusion that *Kudzu* and *It's Grits* are extremely serious films, but nothing could be farther from the truth. Short and Woodward exercise a keen sense of wit in their selection of subjects and settings. We are entertained by a variety of famous people, from Jimmy Carter and James Dickey in *Kudzu* to Craig Claiborne and Strom Thurmond in *It's Grits*. The stars of these films are not the nationally recognized public figures, but rather the Southern hams and country folk, like Atlanta resident James H. Jordan, Queen of Kudzu Martha Jane Stuart Wilson, *Athens Observer* columnist Tifton Merritt in *Kudzu* and linguist

Raymond O'Cain, *Columbia Record* columnist Bill McDonald, the woman who eats 'possom and 'coon, and the grist mill owner who whistles his ss's through his missing teeth in *It's Grits*. Interestingly enough, and much to the filmmakers' credit, we usually laugh with, not at, these people, whose wit and sincerity reflect many Southern qualities.

"Kudzu, city life, and moskeeters," declares Atlanta resident James H. Jordan, "go hand in hand to make your life miserable. We should export kudzu to Russia instead of sending them our precious grain." "You can see that I've maintained the Kudzu tradition," remarks slightly overweight Martha Jane Stuart Wilson, the 1930s Kudzu Queen of Greensboro, Alabama, "by spreading out in all directions myself." *Athens Observer* columnist, Tifton Merritt, plays his own tongue-in-cheek version of Horace Greeley by walking along a railroad track and encouraging a young man to acquire property and grow kudzu. It may not have any commercial value, but at least it doesn't do any harm, he suggests, "which is more than can be said for any other crop, since the Republicans took over the farm program." Perhaps, he adds optimistically, the government will eventually subsidize kudzu and then pay us not to grow it.

In *It's Grits* a recent immigrant to Atlanta proudly displays his "grits permit" to filmmaker Stan Woodward and, with a distinct Northern accent, explains his ambivalence about its meaning and seriousness. The permit, signed by the governor of Georgia, entitles the bearer to cross the Mason-Dixon line with five pounds of grits without having his suitcase searched. The recipient of this official permit cannot decide whether the plump cherubs displayed on the permit are smiling because they've just had grits or because they're looking forward to having grits in the future. A native Southerner describes his ribbing of a gullible Yankee en route to Florida, who accepts the improbable idea that tobacco plants sprouting blossoms are grits bushes. A grits fanatic offers Stan Woodward a frozen gritsicle with peanuts inside and then proudly displays a wooden gritsicle mold with leather straps that "carbon dating would place at about 1861." The ostensible purpose of his gritsicle enterprise is to help people return to the rich Southern customs and traditions that the gritsicle represents. Finally, when asked by Woodward to explain what kosher grits, which appear on the menu at South of the Border restaurant, consist of, a sprightly waitress explains that South of the Border is really a kosher restaurant with a Mexican motif. The manager, of course, has previously indicated that the kosher grits is a gimmick designed to attract the attention of Yankees traveling through South Carolina.

Turning from the ridiculous to the sublime, filmmakers Short and Woodward infuse certain sections of their films with cinematic poetry. Short's images of roads, telephone poles, and abandoned automobiles engulfed by kudzu give concrete realism to poet James Dickey's verbal abstractions. An incident that occurs during Tifton Merritt's monologue about the virtues of growing kudzu, in which he picks up a kudzu leaf and spins its stem between his index finger and thumb, acquires aesthetic value when Short abstracts it out of time and context for her opening title. She uses slow motion optical effects accompanied by the music of gently tinkling bells and a xylophone to stimulate our childlike curiosity about her subject. Woodward alternates between rapidly paced visuals photographed and edited to match the beat of Nat Irvin's theme "Grits" and slow paced, beautifully composed black-and-white images that flow over natural and man-made objects, like the grist mill and the water that powers it. The lighting of the mill's interior brings out every texture and kinetic nuance of this cultural treasure. The moving parts of the mill emit percussion sounds timed exactly to the beat of the accompanying music. The conjunction of sounds, music, and visual images in these films about the South is reminiscent of the brilliant films made by the British documentary's poet laureate, Humphrey Jennings, during the 1930s and 1940s, like *Listen to Britain*, *Fires Were Started*, and *Diary for Timothy*.

Although they are equally poetic, the documentary styles of Short and Woodward are quite different both ethically and aesthetically. Short stands back and observes her subjects, who perform for the camera. Woodward, on the other hand, interacts with the people in his film. To some extent the people in *Kudzu* show us only what they want us to know about themselves, while the people in *It's Grits* are sometimes coaxed into revealing more than they may really want us to know about them. There is both an ethical and an aesthetic dimension to these differences in documentary styles. Short, for example, edits segments of various interviews into a rapid succession of opinions near the conclusion that radically changes the meaning of each segment from what it would have been in the context of that person's entire interview. The effect she achieves is extremely humorous and entertaining to be sure, but she also treads a fine line between laughing with and laughing at some people who appear in her film. Woodward can be accused of treading the same fine line between encouraging audiences to laugh at or laugh with many of the people in his film, especially those whose tastes in food, like gritsicles, peanut butter, hot Mexican grits, or grits with 'coon and 'possom, run to extremes. In Woodward's case the aesthetic dimension of the filmmaker as a participant observer both decreases the chance that we will laugh at people with whom the filmmaker interacts (because of his obvious appreciation and affection for them) and increases the chance they will divulge more about themselves than they would if the filmmaker were a distant observer. The ethical problems of *Kudzu* stem from postproduction rather than production techniques, for Short's documentary style emphasizes editing, while Woodward's emphasizes cinematography.

Despite their rather minor ethical problems and aesthetic differences, *Kudzu* and *It's Grits* are films which will undoubtedly maintain their value as cultural documents and cinematic works of art, for Marjie Short and Stan Woodward have used a full palette of film techniques to assess the practical, cultural, and aesthetic value of two of the South's most plentiful and fascinating agricultural products, kudzu and grits.

*Kudzu* (1976)

Produced and Directed by Marjie Short
Camera by Peter Rosen
Sound by Christine Reynholds
Film Editing by Loren S. Miller and Marjie Short
Music Composed and Conducted by Philip Griffin
Partially funded through a grant from L. Ricker MacAllister, III and from the National Endowment for the Arts.
Distributed by Pyramid Films
Color 16 minutes
Academy Award for Best Live Action Short in 1977

*It's Grits* (1978)

Produced and Directed by R. Stanley Woodward
Camera by R. Stanley Woodward
Sound by Claudia Williams
Editing by R. Stanley Woodward
Grits theme and original score written, arranged, and conducted by Nat Irvin, Jr.
Vocals by "The Uplifters"
Additional sound and Interior Mill Lighting by William Olsen
Supported by the South Carolina Arts Commission and the National Endowment for the Arts
Distributed by Weston Woods
Black and White 45 minutes

# Appalachia on Film:
## *The Making of* Sergeant York

DAVID D. LEE

One of the most successful films of 1941 was *Sergeant York*, the screen biography of a Tennessee farmer who won national acclaim by single-handedly out-shooting an entire German machine gun battalion during the last days of World War I. On October 8, 1918, in the midst of the American drive through the Argonne Forest, Alvin C. York killed twenty-five Germans, captured 132, and silenced thirty-five machine guns while armed only with a rifle and a pistol. Six months later, war correspondent George Pattullo made York into a folk hero with a long piece in the widely circulated *Saturday Evening Post*. Pattullo explained that York, a product of the Appalachian Mountains, foreswore a rowdy past to become an elder of the staunchly fundamentalist Church of Christ in Christian Union. When the United States entered World War I, he requested exemption as a conscientious objector, but his plea was denied and he was drafted. Sympathetic army officers who were convinced of his sincerity gradually persuaded him that his nation's cause was just and he could best serve God by taking up arms. As a result, Pattullo concluded, York became a veritable soldier of the Lord battling Teutonic evil on the side of American righteousness. York's return to the United States shortly after the article appeared prompted an enormous outpouring of public affection as he toured New York and Washington before he finally returned to the small hamlet of Pall Mall in his native Fentress County.

The Pattullo article placed York squarely in the midst of a popular set of stereotypes about Appalachia. As historian Henry Shapiro has written, around the turn of the century Americans began to develop contradictory attitudes about the region. The source of this dichotomy

207

was the Industrial Revolution, which was rapidly destroying the old rural America and replacing it with a new, urbanized society geared to mass production. Amid such rapid change, Americans worked to create a new order as they simultaneously expressed nostalgia for the old one. Hence, in one sense Appalachia was a tragic aberration within the American success story because its poverty and isolation contrasted sharply with the prevailing notion that industrialization and urbanization were the standards of economic progress. According to this view, the typical mountaineer was violent and anti-social in his behavior, ever ready to start a family feud or shoot a revenue agent. A countervailing idea that grew up almost simultaneously cast Appalachia as the last repository of the traditions that were truly American—individualism, hard work, and the English legacy in politics and culture. From this perspective, a mountaineer was slow to anger yet skillful with weapons, plain-spoken, religious, patriotic, and something of a child of nature who, despite his innocence and lack of sophistication, naturally did the right thing.[1]

The York whom George Pattullo introduced to the country represented the latter tradition. Patriotism, Pattullo assured his readers, "was stronger in the Tennessee mountains than any other impulse." The British Enfield rifle and the .45 pistol York had used in the Argonne became "particularly American weapons," and the "big red-head is sure death with either," although Pattullo quickly added that "they won't stand for moonshining or lawlessness in Pall Mall. . . ." York's "unflustered" manner and "unhurried, half-indolent" gait reflected "absolute sureness of self." Answers to the journalist's questions came back "like the crack of a whip." Pattullo marveled that the poorly educated "Tennessee mountaineer seems to do everything correctly" by "intuition" and he quoted an army officer saying "no amount of military training could have improved his tactics" but the unschooled York had acted entirely by "instinct." In Pattullo's hands York became the frontiersman reincarnated in the machine age to slay not only the enemies of the republic but also to reaffirm the validity of traditional American values in a time of upheaval.[2]

York's own actions after his return tended to enhance that image. Almost completely indifferent to the honors of industrial society, York asked only for a subway ride when his welcoming committee placed the city of New York at his disposal. Offered nearly a half million dollars in endorsements and entertainment contracts, he rejected everything, saying he could not commercialize fame won in serving a holy cause. Instead, he returned to Pall Mall, married his sweetheart, and settled down to the life of a farmer. His wartime experience had convinced him of the need for better education in the mountains, so he spent the 1920s and 1930s building and administering a new high school for the children of Fentress County. Living quietly, York gradually faded into obscurity during the interwar period.[3]

The deteriorating international situation of the late 1930s made Alvin York a prominent figure once again. Americans were appalled by the evils of totalitarian governments in Europe and Asia but hoped the United States could escape involvement in a second global war. These contradictory feelings fostered a renewed interest in the story of America's reluctant doughboy whose hard choice between peace and justice in 1917 suddenly seemed so pertinent to the decisions facing the entire nation. For York himself, the new war placed him in a dilemma just as that earlier conflict had because it forced him to choose between his cherished privacy and his conviction that he must speak out for his beliefs.

The man who put York in this predicament was Jesse L. Lasky, a Hollywood motion picture producer fallen on hard times. The son of a San Francisco shoe-seller, Lasky started in show business as a cornet player with a traveling medicine show but rose to head his own motion picture company, Famous Players—Lasky, which later became the core of Paramount Pictures. Forced out of the company he had helped found during an executive shake-up in 1932, he was left nearly bankrupt due to a collapse in Paramount stock. After three years with Twentieth Century-Fox and three more with Pickford-Lasky Corporation, he was reduced to producing radio shows when the latter folded in 1938. Lasky had wanted to do a film about Alvin York ever since he watched him parade through the streets of New York in May 1919. Struck by the intense reaction of his own employees to the mountaineer hero, Lasky immediately dispatched a representative to the Waldorf-Astoria to make him an offer. York refused but the persistent Lasky contacted him again some ten years later only to find York still opposed to the idea.[4]

Realizing the timeliness of the story and desperately in need of a vehicle that would enable him to re-enter the motion picture business, Lasky turned once more to the York project in 1939. He sent a letter to York tactfully suggesting the possibility of a film but York did not reply. Undeterred, Lasky then dispatched a telegram asking for a conference to discuss "a historical document of vital importance to the country in these troubled times." Aware his man would not accept a proposal that smacked of commercialism, Lasky's strategy was to create a conflict of values in York's mind by challenging his aversion to self-aggrandizement with his sense of duty to religious and patriotic causes. Predictably, the appeal to his patriotism struck a responsive chord with York because he was a strong advocate of preparedness in the face of the growing foreign threat. Also, Lasky's proposal came at a time when York was in the planning stages of an interdenominational Bible school designed to "prepare its pupils to live and practice a full Christian life." Envisioning a school where the "pioneer faith will be kept burning," York intended to construct the facility in Fentress County as a complement to his high school, the York Agricultural Institute. Needing money for the project, York was now willing to reconsider a position he had staunchly held for twenty years, and he agreed to see Lasky.[5]

The two men met in a Crossville, Tennessee, hotel on March 9, 1940. To York's surprise, the press was waiting for him when he strode into the lobby. Wincing as photographers snapped his picture, he said apologetically, "I don't have my Sunday clothes on," and explained that he and Lasky were simply "renewing an old acquaintance," although reporters noted that neither man recognized the other until they were introduced. They conferred briefly in private before York took his visitor on a tour of Fentress County with special stops at the York Agricultural Institute and the site of the future Bible school. Getting the producer interested in his schools was important, York told interviewers, because "$50,000 to men like Lasky is the same as 50¢ to me." York was less explicit on the details of the negotiations. "All I know about this movie job," he said, "is that Mr. Lasky visited me . . . , went with me to the old home place where I am planning to start work on my new Bible school soon, and left after making me an attractive offer which will not require a great deal of my time away from home."[6]

By Thursday, March 14, Lasky was back in Tennessee to meet York and Jamestown attorney John Hale at the Hermitage Hotel in Nashville. "What we want," Hale told Lasky, "is a plain old Tennessee contract that simply says what you shall do and what the sergeant shall do." York was equally direct. "You know there isn't a great deal of difference between trading for a mule or a movie contract," he said. "What really counts is the trader." York's major concern was achieving a financial arrangement that would provide enough money to build the Bible school. Lasky initially offered $25,000 and then $50,000, but York insisted on a percentage of the gross receipts as well. During a brief interlude in the discussions, Lasky and York strolled up to the Capitol to visit York's friend and informal advisor, Governor Prentice Cooper. "He urged Sergeant York to go ahead with it and gave the picture his blessing," Lasky reported, but the two sides still could not reconcile their differences. Periodically the sergeant would leave Lasky's room and mysteriously vanish down the hall while the argument sputtered on. Curious, Lasky at last followed him and discovered York kneeling in prayer. Impressed by York's piety yet frustrated by his stubbornness, on Saturday Lasky returned to Hollywood to weigh the matter. Finally, a week later, Lasky made another trip east to accept York's terms and join him in a contract signing ceremony in Governor Cooper's office. York would receive $50,000 plus two per cent of the gross, a figure that was expected to be roughly $100,000.[7]

Both York and Lasky made it clear that they intended the film to be a special one despite the different perspectives they had on the project. "I wish to emphasize that this is in no sense a war picture," Lasky said, although he definitely saw the propaganda value of the York story. Describing the film as an example of "the historical medium of the future," Lasky termed it "a story Americans need to be told today." York's biography "will be a document for fundamental Americanism" and "the story of a great personality from which Americans will draw inspiration." York, however, expected a film that would use his experiences to tell the story of the mountain people. "Actually its going to be more a story of our people up there in the mountains than it is of me," he said. "It's going to show how education has been taken into the mountains and how we're training our young people now to be good citizens." Asserting he did not like "war pictures," York said, "My part in the war should be presented only as an incident in my life. They way I've lived since then, the contributions I've made to my community, are the things I'm really proud of."[8]

Implicit in the remarks of each man is the notion that Appalachia is somehow a special depository of "fundamental Americanism." As an editorial in the Nashville *Tennessean* put it, ". . . the time is ripe for a reminder that the pioneer spirit still survives." To Jesse Lasky and millions of other Americans, Sergeant York and his neighbors were the contemporary heirs of the spirit that had made America great.[9]

The filming of *Sergeant York* presented Lasky with a number of perplexing problems, the most immediate of which was finding a studio that would take it on. As proof of good faith, Lasky gave York a postdated check for $25,000, ignoring the fact that his financial situation was so precarious he had to borrow on his life insurance to cover it. With the rest of the $50,000 due sixty days after the signing, Lasky criss-crossed Hollywood in search of a backer, but his efforts were unsuccessful because war movies were usually weak at the box office. Finally a friend suggested that Harry Warner of Warner Brothers was particularly susceptible to projects with a patriotic theme. Warner was intrigued by the idea and promised to give it serious consideration if Lasky could line up some talent. Encouraged, Lasky invited Howard Hawks to direct. Uninterested in screen biographies, Hawks was reluctant to accept until Lasky convinced him that *Sergeant York* would not follow the standard success-story format for such films. Disavowing the usual cliché-ridden, one-dimensional approach, Lasky told Hawks that he was planning a character study of York rather than a simple description of his life. As Hawks explained the technique, "I don't attempt to preach or prove anthing. I just figure out what I think was in the man and tell it." Persuaded by Lasky, Hawks cancelled his commitment to direct *The Outlaw* for Howard Hughes and signed for *Sergeant York*. With Hawks aboard, Warner Brothers accepted the film and added Hal Wallis as co-producer with Lasky.[10]

Casting the part of Alvin York was particularly difficult. Most press speculation centered on four actors—Gary Cooper, Henry Fonda,

Raymond Massey, and Spencer Tracy—although columnist Louella Parsons cautioned her readers not to "faint from surprise if it turns out to be Jimmy Cagney." Pondering the idea of Cagney as the lanky mountaineer moved the *Tennessean* to editorialize, "We'll faint if it's Jimmy." From the first, though, Lasky wanted Gary Cooper for the lead and set out to trap the cowboy star. Leaving Nashville after

Gary Cooper meets with Sergeant Alvin York, whom he portrays in the film. (Courtesy of Musuem of Modern Art/ Film Stills Archive)

signing the contract with York, Lasky hastily composed a telegram to Cooper: "I have just agreed to let the motion picture producer Jesse L. Lasky film the story of my life, subject to my approval of the star. I have great admiration for you as an actor and as a man, and I would be honored, sir, to see you on the screen as myself." He signed York's name to it and sent it off, thereby planting the idea that Cooper was York's personal choice for the role.[11]

The offer brought Cooper what he later called "my first big struggle with my responsibility to the movie going public." Aware of the patriotic merit of the movie, he nevertheless believed that York was too complex a man for him to portray adequately. "Here was a pious, sincere man, a conscientious objector to war, who, when called, became a heroic fighter for his country," Cooper wrote later. "He was too big for me, he covered too much territory." Still he realized that with the "clouds of World War II piling up fast, . . . what had happened to Sergeant York was likely to happen all over again." Cooper's worries were compounded by the fact that York, unlike most subjects of screen biographies, was still alive and very concerned about the accuracy of the finished film. His attitude precluded what Cooper called the "romantic leeway" that was customary in "screen biographies dealing with remote historical characters." Cooper concluded that he "couldn't handle it."[12]

Undeterred by his refusal, Hawks and Lasky pressured Cooper to change his mind. Hawks reminded him that Lasky had helped launch the actor's career while an executive at Paramount, and Lasky arranged a series of "chance" encounters with Cooper that gave him an opportunity to discuss the matter at length. At last Cooper agreed providing MGM, the studio that held his contract, would release him temporarily to Warner Brothers, a deal completed in early September when Sam Goldwyn agreed to loan Cooper to Warner Brothers in exchange for permission to use Warner star Bette Davis in *The Little Foxes*. Aside from the title role, York was concerned only with the casting of the part of Gracie Williams, his sweetheart and future wife. He and Mrs. York insisted the actress selected to portray her must not smoke or drink, a potentially tough order to fill in jaded Hollywood. Lasky wanted Jane Russell, an actress still awaiting her first screen role, but Warner Brothers chose one of its own contract players, a sixteen-year-old fledgling named Joan Leslie. She was joined by Walter Brennan as York's minister, Pastor Rosier Pile, and Margaret Wycherly as his mother, the other leading characters.[13]

Because *Sergeant York* was about a living man, its shooting presented a unique problem, namely the need to obtain releases from all the people it would portray who were still alive. William Guthrie, location manager for Warner, travelled 10,000 miles tracking down the members of York's squad. He managed to find ten of them holding such diverse jobs as insurance salesman, honky-tonk waiter, and orange grower. One man was eking out a five-dollar-a-week existence by salvaging metal from the Philadelphia city dump while another was wanted by the police and had to be contacted through a newspaper advertisement. Guthrie paid each one $250 for permission to portray him on the screen. York's friends and relatives in Fentress County negotiated shrewdly with Guthrie, some winning fees as high as $1500 for their cooperation. York's father-in-law, however, refused to sign, and his character was deleted from the script.[14]

Lasky and Warner Brothers took great pains to satisfy York's demands for accuracy. On April 21, barely a month after the contract was signed, Lasky, a cameraman, and two writers arrived in Pall Mall to collect background information on their subject. They stayed a week, visiting a shooting match and interviewing two hundred people. A few months later, Lasky brought York to Hollywood where he previewed the script and then called on Gary Cooper to give the actor a chance to become better acquainted with the character he would have to recreate on the screen. As York and Cooper sat silently in the latter's living room, the gregarious Lasky desperately tried to spark a conversation. "If we'd had Calvin Coolidge there," Lasky remembered, "it would have been a three-ring wake." Finally Lasky mentioned Cooper's gun collection and then sat back as the two hunters eagerly discussed the relative merits of their favorite weapons. "Sergeant York and I had quite a few things in common . . . ," Cooper later wrote. "We both were raised in the mountains—Tennessee for him, Montana for me—and learned to ride and shoot as a natural part of growing up." Asked his opinion of the westerner, York simply replied, "He's a good shot."[15]

Their field work done, Lasky's production team set out to recreate a slice of Fentress County life in a Hollywood sound studio. The 123 sets were a record number as was the number of living people being portrayed, and the script included more speaking parts than any picture up to that time except *Anthony Adverse*. The crew took over the largest stage in town, building a forty-foot mountain made of timber, cloth, plaster, rock, soil, and 121 live trees. Mounted on a turntable, it had sixteen faces and was equipped with spare peaks and precipices to replace any that might break. An unexpected problem developed with the score because it called for a baying dog, but Warner Brothers discovered to its dismay that none of its trained animals bayed in the required key of A. Fortunately, a hastily arranged screen test at the local pound resulted in the "discovery" of a suitably talented canine. The battle scenes were filmed in a field forty miles away where, Cooper said, "We blew up enough land . . . to make a good-sized farm in Iowa." The hectic ninety-day shooting schedule was made even more frenzied by the lack of a completed script. The original script by Abem Finkel and Harry Chandlee was later revised by John Huston and Howard Koch, although in the end Hawks said he and Huston "threw away the written script and did what Jesse Lasky told us about the real Sergeant York." The two "just kept ahead of shooting," according to Hawks, leaving the director uncertain how the finished product would look, especially since, as he put it, the film "follows no patterns."[16]

The publicity connected with the filming catapulted York into the limelight and gave him an opportunity to express his views on national defense and foreign policy. Like many people, he believed that, if America simply supplied arms to Great Britain, John Bull could dispose of Hitler and Germany without any direct intervention by the United States. On May 30, York gave the Memorial Day Address at the Tomb of the Unknown Soldier, the anonymous symbol of the nation's war dead whom York had served as pallbearer some twenty years earlier. In his widely reported remarks he launched a fierce attack on the isolationists, particularly Senator Burton K. Wheeler, whom York disdainfully nicknamed "Neville" after the discredited British prime minister Neville Chamberlain. "The senator ought to know by now," York declared, "that you can't protect yourself against bullets with an umbrella." A few months later York noticed with pride that Roosevelt quoted him extensively in the President's Armistice Day remarks to the nation.[17]

The glittering New York premiere of *Sergeant York* provided York with yet another chance to urge preparedness. He arrived in New York on July 1 for a five-day visit studded with frequent press conferences. Once again he had harsh words for the isolationists saying, "I think any man who talks against the interest of his own country ought to be arrested and put in jail, not excepting senators and ex-colonels," explicit references to Wheeler and America First spokesman Colonel Charles A. Lindbergh.[18]

*Sergeant York* opened July 2 at the Astor Theater where several hundred people cheered York's arrival and an enthusiastic audience gave him a fifteen minute ovation after the show. Asked to say a few words, the sergeant expressed his hope that the film would contribute to "national unity in this hour of danger" when "millions of Americans, like myself, must be facing the same questions, the same uncertainties, which we faced and I believe resolved for the right some twenty-four years ago."[19]

A month later, on July 30, York, Lasky, Gary Cooper, and Tennessee Senator Kenneth McKellar visited President Roosevelt at the White House during the film's Washington premiere. Eager to identify his controversial foreign policy with a popular hero, FDR said he had had a special preview ten days earlier and was "really thrilled" by it. "The picture comes at a good time," the President continued, "although I didn't like that part of it showing so much killing. I guess you felt that way too." "I certainly did," York replied. The President puckishly expressed his regret that "old Cordell," meaning Cordell Hull, now Secretary of State, could not have played his own part as the former Congressman from York's district. The ten minute session ended with York, to Roosevelt's obvious delight, assuring the chief executive that the people of Tennessee were solidly behind his policies.[20]

Contemporary reactions to the film were strongly influenced by the bitter debate over foreign policy. Preparedness advocates hailed it as a vital and important film. "Like the clear notes of reveille at summer sunrise," said *Variety,* "*Sergeant York* is a clarion film that reaches the public at a moment when its stirring and patriotic message is probably most needed." The show business weekly predicted *York* "will hit box offices like a hand grenade." Labelling Jesse Lasky "as sincere a movie maker as Hollywood ever knew," *Life* explicitly connected York's experience with the events of 1941 saying, "York, as played by Cooper, had to solve certain personal problems about the last World War, just as other Americans must solve personal problems about the war of today." *Time* called it "Hollywood's first solid contribution to the national defense," and Senator McKellar told his colleagues, "I believe it will be of enormous benefit to citizens of the United States of America to see the picture. . . ."[21]

By contrast, isolationists were sharply critical of the film. Writing in the *New Republic*, reviewer Otis Ferguson dismissed it as a "stunt picture" about a feat that "did nothing toward winning" a war that "made far greater demands in the way of day-in-day-out heroism." Speaking to an America First rally in St. Louis, North Dakota Senator Gerald P. Nye warned, "The movies have ceased to be an instrument of entertainment," and instead "have been operating as war propaganda machines almost as if they were directed from a single central bureau." Nye noted that Roosevelt himself "after he had forced Congress to pass the lend-lease bill . . . complimented the industry on their 'help' in explaining the bill." Referring to York's visit to the White House, he remarked that if FDR did not like the killing shown on the screen he was nevertheless willing to see the film arouse people to kill.[22]

In spite of the political debate *Sergeant York* provoked, many reviewers found themes in the movie besides preparedness. *New York Times* critic Bosley Crowther called it a "simple and dignified screen biography" that "has all the flavor of true Americana." Howard Barnes of the New York *Herald Tribune* observed that even without the war scenes, *Sergeant York* was "a valiant testament to the American way of life. . . ." Southerners particularly liked the film because it cast the South in such a favorable light. The Nashville *Tennessean* praised *York* as an "antidote for the poison of *Tobacco Road*" and noted "the fresh appreciation of the East for the tale of the Tennessee doughboy. . . ."[23]

York, his family, and friends were quite pleased with the picture. The sergeant pronounced it a "fine job" chuckling, "Gary Cooper had me like I was years ago when I weighed only 170 pounds." The two decades since then had added over a hundred pounds to York's now portly frame. Vehemently denying it was a propaganda film, York said the only people who felt that way were "definitely Nazi inclined themselves." Pastor Rosier Pile was also pleased with the work of Walter Brennan in the role of York's minister. ". . . [T]hat fellow who played me put over what I was trying to get over to Alvin," he said. Least impressed was probably Gracie Williams York. When Joan Leslie telephoned from Hollywood to ask if she was excited by the Nashville premiere, Mrs. York replied, "Oh no, I'm used to this." She admitted that "most of the facts were pretty accurate" and seeing it "sure carries me back," but Mrs. York was a shy, private woman who took little delight in her husband's celebrity status. In fact, she had refused to accompany him to California for fear they might both be killed in an accident and their children orphaned.[24]

York's single objection to the film centered on the portrayal of his religious conversion. During one of their conversations, Howard Hawks asked him how he had gotten religion, and York said he had found it "in the middle of the road," a cryptic comment that the director took literally. The movie shows Gary Cooper being struck by a bolt of lightning while riding to kill a man who has cheated him. The stunned Cooper then wandered into a church and was "saved." York, however understood things differently:

> That weren't the right down facts of it. You see I had met Miss Gracie. Miss Gracie said that she wouldn't let me come a-courting until I'd quit my mean drinking, fighting, and card-flipping. So you see I was struck down by the power of love and the Great God Almighty, all together. A bolt of lightning was the nearest to such a thing that Hollywood could think up.

Despite the misunderstanding, neither York nor his wife was perturbed by the scene because, as Miss Gracie put it, "that was just demonstrating the power of the Lord."[25]

*Sergeant York* brought important benefits for many of the people connected with it. His career rejuvenated, Jesse Lasky made roughly $500,000 from his brainchild. For Howard Hawks, it was his greatest commercial success and earned him the only Academy Award nomination he ever received. Even more fortunate was Gary Cooper, who drew high critical acclaim and won the first of two Oscars for best actor. ". . . I put all I had into the role," Cooper admitted, but he insisted, "I didn't win that award. Sergeant York did, because to the best of my ability I was him." Alvin York's rewards were less spectacular yet equally gratifying. The $150,000 the film earned for him stabilized his financial situation and enabled him to begin the preliminary work on his Bible School.[26]

The overwhelming response to *Sergeant York* illustrates the enduring importance of the "idea" of Appalachia in modern America. As a propaganda device, the film was very effective and made Alvin York a legend, but it achieved these ends by portraying Appalachia in extremely idealized terms. Despite York's initial insistence that the film would be "a story of our people up there in the mountains," it instead manipulated popular stereotypes about the mountains to arouse nationalistic fervor. Ignoring the complexity of the mountain experience, the filmmakers show Appalachians as religious and patriotic people whose poverty is simultaneously picturesque and ennobling. These quasi-pioneers represent the lasting validity of the American value system even in times of chaos and upheaval, and Sergeant York became the embodiment of these virtues. As a consequence, *Sergeant York* tells us less about Appalachia than it does about the larger society which applauded it.

## NOTES

I would like to thank the Western Kentucky University Faculty Research Committee for a grant which enabled me to prepare this article.

[1] Henry Shapiro, "Appalachia and the Idea of America," in *An Appalachian Symposium*, ed. J. W. Williamson (Boone: Appalachian State Univ. Press, 1977), pp. 43–55. For a fuller discussion see Shapiro, *Appalachia on Our Mind: The Southern Mountains and Mountaineers in the American Consciousness, 1870–1920* (Chapel Hill: Univ. of North Carolina Press, 1978).

[2] "The Second Elder Gives Battle," *Saturday Evening Post* April 26, 1919, pp. 3–4, 71–75.

[3] Tom Skeyhill, ed., *Sergeant York: His Own Life Story and War Diary* (Garden City: Doubleday, Doran, 1928), pp. 293–302.

[4] Hector Arce, *Gary Cooper: An Intimate Biography* (New York: William Morrow, 1979), pp. 169–170; Philip Frend, *The Movie Moguls: An Informal History of the Hollywood Tycoons* (Chicago: Henry Regney, 1969), pp. 145–46; Jesse Lasky with Don Weldon, *I Blow My Own Horn* (Garden City, Doubleday, 1957), pp. 252–253; Frances Marion, *Off with Their Heads: A Serio-Comic Tale of Hollywood* (New York: Macmillan, 1972), p. 8; Larry Swindell, *The Last Hero: A Biography of Gary Cooper* (Garden City: Doubleday, 1980), p. 232; Norman Zierold, *The Moguls* (New York: Coward-McCann, 1969), pp. 163–64; *Nashville Tennessean*, 8 Sept. 1940; *New York Times*, 29 June 1941.

[5] Arce, *Cooper*, p. 170; Lasky, *Horn*, p. 253; Nashville *Banner*, 3 Aug. 1939.

[6] Nashville *Tennessean*, 10, 11, 14 March 1940.

[7]Lasky, *Horn*, pp. 254–56; Nashville *Tennessean*, 15, 17, 24 March 1940; *New York Times*, 16, 24 March 1940; *Variety*, 27 March 1940.

[8]Nashville *Tennessean*, 15, 24 March, 20 April 1940; *New York Times*, 16 March 1940; *Variety*, 27 March 1940.

[9]Nashville *Tennessean*, 16 March 1940.

[10]Arce, *Cooper*, pp. 171–75; Lasky, *Horn*, pp. 257–58; Swindell, *Last Hero*, pp. 232–33.

[11]Arce, *Cooper*, p. 171; Lasky, *Horn*, p. 257; Nashville *Tennessean*, 24 March, 5 April 1940.

[12]Gary Cooper as told to George Scullin, "Well, It Was This Way," *Saturday Evening Post*, 7 April 1956, p. 120.

[13]Cooper and Scullin, p. 120; Rene Jordan, *Gary Cooper, A Pyramid Illustrated History of the Movies* (New York: Pyramid, 1974), pp. 92–94; Nashville *Tennessean*, 7 Sept. 1940; *New York Times*, 16 Feb. 1941; Howard and Betsy Ross York Lowry, son-in-law and daughter of Alvin C. York, interview with the author and Professor Joseph Boggs, 27 June 1978, Bowling Green, Kentucky; Lasky, *Horn*, pp. 259–60.

[14]Lasky, *Horn*, p. 259; Nashville *Banner*, 10 Jan. 1941; Nashville *Tennessean*, 5 July 1941; *New York Times*, 16 Feb. 1941.

[15]Arce, *Cooper*, p. 176; Lasky, *Horn*, p. 260; Nashville *Tennessean*, 22, 25, 27, 28 April 1940.

[16]Arce, *Cooper*, pp. 172–73; Cooper and Scullin, p. 120; Nashville *Tennessean*, 10 Feb., 29 June 1941.

[17]Samuel Rosenman, compiler, *The Public Papers and Addresses of Franklin D. Roosevelt: The Call to Battle Stations* (New York: Harper and Brothers, 1950), pp. 485–87; *New York Times*, 7 Jan., 18 May, 31 May, 12 Nov. 1941.

[18]*New York Times*, 2, 3, 4 July 1941.

[19]Nashville *Tennessean*, 3 July 1941; *New York Times*, 3 July 1941.

[20]Nashville *Tennessean*, 31 July 1941; *New York Times*, 31 July 1941; Arthur S. Bushing, Jr., friend of Alvin C. York, interview with the author, 11 July 1978, Maryville, Tennessee.

[21]*Congressional Record*, 77th Congress, 1st Session, p. 6411; *Life*, 26 Aug. 1941; *Time*, 4 Aug. 1941; *Variety*, 2 July 1941.

[22]Otis Ferguson, "In the Army Aren't We All," *New Republic*, pp. 403–04; *New York Times*, 2 Aug. 1941; *Variety*, 6 Aug. 1941.

[23]Nashville *Tennessean*, 4, 7 July 1941; *New York Times*, 3 July 1941.

[24]Nashville *Tennessean*, 14, 18 Sept 1941; *New York Times*, 4 July 1941; Mrs. Gracie Williams York, interview with the author and Professor Joseph Boggs, 1 July 1978, Pall Mall, Tennessee.

[25]Arce, *Cooper*, p. 176; *Time*, 11 Sept. 1964; Mrs. Gracie Williams York, interview with Dr. Jospeh H. Riggs, WMC-TV, Memphis, Tennessee, 28 Feb. 1969, transcript in Memphis Public Library, pp. 7–8.

[26]Robin Wood, *Howard Hawks* (Garden City: Doubleday, 1968), p. 165; Andrew Sarris, "The World of Howard Hawks," in *Focus on Howard Hawks*, ed. Joseph McBride (Englewood Cliffs, N.J.: Prentice-Hall, 1972), p. 49; Cooper and Scullin, p. 120; *Variety*, 23 July 1941.

# A FILM ON THE
# LIFE OF JAMES AGEE

**WITH John Huston, Robert Fitzgerald, Walker Evans, Dwight MacDonald, Mia Agee, Father James Flye, Olivia Wood, "Annie Mae Gudger", "Margaret Ricketts", Alma Neuman, Robert Saudek, and President Jimmy Carter.**

## A FILM by ROSS SPEARS

CINEMATOGRAPHY .....ANTHONY FORMA     VOICE .................EARL McCARROLL
MUSIC .......................KENTON COE     ASSOCIATE PRODUCER......JUDE CASSIDY

# Regional Filmmaking:
## *The James Agee Film Project*

ROSS SPEARS

> We shall not cease from exploration
> And the end of all our exploring
> Will be to arrive where we started
> And know the place for the first time.
>
> *Little Gidding*, T. S. Eliot

I like to think that a giant vacuum in American film production is slowly being filled at the moment and that the James Agee Film Project is contributing to the process. The vacuum I refer to is the absence of regionally inspired and regionally produced film work. Among the arts this situation may be unique to film. In literature there are great regional writers like William Faulkner; in visual arts there are painters like Thomas Hart Benton; in music, composers like Charles Ives. Who are the great regional filmmakers in America, filmmakers who use the raw materials of a specific *place* to create a microcosm? I think there may be none.

This loss is not a trivial one. It was William Carlos Williams's assertion that "all art is local," which I have always taken to mean that art springs from the deeply personal, extraordinarily subjective experience, from what we know "in our bones," from subjects and places "close to home" wherever that might be. Many of the great European and Asian films have had this quality. I think of Rossellini and Olmi in Italy, of Satyajit Ray in India, and of François Truffaut of France. I think of films such as *Shoeshine, Ikiru, Zero for Conduct*, and *Battle of Algiers*. Much of the power and poetry of these films derives from their strong sense of place.

The strong points of American films, on the other hand, have always been their superb craftsmanship and entertainment value, from the virtuosity of the silent comedies to the fast-paced scripts of the 30s and

40s, and such technological achievements as technicolor, cinema-scope, and computerized camera movements. What American films have lacked most often are images which ring true to the poetry of real life. And real life begins with *place*.

This problem is certainly not caused by any lack of talent, but by the unfortunate conditions under which films are made. The pressure to make profitable films is less a serious hurdle in this regard than the centralization of filmmaking in Hollywood and New York. To see Knoxville, Tennessee through the eyes of a Los Angeleno or Topeka, Kansas through the eyes of a New Yorker not only precludes accuracy, it robs a film of any chance to be true to the human condition, which is after all one of the chief aims of art. Woody Allen can make *Manhattan*, and Billy Wilder, *Sunset Boulevard*, but those two cities are not the Alpha and Omega of human experience, not even American experience.

Indeed, there is a place called Johnson City, Tennessee, which is located in upper East Tennessee on the edge of the Appalachian Mountain range, near the headwaters of what becomes the Tennessee River. Nearby is Jonesboro, the oldest town in Tennessee. It is surrounded by farms and TVA lakes and hardwood manufacturers. There are as many hogs in the county as people, although more than 1.5 million people live within 50 miles. Johnson City is where the James Agee Film Project makes films. For the first time ever, thanks to the catalytic influence of the National Endowment for the Arts, the National Endowment for the Humanities, the Public Broadcasting System, and the state arts and humanities councils, regional feature films are being created. Some beauties have already been made in places like Florida, North Dakota, Missouri, and, yes, Tennessee.

The James Agee Film Project was founded in 1974. Its first major project was a feature documentary on the life of James Agee. *Agee* was completed in 1979 and won the Blue Ribbon for Literature at the 1980 American Film Festival. The film project is now making a long documentary about the evolution of the Tennessee Valley Authority, America's largest energy producer and a powerful force in the Tennessee Valley. A film about the Civil War is in the works. The Film Project is working on documentaries at the moment (so many real stories to tell), but fiction films seem not far away. They will very likely be works of pure imagination based on real people and real places, and shot in East Tennessee. The aim of the James Agee Film Project is to create work that will fit James Agee's description in 1947 of "the best direction movies might take": "I . . . mean that the theme or story needs to be passionately felt and intimately understood, and that it needs to be a theme or story worthy of such knowledge or passion. I also put my deepest hope and faith in the future of movies in their being made on relatively little money, as much at least by gifted amateurs as by professionals, in actual rather than imitated places, with the binding energy, eye, conviction, and delight in work which are fostered in good-enough people by that predicament. . . ."

## *Agee:*
## *A Film*

### CHARLES MALAND

James Agee was equally devoted to writing and to living. As a twenty-year-old Harvard student, he wrote in a letter, "So far as I can tell, I definitely want to write." In choosing writing over his other two loves—music and movies—Agee added, "Nothing else holds me in the same way."[1]

Yet later Agee wrote, "I know I am making the choice most dangerous to an artist, in valuing life above art."[2] Deeply engaged in living and in transforming his experiences onto the written page, Agee lived a life of intensity, boundless (almost destructive) energy, and profound sensitivity. Ross Spears's ninety-minute documentary, *Agee: A Film*, gives us a vivid picture of the life Agee lived and the environments which helped shape it.

Spears obviously offers the film as a labor of love. In many ways, Spears and Agee are similar. Both grew up in East Tennessee, both spent time in New York, and both were drawn to California by an interest in the movies. Spears even physically resembles Agee: in one of the film's dramatizations of Agee sitting on a sharecropper's porch, struggling with *Let Us Now Praise Famous Men*, the camera captures Spears playing Agee through a screened window.

The film is framed with readings by Father Flye, the Episcopal priest who knew Agee at St. Andrews School in the Cumberland Mountains from 1919 to 1925 and who maintained correspondence with Agee for the rest of Agee's life. Following Flye's first reading, Jimmy Carter comments on how much he has admired Agee's work, especially *Let Us Now Praise Famous Men*. From then on the film divides into four chronological sections.

In the first, "Father Flye and Tennessee," we learn of Agee's childhood in the Fort Sanders neighborhood in Knoxville; his family's "cultivated" background; the death of his father when James was only six; and his education first at St. Andrews, and later at Phillips Exeter Academy. The second section, called "Olivia, Harvard, and New York," traces Agee's life from his entrance to Harvard in 1928 to the mid-1930s. During this period he worked on the Harvard *Advocate*, graduated, got a job in New York as a *Fortune* staff writer, published a volume of poetry, *Permit Me Voyage*, and in 1933 married Olivia Saunders. In "Alma and Alabama," the third part, we learn of Agee's experiences from the time *Fortune* assigned Walker Evans and him to do an article on poor Southern sharecroppers until the publication of *Let Us Now Praise Famous Men* in 1941. During this period, Agee married for a second time. The last section of the film, "Mia and the Movies," traces Agee's life with his third wife, Mia Fritsch, whom he married in 1946. It also treats his involvement with the movies—first as reviewer for *The Nation* from 1942 to 1948, later as a screenwriter for directors like John Huston (*The African Queen*)—and his other projects until his death by heart attack in a taxicab in New York City in 1955.

It's hard to make an interesting and honest biographical film about a man not often in the public eye, but Spears provides a kaleidescopic variety of visual and aural information to engage the viewer. Besides interviewing Carter and Father Flye, Spears interviews all three of Agee's wives, his Harvard roommate Robert Saudek, poet Robert Fitzgerald, critic Dwight Macdonald, and film director John Huston. We also hear tapes of Walker Evans describing Agee in Alabama, Agee himself talking to Father Flye in 1953, and "Margaret Ricketts" and "Anna Mae Gudger," two of the women Agee wrote about in *Let Us Now Praise Famous Men*. ("Margaret" describes how kind Agee was, even though his "Northern kind of talk" was hard to understand.)

These interviews do much to provide a composite portrait of Agee. Macdonald says, "He was oceanic." Fitzgerald concurs: "Agee was immoderate in every way." For Huston, "Jim was utterly congenial," a man who "inspired hope in people that the world would come to terms with itself." "Anna Mae" remembers crying when Agee and Evans left Alabama "because I got attached to them." Olivia Saunders Agee tells us wistfully, a little sadly, "writing was the master of his life."

But we see much more in the movie. There are dramatizations shot in Knoxville, in Alabama, and at St. Andrews, usually accompanied by Earl McCarrol's reading from Agee's work. There is documentary footage of the Depression and the Hollywood Ten trials. We see a rich variety of still photographs from throughout Agee's life, which accurately present how Agee matured physically, then began to deteriorate in his final years. One particularly effective use of the stills comes when Spears almost animates several pictures of Agee and Mia playing a piano duet by cutting rapidly from one detail of the pictures to another, all rhythmically cut to the music on the sound track. Besides other visual imagery—newspaper headlines, covers of magazines and books, a segment from *The African Queen*—one of the electric moments in the film is when we actually see Agee talk and move in his bit part as the jailbird in *The Bride Comes to Yellow Sky* (1952). All this, along with Kenton Coe's sensitive score, makes *Agee* a fascinating attempt to capture the being of Agee, however fleetingly, in a documentary film.

The film seconds Geneviève Moreau's view in a recent biography that Agee's life was a "restless journey." Of course the film, because of its brevity, leaves out many details of that journey, but the general contour is there. Agee was an introspective, deeply humanistic, talented man who made huge demands on himself. Though he had difficulty focusing his energies, when he did, he wrote some of the most beautiful and penetrating passages in twentieth-century American literature. Though we haven't yet gotten a definitive biography of

Agee, this film joins David Madden's collection, *Remembering Agee* (1974), and Moreau's biography, *The Restless Journey of James Agee* (1977), as an essential document for those interested in the life of Agee. I hope we will sometime soon have the definitive biography. I also hope that the biographer will remember Agee's words from *Let Us Now Praise Famous Men*. Pondering the difficulties, perhaps impossibilities, of conveying the truth of any person's life to another person in words, Agee wrote of his book: "I must say to you, this is not a work of art or of entertainment, nor will I assume the role of artist or entertainer, but is a human effort which must require human co-operation."[3]

## NOTES

[1]*Letters of James Agee to Father Flye* (New York: Braziller, 1962), p. 45.

[2]Quoted in Geneviève Moreau, *The Restless Journey of James Agee*, trans. Miriam Kleiger (New York: Morrow, 1977), p. 17.

[3]*Let Us Now Praise Famous Men* (1941; rpt. New York: Ballantine, 1966), p. 102.

# Fawn Bites Lion:
## Or, How MGM Tried to Film The Yearling in Florida

WILLIAM STEPHENSON

When Metro-Goldwyn-Mayer bought the film rights to Marjorie Kinnan Rawlings's novel *The Yearling* in May 1938, the studio heads knew they had an important property. The story of Jody Baxter, a lonely little boy in the nineteenth-century Florida wilds who made a beloved pet out of a fawn, only to see it sacrificed to his family's need for survival, was not just another tear-jerker. It was a story that touched on the basic realities of nature. It could be a great artistic success as well as a box-office success. "The word came down to go all out on it, to make it cost at least three million dollars and not to crap it up," wrote John Marquand in an ironic account of his brief association with the film. "It had to be real and artistic, in technicolor, long shots of sunsets, plain simple southern folk with dialect and overalls. It was good for the Academy Award."[1] In the end, that was exactly the kind of film MGM produced. What no one foresaw in 1938 was that seven years would pass, not to mention several directors and sets of leading actors, before the film would be completed.

The source of the difficulty was the decision that the film must be shot on location in Florida. "The main thing they wanted to do was to make it absolutely real," said Marquand (p. 15). The production had to capture on film the reality of man's relation to nature or the essence of the novel would be lost. Visually, the camera had to show the actors relating to real animals in a real forest against the real light, misty and luminescent, of the Florida wilderness. Unfortunately, Hollywood people in the 1930s were more accustomed to re-creating and heightening reality on their studio stages than to capturing it unadorned on location. MGM especially was renowned for the glossy perfection of its visual product, the result of hundreds of studio technicians labor-

229

ing beforehand to smooth every detail. Filming real animals in a real forest called for some compromises of technical standards the MGM workers were not prepared to make. They expected to film life in the wilds with as much perfection of style as was the rule back at the studio—which set the scene for as pretty a showdown between art and nature as anyone could hope to find.

With producer Sidney Franklin in charge, a preliminary script was soon brought forth by the studio's writers. The lead role of Penny Baxter, the boy's father, was tailored to fit one of MGM's top stars, Spencer Tracy. Then the long business of figuring every detail of what would be needed for the location shooting, and how to provide it from Hollywood, was begun. Though movies have been shot in Florida from time to time since the early days of filmmaking, no permanent set-up to facilitate production ever evolved there. The lists sent in to the producer grew longer and longer, with more and more technicians involved. Much time would be needed before everything was ready.

First, the studio had to provide an authentic Florida farm of two generations past for the boy and his family to live on. Months of painstaking work went into that. The MGM people discovered that Rawlings's story was from life, that there had once been a real boy like Jody Baxter and a farm like Baxter's Island in the book. ("Island" is a local word for a farm clearing in the Florida scrub forests.) The real Jody was long since dead, and the farm gone back to wilderness. But a brother was still living, at the age of eighty-five, in Jacksonville. An MGM crew went to him and worked with him until, in the middle of the Ocala State Forest, "the whole Baxter farm was restored just as Jody Baxter's brother remembered it, the old slab cabin, the barn, the corn crib and the backhouse" (Marquand, p. 15). The crew found, still standing on another farm, a perfect old weathered split-rail fence to go around Baxter's Island. But the farmer didn't want to sell it. To get the fence, MGM bought his whole farm. Then the old fence rails made the studio-built farm buildings look too new, so the buildings had to be aged by hand. To get the dirt paths to look as worn as the rest of the quarters, then, they had to hire a couple to live there full time. In all, it took one hundred people six months to produce Baxter's Island as a set, down to its last gourd ladle.

That was only one set out of the thirty-seven location sites the script called for. MGM had to carve all of them out of the untouched forest along the St. John's River and connect them by passable roads over the many acres they covered. Trees figuratively had to be "combed back to let one hard-surfaced road through" for the heavy equipment of Technicolor filming.[2] With roads to be built even before any other preliminary work could be done, it is no wonder two years passed before the location site was ready for filming.

A number of the outdoor sets were fields of corn in all stages of growth, for "in *The Yearling* much of the action takes place around a meager cornfield, the main sustenance of the young lad and his family. The boy's pet deer must be done away with when it repeatedly jumps the fence and destroys a portion of the crop."[3] This made more complications when filming began in the spring of 1941. The scenes of the script would be shot out of sequence, to allow the director to make most economical use of the actors and crew required. Thus for one scene the director might need a field with corn plants two feet high one day, and the next day a field at its full growth. The production department had to have fields ready at every height. A corn production line began. Every few days tiny corn plants were started in tin cans. As they grew larger, they were transferred to regular fields. After another few days, another field would be set out the same way. King Vidor, who became the film's second director, notes that when he took over he found the production department had seventy-five thousand corn plants in one stage of growth or another. Vidor knew a simpler way it could have been done: "In *Our Daily Bread* we didn't have much money, so we just worked backward, using a mature corn field to begin with, and cutting the stalks off as we went along. When the film was finally assembled in its proper order it appeared that the corn grew with each sequence. But this was too simple for a big operation like MGM."[4]

Manipulating the basic rules of nature to get the effects the script called for was difficult enough in the case of the cornfields. Even more trouble arose when the technicians tried to line up nature's animal population, both domestic and wild. The biggest problem was to provide a suitable fawn for the boy to love. The fawn's growth to marauding maturity was central to the story, so it was necessary to have a number of fawns at every stage of growth ready for filming at all times, to be used in whatever scene was being shot that day. A fawn production line came into being. It could not be started until spring, since does have a limited yearly breeding season, but soon there were fawns of every size available, "with the right number of spots and properly trained to romp with the little boy" (Marquand, p. 16).

As far as possible, the wild animals to be used in the film were brought from Florida to the Hollywood studio beforehand for a domesticating treatment that would get them used to cameras and lights. Then they were shipped back to Florida when location shooting began. It was a project almost worthy of Noah's Ark. The *New York Times* reported the film was using "twenty-four deer, six bears, a bobcat, eight coons, two foxes, twenty squirrels," and uncounted numbers of wild fowl from doves to buzzards.[5] That was beside the domestic animals of the Baxter farm, numerous pigs, chickens, hounds, and a family horse and cow.

Even with six Hollywood bears, reality had to be bent a bit for the bear hunt of Old Slewfoot in the film. Real dogs attacking a real bear could not be filmed because S.P.C.A. regulations decreed animals could not be subjected to cruelty on screen. So a special animal imitator, inside a rubber suit fashioned to look exactly like a real bear, was used instead (Marquand, pp. 13–14). The dogs in the scene were driven to the proper barking frenzy by an animal trainer who ran ahead of the camera dragging the film's bobcat snarling in a gunny sack.[6]

A kind of domesticating treatment was also used on the little boy who played Jody. His name was Gene Eckman. In their drive for absolute reality, the studio heads declared that no professional child actor would be used. It would be a true Southern boy who played the role, with real freckles and a real Southern accent. They found twelve-year-old Eckman in Atlanta in 1940, after a casting department search that involved thousands of interviews. Having found a real Southern boy, MGM next brought him and his mother to Hollywood, where he had his teeth straightened and had acting lessons from MGM's drama coach. But the studio felt his purity was being protected: "when he was there he couldn't play with the other little kids because he might lose his southern accent, so they kept him in a suite alone with his mother except when he went to the Zoo to get used to deer" (Marquand, p. 17).

Filming began in Florida in late April 1941. The Hollywood people descended en masse on Ocala, where they lived during the shooting. They made quite an impression on the town of twelve thousand. There was Victor Fleming, the first of the film's directors, looking overwhelmed by his responsibility to lead MGM through the wilderness. There was Gene Eckman, accompanied by his entire family, all on the MGM payroll down to younger brother Harold as Gene's stand-in.[7] There were about 275 other crew members, and forty tons of equipment, not to mention all the animals and their handlers. "Signs of 'no vacancy' hang on doors of hotels and tourist camps," reported a newspaper. "Hollywood station wagons are conspicuous on the streets, where four stoplights punctuate the corners of a court house square." Members of the movie crowd "are easily recognized by the slack suits, moccasins and sun helmets they affect." The crew had been given printed instructions before they left Hollywood on how to avoid everything from alligators to sunstroke. The weather was not yet really hot in April, but "the townspeople are greatly impressed by the rumor that an air-conditioning system was installed in the hotel for Spencer Tracy."[8]

Spencer Tracy, as the star of the production, was on everyone's mind, the Hollywood personnel as well as the townspeople. He had been assigned the role of Penny Baxter because he was famous for playing fatherly parts, the "big strong kindly man whom you see so often giving up a drop of water and his life for a pal." He had won two Academy Awards, in *Boy's Town* and *Captains Courageous*, for playing fatherly men. But offscreen, even at MGM, a studio famed for pampering its stars, Marquand rated Tracy "about as spoiled and temperamental as any star in the business" (p. 17). In April 1941, Tracy wasn't at all sure he liked his role, or Victor Fleming, or the whole idea of filming in Florida. The air-conditioning in the hotel was there because Tracy absolutely refused to go on location until it was put in.

Having a discontented star is no very good way to begin location shooting, and matters did not get better as the filming progressed.

Everything seemed to go wrong at the location, despite the filmmakers' most careful plans—as if there were a primadonna Nature somewhere saying, "So you think you know how to handle me?" Each day began with long rides to location sites over roads where "many a smart Hollywood station wagon snorted and struggled in the grip of the sand." When the crew arrived, millions of mosquitoes and other insects were waiting to pounce, and there was the threat of poisonous snakes. The first days were ruined by a long dry spell that withered the carefully-tended corn fields. Then there was a period of heavy rain that made filming impossible. Then high winds interfered with sound recording. Finally the heat began soaring, and before May was over was hitting 102 to 104 degrees in the shade. There was no way to air-condition the Ocala Forest, whose "impenetrable thickets of scrub and palmetto hold heat like a cup."[9] Exhaustion began to set in as the struggle for filming perfection continued.

There was an endless, and maddening, series of wasted takes because animals used in the film wanted to do what nature told them rather than what the studio did. They didn't pick up their cues. Instead, they made loud noises. They defecated on camera. They broke loose in the middle of scenes. The worst came in a scene where about twenty buzzards were supposed to be seen around the carcass (simulated) of a wild deer. They were brought on the set fed and deodorized, and hobbled in place around the prop carcass. What no one remembered was that buzzards by nature have "a disagreeable habit of disgorging carrion when disturbed, preferably on their enemies. Some of the natives, led by a brave and unknowing cameraman from Hollywood, rushed in to excite the birds and cause them to fly into the branches of a nearby tree. With one movement all the buzzards turned and aimed their anger at their tormentors. The camera . . . clearly portrays Californians and Floridians joined in one great upheaval, definitely outdoing the birds."[10]

There was trouble with the local Floridians, as time went on. These people, the *New York Times* noted in its article, "are very little different from the backwoodsmen of fifty years ago. Clannish and independent, their contacts with the outside world are limited to the hunting parties they guide."[11] The country folks simply could not understand the Hollywood people, to whom the local region was only a realm for make-believe scenes. The Floridians could not comprehend the ways of people whose entire working lives seemed to be bound up with fantasy, and for whom putting fantasy on film was reality. In one case, the production department hired an eighty-four-year-old master canoe carver to make a hand-hewn cypress log canoe for the film. The old man made it slowly, with care and love, as he had made others all his life. As soon as he was finished, the art director took an axe to it and splashed brown paint on it, to make it look aged. The canoe maker burst into tears.

Spirits began to plunge as the heat continued and filming crawled. The isolated Hollywood people began to be truly worried about the progress of the film and desperate for any relief from their circumstances. One story shows both feelings at work. The animal trainers were upset about how the fawns kept growing regularly until they were too big for further use. They heard some local lore that the growth of fawns could be retarded by giving them a little moonshine to drink. They requested from the supply chief, and got, a bottle of bourbon every day for that purpose. That was the worry part of the story. The relief part was that they requested a whole quart of bourbon every day, and gave each fawn exactly one teaspoonful of it each evening. The rest of the quart mysteriously evaporated among the crew.[12]

At the head of the plunging spirits were Victor Fleming and Spencer Tracy, whose studio careers would be most affected by a failure on the film. Florida was just as uncongenial as Tracy had thought it would be. He sat on the set and brooded about the heat, and the hours that were lost while everybody coped with some animal disaster. He reflected on how much he disliked his part, and what kind of picture he would present his fans as Penny Baxter, dressed in floppy hat and sagging overalls, a wad of tobacco in his mouth. Most of all he worried that next to young Gene Eckman's authentic Southern accent, his own attempts sounded about as real as a four-dollar bill. Victor Fleming brooded about how far behind schedule the film was getting, at a cost of about twenty thousand dollars a day to MGM. After enough brooding on each side, the explosion came. Tracy told Fleming he wanted out of the picture, that "he was God damned if he would act with any little boy with an accent like that, that it was too hot anyway and the whole thing was corny and would ruin his reputation." At that, said Marquand in his account, "Mr. Fleming, who I am sure had ulcers at the very beginning, suffered from a nervous breakdown and Spencer Tracy flew back home" (p. 17). Fleming flew back to Hollywood too, leaving a lot of stunned production workers to their own devices in Ocala.

Next, orders came from the studio to pack everything and everybody but a maintenance crew and take the train back to Hollywood. Shooting would come to a temporary halt while things were sorted out at the studio. At first, it was thought that matters could be patched up between Fleming and Tracy. Louis B. Mayer, MGM's chief executive, was legendary for being able to wheedle fractious stars and directors into doing things they didn't want to do. But, director King Vidor wrote, "after a week's layoff when it was certain that their differences could not be amicably resolved, I was called in to take over the direction of the film."[13] In fact, he was yanked off preparations to film Marquand's novel about a Boston aristocrat, *H. M. Pulham, Esq.*, and told to get working on a lot of Florida farm people and animals.

To take over *The Yearling*, Vidor had to look at all the film shot to date, and study all the preparations made by the crew. He had to ask for changes in the script where he felt as director there were things he could not work with. It was a tremendous undertaking. Vidor clung to Marquand, who turned out to be the only man at the studio who had read the Rawlings novel. But MGM, with the overhead mounting up every day, wanted Vidor to get the job done in no time. "It was proposed that photography should begin again in a week or ten days, but I knew this was impossible." So Vidor was caught between the demands of the production and of the studio executives. Every day brought pressure. It might be from a technician, as when an assistant production manager called long-distance from Florida for instructions: "We have forty-five thousand corn plants growing in tin cans. What shall we do with them?" "Water them," said Vidor, and hung up.[14] Executives got the same short shrift from Vidor when they called. Without preparation and a script he liked, he told Mayer, "he was damned if he would get a sunstroke in any swamp" (Marquand, p. 18).

Back in the Ocala Forest, things were very quiet as June went on—a big contrast to the frenzy of the studio. The heat kept rising, the corn in all those cans went on growing, fawns were born and nuzzled close to their mothers. But then in the middle of the serenity, nature ordered a shutdown that was nowhere on the production schedule. It got to be the middle of June and the does' mating season was over. There would be *no more* newborn fawns until next spring. That, said nature, is that. "Oblivious to the screams of top studio executives, the fawn production line suddenly came to a halt. The does refused, even for M-G-M, to change the course of nature."[15]

There stood Baxter's Island, beautiful and ready. The script was refurbished. The crew and the actors and the trained animals were waiting to go again. The air-conditioning hummed in the Ocala hotel rooms. But without more fawns, no one could continue the picture. On June 22, 1941, the *New York Times* carried the notice that "the studio has been forced to shelve its titanic production of 'The Yearling.' . . . the primary cause for all the trouble can be traced to the fact that fawns grow faster than M-G-M could operate. . . . Next year, it is said, Metro will probably try again. . . ."[16]

Of course the studio was not going to give up. If they did, all the money invested in the picture, which came to about a million dollars, was as good as poured down the St. John's River. They would start again next spring. The animals were housed in various parts of the studio back lot. The props were stored. The sets were left to weather some more in Florida. Vidor got to go back to *H. M. Pulham, Esq.*, and Spencer Tracy went on to a new assignment. In fact, it was no bad thing for Tracy that *The Yearling* was shelved. With his time unexpectedly free, he was cast next in a romantic comedy, *Woman of the Year*. His co-star was Katherine Hepburn. The two had never met, never made a picture together. Thanks to *The Yearling* shutdown, they did. The rest, of course, is Hollywood history. The only real loser by the delay was Gene Eckman. Nature kept pushing the thirteen-year-old toward gawky, broken-voiced adolescence. By next spring he might be already too old to play Jody.

But the next spring was 1942, when America had entered World War II. The public taste had shifted to other kinds of entertainment, even if location shooting had been possible with transportation and housing and food shortages. The *Yearling* project was indefinitely delayed. It was 1945 before all the mechanism for location shooting could be wound up again. About that time, Eckman was inducted into the United States Army.

The studio casting office in 1945 went through another gigantic search to find a little Southern-accented boy to play Jody. This time they cast a ten-year-old, Claude Jarman of Nashville, to play the thirteen-year-old. By starting him that young, even if Jarman grew like a weed, there would be time to spare before he outgrew the part. The studio assigned the film to one of their veteran directors, Clarence Brown, and put in a whole new cast beginning with Gregory Peck as the father. The report was that "this Hollywood company—even to star Peck—was hand-picked for *The Yearling*—not just for technical reasons, but because they are supposed to have reasonably good dispositions."[17]

They all went back to Florida to try again. The weather was no better than before. There were more delays as sets were changed. Director Brown decided he did not like the look of the original Baxter cabin, and the only one that would suit him was Marjorie Kinnan Rawlings's own cabin that she had lived in while writing the book. Fifty laborers took apart her cabin, carried it piece by piece to the movie site, and reassembled it there for the filming.

But this time the film kept pretty well to schedule. It was as though now the perfectionist crew members realized the film had to work by nature's timing as well as the studio's drive for technical gloss, and that nature's schedule allowed for no artificial hurrying things up or holding them back. There was one piece of film the crew loved, though it was never used in the picture, that put this message across vividly. It was from the bear-hunt footage. "Bears are very unpredictable animals, even those raised on bottles as the real Slewfoot of this picture was. With permission of the S.P.C.A., a slingshot was used to hurry Slewfoot through a chase scene: he wanted to stop and play with old Julie, chief bearhound in the picture. With cameras grinding expensive film away, Slewfoot was urged along with BBs until he was halfway across a shallow stream. Then he calmly sat down in the water, held up a paw as if asking for time out, and proceeded to turn his bottom to the lens while he picked the BBs out. During the showing of rushes of this scene," with the bear placidly mooning the camera, "Slewfoot brought down the house."[18]

The happy ending for the studio was that they did get the picture completed on location this time. The effort and the investment did produce results, after all. *The Yearling* went on to be an artistic and a box-office success. It even won three Academy Awards. But first the studio, whose proud trademark was a roaring lion, had to learn a lesson from the way Nature twisted Leo's tail back in 1941.

## NOTES

[1]John Marquand, "Hollywood," pp. 14–15. Talk delivered to the Tuesday Night Club, Newburyport, Mass., 9 Dec. 1941. Manuscript now in the Collection of American Literature, Beinicke Rare Book and Manuscript Library, Yale University. Quoted by permission. Subsequent references to this source appear in the text.

[2]*New York Times*, 25 May 1941, Sec. 9, p. 3:3.

[3]King Vidor, *A Tree is a Tree* (New York: Harcourt, Brace, 1953), p. 247.

[4]Vidor, p. 248.

[5]*New York Times*, 25 May 1941.

[6]John Maloney, "Them Hollywood Nuts," *Liberty Magazine*, 16 Nov. 1946, p. 80.

[7]*Florida Times-Union*, [Jacksonville, Fla.], 23 April 1941, p. 8:4.

[8]*New York Times*, 25 May 1941.

[9]*New York Times*, 25 May 1941.

[10]Maloney, p. 80.

[11]*New York Times*, 25 May 1941.

[12]Maloney, pp. 80–81.

[13]King Vidor, *King Vidor on Film Making* (New York: David McKay, 1972), p. 34.

[14]Vidor, *A Tree*, p. 247.

[15]Vidor, *Film Making*, p. 34.

[16]*New York Times*, 22 June 1941, Sec. 9, p. 3:6.

[17]Amy Porter, "Growth of *The Yearling*," *Collier's Magazine*, 29 Sept. 1945, p. 77.

[18]Maloney, p. 25.

# The Image of New Orleans on Film

## H. WAYNE SCHUTH

"Before I moved to New Orleans," a friend said to me, "my impressions of the city came basically from film and television. I expected New Orleans to look mostly like the French Quarter, with narrow streets, courtyards, fountains, magnolias, balconies, and jazz. I drove in on the Interstate and was surprised to see from a bridge the buildings, industries and neighborhoods of a typical American city." The image of New Orleans, for my friend and for many people, has been created by the more than fifty major American motion pictures and television series in which the city is used as a setting.

In some of the films, New Orleans is a character, essential to the structure of the film itself. In others, it is merely in the background for beauty, mystery, and excitement. The city may appear throughout a film, or in just a small part. Whether the film is set in the historical past (*Pretty Baby, Band of Angels*) or in contemporary times (*Let's Do It Again, Live and Let Die*), whether in a filmed television series (*Yancy Derringer, Longstreet*) or in feature films made for television (*Concrete Cowboy, Sparrow*), whether in theatrical films (*The Cincinnati Kid, Easy Rider*) or in non-theatrical films (*Always for Pleasure, Three New Orleans*), whether in famous films (*Streetcar Named Desire, Panic in the Streets*) or in obscure films (*Mirrors, French Quarter*), New Orleans has a personality all its own.

Film is a complex symbol system, made up of images, words and sounds. Filmmakers often choose the physical reality of New Orleans, but they ultimately create a symbolic reality colored by a personal vision and the manipulation of the elements of the symbol system.

The image of New Orleans in a film, therefore, does not depend on location shooting. There are films with New Orleans settings that are

240

not shot in New Orleans but in studios and Hollywood backlots. There are films that use a few shots of New Orleans photographed in the city, but for which the majority of the production takes place in the studio. There are films which are shot in their entirety in New Orleans. The image of the city depends on what the image maker selects to include, real or not, and how he or she chooses to present it. What matters is not how authentic the image of the city is, but how the image shapes the viewer's total idea of what New Orleans is like. There is a cumulative effect of recurring images and stereotypes that create for each individual a private impression of the city.

One of the most prevalent stereotypes of New Orleans is the portrayal of jazz as the only form of music in the city. There is jazz, but there are lots of other forms, too. Such images and stereotypes as jazz, the French Quarter, and waterfront docks are found in most films that use New Orleans as a setting. Other stereotypical images that appear now and then, each contributing to a composite image, are sternwheelers, ferries, freighters, iron grillework, courtyard apartments, the Pontalba apartments, balconies, St. Louis Cathedral, courtyard restaurants, Jackson Square, strip joints, jazz funerals, horse and carriages, redneck policemen, crabs, shrimp, crawfish, Dixie beer, questionable politicians, Victorian mansions, voodoo, spanish moss, sex, violence, Bourbon Street, Creoles, Cajuns, the St. Charles streetcar, cemeteries, the Superdome, the Royal Sonesta Hotel, the Royal Orleans Hotel, Cafe Du Monde, Mardi Gras, swamps, fans, French accents, Southern accents, prostitutes, fountains, magnolias, black children dancing, and Lake Pontchartrain. I'm sure there are many others.

To a great extent, the degree of stereotyping of New Orleans in film depends upon the type of film. When New Orleans is found in a fiction film made for television or in a filmed television series, the image maker normally relies very heavily on stereotypes. Television is a medium that, because of its basic characteristics, encourages stereotyping. There is a rigid time frame of thirty, sixty, ninety or one hundred and twenty minutes which must include breaks for commercials. There is a limited screen size. There is the widest range of audience to aim for, in terms of age and intelligence. Films for television are shot quickly, and many are put together by a committee. There is usually little time for complexity.

In theatrical fiction films made for first exhibition in theatres, the image makers may not rely so heavily on stereotypes. There is flexibility in the length of the film. There is the big screen. There are specific audiences that the film can be aimed to. And there is more control by the image maker who often wishes to present a complex, personal statement. In non-theatrical and documentary films, where the emphasis is often on realistic images, fewer stereotypes can be expected.

Image makers manipulate New Orleans for artistic purposes. In the television film, *The Savage Bees*, a girl is trapped outside the city in a car on which the bees have settled. She is to drive the car to the Superdome. Once inside, the building's air conditioning can be used to cool and thereby kill the bees. In reality, the Superdome is in downtown New Orleans, and there are several ways to get there which would involve encountering a minimum number of people; but in the film, the car is directed through the crowded, congested French Quarter in order to use this stereotyped location. The majority of the television audience, not knowing the geography of New Orleans, assumes that the Quarter is the quickest and safest route to the Superdome. In *King Creole*, Elvis Presley stands on a balcony on one street and looks down. There is a cut to his point of view, an image of another street, that is in reality several blocks away. Of course, the street depicted in the film is a better setting for the action which follows.

Reality is manipulated in ways other than geographic. In *Voyager*, Lassie wanders into the Court of the Two Sisters courtyard restaurant looking for her master. Neither waiters nor patrons show much concern about a collie in their midst, even when she starts barking and running through the tables to greet him. In *Docks of New Orleans*, Charlie Chan's car stops in the middle of a narrow Quarter street and Chan gets out to question a man. No one behind the car honks or shouts.

When New Orleans is chosen as the setting for a film, it often has some relation to plot and structure. For example, *Louisiana Purchase* is a Bob Hope vehicle which uses the city's political folklore for its spoof on Southern politics and the city's Mardi Gras for its lavish production numbers. *New Orleans Uncensored* employed the city for its waterfront story of gangsters attempting to take over an incorrupt industry. The film used some city officials playing themselves as they attempted to protect the waterfront from the gangsters. *Pretty Baby* drew upon the city's Storyville history for its tale of that milieu as seen through the eyes of a young girl. *Walk on the Wild Side*, which also dealt in part with prostitution, utilized the sultry ambience of the city for its story of good and evil. *Lady from Louisiana* made use of the city for the spectacular ending, in which John Wayne steers a giant sternwheeler into a break in the Mississippi River levee to save New Orleans from a deluge. These films, and many others, had artistic reasons in their original conceptions for the setting in New Orleans. Many times, images other than the usual stereotypes are employed. In fact, two of the most famous and critically acclaimed of all the films set in New Orleans, *Streetcar Named Desire* and *Panic in the Streets* (both directed by Elia Kazan) could not have been set anywhere else with the same impact, as both employed aspects of the city for plot, character development, symbolism, motivation, and believability.

Other films often exploit the city. Although they could have been made in any big city, they use New Orleans as a drawing card for commercial success. For example, in *Docks of New Orleans*, what is seen of the city in this typical Charlie Chan murder mystery is the river at the beginning of the film and Canal Street in rear projection behind Chan's car. The plot has nothing to do with New Orleans and no one in the film even has a trace of a New Orleans accent. In *Superdome*, the murder and chases could have been staged at the Astrodome, or in any large indoor stadium. In *Live and Let Die*, any exotic location would do for the famous James Bond chases and fights. *The Savage Bees* could attack any major American city. Bill Cosby's and Sidney Poitier's very funny comedy *Let's Do It Again*, has much more to do with character and situation than it does with the city itself. In *Mississippi Gambler*, the fencing academies could be found in any large Southern city.

The image of New Orleans for the viewer, however, does not always depend upon how essential or gratuitous the city is to the structure of the film. Elements and stereotypes unique to New Orleans recur again and again, while elements common to any city are often omitted, in fact, are taboo. These recurring images contribute to the viewer's private, composite image of the city.

The real New Orleans is both typical and different. The French

Quarter exists alongside a modern downtown and there are Victorian mansions as well as suburban ranch houses. In fact, New Orleans is a city of many neighborhoods, each with its own architecture, culture and style. When shooting on location in the city, however, directors are very selective. They usually prefer to shoot in the garden district rather than the central business district. They prefer Bamboo Lane to Lookalike Lane. They choose New Orleans for what is unique, not similar, and they often rely on what they think the viewer expects New Orleans to be like. The image makers amplify, dramatize, and repeat certain images of the city until these images become part of our personal map, which doesn't necessarily fit the entire territory.

The universe created in the films not only includes recurring locations, props and events, but consistent faces. Local actors and actresses are often used in small roles when film companies shoot on location in New Orleans. If you look at enough of these films, you will recognize Louis J. Dezseran, George Wood, Rebecca Davis, Orlando Taylor, and others in a variety of roles in a variety of films.

Marjorie Roehl writes in the New Orleans *Times-Picayune* (8 June 1980), "Forget that picture of New Orleans as a wicked old city—a bawdy gal with a lace handkerchief in one hand and two bottles of bourbon in the other. The word from Le Fete de la Nouvelle Orleans is, 'Come to the party and bring the kids.' New Orleans, they say, is a family oriented town and the festival movers and shakers plan to present it as such to the nation." It is true that parts of New Orleans are indeed family oriented. There are lovely parks, a zoo, fast food restaurants, an amusement park (Pontchartrain Beach), many fine churches, a symphony orchestra, and several university and community theatres. But one wonders if the nation really wants to see these images of the city.

Voodoo, although very few people practice it, seems much more mysterious than Catholicism, which is the major religion in the city. Tiny French Quarter shops and apartments are much more atmospheric and exciting than the huge, sprawling modern shopping centers and apartment complexes. Antoine's Restaurant and the Columns Hotel seem more atmospheric than taco restaurants and budget motels. Spanish moss and magnolias seem much more romantic than pine trees and sunflowers. I suspect that the typical movie viewer

would be a bit disappointed if he or she went to a movie about New
Orleans and it did not include some of the comfortable stereotypes.

My favorite image of New Orleans appears at the beginning of *King
Creole*. Peddlers of all sorts are in horse-drawn carriages singing
hauntingly about their wares at dawn in the French Quarter. The
image reflects a New Orleans so touching and beautiful that it matters
little whether it existed in reality.

The reel world can never completely mirror the real world, and
there is a huge heritage of images about New Orleans that help create
our mental mosaic of the city. One hopes that image makers in the
future will move beyond some of the familiar patterns and enable
viewers to see the city and its people in richer and more varied ways.

Hollywood evokes New Orleans: Elvis Presley against the
cast iron decorations of a Bourbon Street bar. (Courtesy of
Museum of Modern Art/Film Stills Archive)

# Notes on Contributors

MICHAEL ADAMS teaches in the English department at Louisiana State University at Baton Rouge and has reviewed films for newspapers in Alabama and Pennsylvania.

ROBERT A. ARMOUR is a professor of English at Virginia Commonwealth University, Richmond, and the author of *Fritz Lang* (1978) for the Twayne Theatrical Arts Series and *Film: A Reference Guide* (1980).

WADE AUSTIN teaches courses in film and popular music at the Florida Institute of Technology, Melbourne.

JACK BARBERA teaches film and literature at the University of Mississippi (Oxford) and is working with William McBrien on a biography of British poet Stevie Smith.

EDWARD D. C. CAMPBELL, JR., is director of the Museum of the Confederacy, Richmond, Virginia, and the author of *The Celluloid South: The Old South in American Film, 1903–1978* (University of Tennessee Press, 1981).

TRISHA CURRAN is director of the Film Program at Fordham University, author of *A New Note on the Film* (Arno, 1980), and a regular contributor to *Films in Review*.

EVELYN EHRLICH is currently a visiting assistant professor at the University of Vermont and is completing her Ph. D. in cinema studies at New York University.

JEFFREY J. FOLKS teaches American literature at Tennessee Wesleyan College, Athens, and has written other articles on William Faulkner.

WARREN FRENCH teaches film courses for the English department at Indiana University, Indianapolis, and edits the Twayne Theatrical Arts Series, devoted principally to detailed studies of the work of film directors.

IDA JETER has recently moved from Wisconsin, where she did her research on *Jezebel*, to teach at St. Mary's College, Moraga, California.

GORHAM KINDEM is an assistant professor of radio, television and motion pictures at the University of North Carolina at Chapel Hill.

DAVID D. LEE is a member of the department of history at Western Kentucky University.

CHARLES MALAND teaches film and American literature in the English department at the University of Tennessee—Knoxville, and is the author of two books on film, the most recent being *Frank Capra* for the Twayne Theatrical Arts Series.

MARTIN F. NORDEN is an assistant professor of communication studies at the University of Massachusetts—Amherst.

VICTORIA O'DONNELL teaches on the faculty of the department of speech, communication and drama at North Texas University and is program chair for the 1981 Conference of the University Film Association at the University of South Dakota, Vermillion.

GERARD PLECKI is spending the year at Clemson University as a visiting lecturer on film. His book, *Robert Altman*, for TTAS, is a revision of his University of Illinois dissertation.

H. WAYNE SCHUTH teaches film history and criticism, filmmaking and television production at the University of New Orleans. He is the author of *Mike Nichols* (Twayne, 1978).

JOAN L. SILVERMAN teaches American history at New York University and serves as a consultant to Citibank.

ROSS SPEARS is director of the James Agee Film Project, a non-profit corporation in Johnson City, Tennessee, which is currently filming "The Valley," a history of the TVA.

LENORA CLODFELTER STEPHENS is associate professor of mass communications at Clark College, Atlanta.

WILLIAM STEPHENSON, a professor at East Carolina University, is especially interested in eighteenth-century British literature and modern American film.

J. P. TELOTTE teaches film for the department of English at Georgia Tech and is working on a study of the films of Val Lewton, part of which has appeared in *American Classic Screen*.

HART WEGNER is an associate professor of German and comparative literature and coordinator of film studies at the University of Nevada, Las Vegas.

# A Chronology of the Evolution of "The Southern"

These films and the seven periods into which they have so far fallen chart, regardless of the artistic quality of the works, the evolution of "The Southern" to 1980. Some important films discussed in this book, like *The Yearling* and *Sergeant York,* are not included here, because they are exotics, more concerned with the portrayal of powerful characters than the creation of an ambience. Only the progenitors of subgenres (*Mississippi, Mountain Music, Mandingo, Obsession,* for example, are listed, despite the prominence of some other plantation musicals, hillbilly films, blaxploitation films and neo-Gothic horror tales.) Film directors are noted parenthetically. Though no director has dominated "The Southern," since D.W. Griffith, the recurrence of a few names like Michael Curtiz and and King Vidor is noteworthy.

## I. *D. W. Griffith Creates the Myth*

1909    "In Old Kentucky"
1911    "His Trust" and "His Trust Fulfilled"
1915    *The Birth of a Nation*
1919    *A Romance of Happy Valley*

## II. *The Myth Questioned* (Before the Tightening of the Production Code)

1926    *The General* (Buster Keaton and Clyde Bruckman)
1929    *Hallelujah!* (King Vidor)
1932    *Cabin in the Cotton* (Michael Curtiz); *I Am a Fugitive from a Chain Gang* (Mervyn LeRoy)

1933    *The Story of Temple Drake* (Stephen Roberts); *Wild Boys of the Road* (William Wellman)

## III. *The Myth Renewed* (After the Tightening of the Production Code)

1935    *Little Colonel* (David Butler); *Mississippi* (Edward Sutherland); *So Red the Rose* (King Vidor); *Steamboat Round the Bend* (John Ford)
1936    *Showboat* (James Whale)
1937    *Mountain Music* (Robert Florey)

## IV. Transition — The Myth Darkened, The Myth Sweetened

248

# Bibliography

Only general studies are listed here. For specialized subjects, consult the notes to the articles and Edward D.C. Campbell's book listed below. Dr. Campbell has also been most helpful in providing material for this introductory list.

Bergman, Andrew. *We're in the Money: Depression America and Its Films.* New York: New York University Press, 1981.

Bogle, Donald. *Toms, Coons, Mulattoes, Mammies and Bucks: An Interpretive History of Blacks in American Films.* New York: Viking Press, 1973.

Campbell, Edward D.C. *The Celluloid South: The Old South in American Film, 1903-1978.* Knoxville: University of Tennessee Press, 1981.

Chappell, Fred. "The Image of the South in Film." *Southern Humanities Review,* 12 (Fall 1978), 303-11.

Cash, Wilbur J. *The Mind of the South.* New York: Knopf, 1941. (The classic study of the culture generally portrayed in Southern films.)

Cripps, Thomas J. *Slow Fade to Black: The Negro in American Film, 1900-1942.* New York: Oxford University Press, 1977.

Flamini, Roland. *Scarlett, Rhett and a Cast of Thousands: The Filming of "Gone With the Wind."* New York: MacMillan, 1975.

Gaston, Paul. *New South Creed: A Study in Southern Mythmaking.* New York: Knopf, 1970.

Kawin, Bruce. *Faulkner and Film.* New York: Ungar, 1977.

Kirby, Jack T. *Media-Made Dixie: The South in the American Imagination.* Baton Rouge: Louisiana State University Press, 1978.

Lambert, Gavin. *GWTW: The Making of "Gone With the Wind."* Boston: Little, Brown, 1973.

Merritt, Russell. "Dixon, Griffith, and the Southern Legend." *Cinema Journal,* 12 (Fall 1972), 26-45.

Silva, Fred, ed. *Focus on "The Birth of a Nation."* Englewood Cliffs, N.J.: Prentice-Hall, 1971. A collection of essays: see especially Everett Carter, "Cultural History Written with Lightning: The Significance of *The Birth of a Nation,"* pp. 133-43; and see also *Focus on D. W. Griffith,* ed. Harry M. Geduld (Englewood Cliffs: Prentice-Hall, 1971).

Soderbergh, Peter A. "Hollywood and the South, 1930-1960." *Mississippi Quarterly,* 19 (Winter 1965-66), 1-19.

# Film Index

251

# General Index

254